# DIRECTING THE DANCE LEGACY OF DORIS HUMPHREY

# Society of Dance History Scholars

The Society of Dance History Scholars (SDHS) advances the field of dance studies through research, publication, performance, and outreach to audiences across the arts, humanities, and social sciences. As a constituent member of the American Council of Learned Societies, SDHS holds wide-ranging annual conferences, publishes new scholarship through its book series and proceedings, collaborates regularly with peer institutions in the United States and abroad, and presents yearly awards for exemplary scholarship.

www.sdhs.org

*SDHS President*: Thomas DeFrantz, Duke University

*SDHS Editorial Board*

*Chair*: Ann Cooper Albright, Oberlin College

Sarah Davies Cordova, University of Wisconsin–Milwaukee
Sherril Dodds, Temple University
Norma Sue Fisher-Stitt, York University
Ellen Graff, The New School
Darcey Callison, York University
Vida Midgelow, University of Northampton
Gay Morris, New York, New York
Yutian Wong, San Francisco State University
Rebecca Rosen, University of Texas at Austin

# DIRECTING THE DANCE LEGACY OF DORIS HUMPHREY

*The Creative Impulse of Reconstruction*

LESLEY MAIN

THE UNIVERSITY OF WISCONSIN PRESS

Publication of this volume has been made possible, in part, through support from the Anonymous Fund of the College of Letters and Science at the University of Wisconsin–Madison.

The University of Wisconsin Press
1930 Monroe Street, 3rd Floor
Madison, Wisconsin 53711-2059
uwpress.wisc.edu

3 Henrietta Street
London WC2E 8LU, England
eurospanbookstore.com

Printed in the United States of America

Library of Congress Cataloging-in-Publication Data
Main, Lesley
Directing the dance legacy of Doris Humphrey : the creative
impulse of reconstruction / Lesley Main.
p. cm. (Studies in dance history)
Includes bibliographical references and index.
ISBN 978-0-299-28584-5 (pbk. : alk. paper) — ISBN 978-0-299-28583-8 (e-book)
1. Humphrey, Doris, 1895–1958 — Criticism and interpretation.
2. Modern dance — Production and direction.
I. Title.   I. Series: Studies in dance history.
GV1783.M28        2012
792.028092 — dc22
[B]
2011015990

This book is dedicated to
PENNY, GABRIEL, AND CELIE,
who share my dance through life,
and to the memory of
DORIS HUMPHREY AND
ERNESTINE STODELLE,
without whom that dance
would be so much less.

When we move we stand revealed for what we are.
—Doris Humphrey

# Contents

# Illustrations

## *Water Study*

## *Passacaglia*

## *With My Red Fires*

## *The Shakers*

# Acknowledgments

I have been fortunate indeed to benefit from the wisdom of some exceptional women in dance. Elaine Macdonald, Pat Mackenzie, Wendy Cook, Ann Hutchinson Guest, Millicent Hodson, and Stephanie Jordan each in their individual ways made me feel that distant aspirations were reachable. I thank my dear friend Alexandra (Sandra) Carter for her unstinting support and encouragement as my writing progressed from the uncertain state of emerging scholar to something deemed publishable. Thanks also to Ann Cooper Albright (SDHS), Raphael Kadushin (University of Wisconsin Press), and the anonymous readers for their editorial guidance and generous support as this volume evolved. My appreciation to photographers Linda Butler, Lisa Green, Jennifer Lester, and Alberto Sachero, whose work enhances my own and collectively illuminates this text. A final and ongoing thank you to the many, many dancers in Great Britain, in Italy, and in the United States who have danced these magnificent Humphrey dances with me along the way, from a fledgling *Passacaglia* in 1982 to its more recent incarnations in Turin and Oak Park, Illinois. And to my parents, Norma and James Main, for seeing most of them.

# DIRECTING THE DANCE LEGACY OF DORIS HUMPHREY

# PROLOGUE

## *Negotiating a Living Past*

Doris Humphrey made dances for America. Her opus is a repertoire of dances that span abstract, thematic, and narrative works. Many of them have breathtaking choreographic design and sociocultural significance or are just simply beautiful to watch and to dance. This legacy is a vital part of American cultural heritage and demands attention not only from the perspective of preservation but also from a contemporary desire to creatively engage the past. Humphrey's dances are more than a body of work; they are theatrical representations of a movement style and philosophy that remain relevant today. Although rooted in the American experience, her work has international appeal. European audiences respond as fervently to the choreography as their American counterparts. Unfortunately, many of Humphrey's masterpieces are not seen enough today. Humphrey's prominence is not where it should be, given her place in the history of American modern dance. Herein lies the task I share with fellow Humphrey exponents — to bring the past back to the present.

My life as a Humphrey dancer began the day I saw Lucy Venable's exceptional film of *Passacaglia*. I clearly recall sitting in the university library watching it over and over, awestruck at the power and magnificence of the choreography. By the end of that afternoon in 1981, I was determined to stage the work myself. An earlier fascination with Labanotation led me to Ann Hutchinson Guest's front door in Holland Park, London. I would sit for hours in her living room, which doubled as a notation library, poring over scores and trying to see the movement patterns in my mind. On hearing I planned to stage *Passacaglia* as my dissertation project, she gently suggested that *Partita in G Minor* might be a less demanding first work. Happily, she did not take offense when I ignored her suggestion, and she gave generous support throughout the staging process.

3

When I look back at the video recording of that first production, I see that the dancing is proficient enough, given the novitiate status of the director and her band of eager if equally inexperienced student colleagues. In retrospect, this can be attributed to our training in Limón technique with Jeanne Yasko, supplemented toward the end of the process by Humphrey classes with Gail Corbin, who was fortuitously visiting London from the United States. Many years on, a number of those dancers still remember substantial sections of the work. The rehearsal period spanned a period of months, but, arguably, it is the quality of the choreography that enables such clear memories. There is a profound clarity in Humphrey's use of choreographic structure, with every movement having a purpose and a connection to what comes before and after. The combination of these aspects, I believe, is what allows it to remain within memory's grasp.

My association with Ernestine Stodelle was a natural progression from that first encounter with *Passacaglia*. The years of Limón training aside, I was drawn to Stodelle's Connecticut studio in 1985 rather than the Limón School in New York City. Stodelle was already regarded as a leading authority on Humphrey's movement philosophy and choreographic repertoire. Born in Oakland, California, in 1912, Stodelle and her family moved to New York when she was a child. She attended an early Humphrey-Weidman concert as a teenager and was deeply inspired by what she saw—much as I was when I first saw *Passacaglia*. She went on to become a member of and soloist in the Doris Humphrey Concert Group and the Humphrey-Weidman Company between 1929 and 1935. Subsequently, Stodelle re-created a number of Humphrey's dances from that period, including *Water Study* (1928), *Air for the G String* (1928), *Quasi Waltz* (1929), *The Call/Breath of Fire* (1929/30), *Two Ecstatic Themes* (1931), and *The Shakers* (1931). She staged these works for dance companies and colleges across the United States, Canada, and Europe, including the José Limón Dance Company, Silo Concert Dancers, Momenta Dance Company, Danskern in Amsterdam, London Contemporary Dance School, and Marianne Forester in Basle, Switzerland.

In 1956 Stodelle established the Silo Studios of Dance in Cheshire, Connecticut, so named because the buildings were born out of a converted silo surrounded by trees. In this remarkable place, she taught dancers from her company, Silo Concert Dancers, alongside classes for children of every age and adults who just loved to dance. One of the most rewarding classes I attended was her women's class, held every Monday, Wednesday, and Friday at 9:30 a.m. sharp. The women ranged in age from forty to seventy-five, and some of them had been coming to her for over twenty-five years. They danced every exercise and study that we did in the professional class, perhaps not with the same technical precision, but certainly matching us in spirit. Stodelle also created a children's technique based on the Humphrey principles. It was exciting to see ten-year-olds performing core stylistic themes such as "hinges," "successions" at the barre, and "diagonals" on the floor with great accomplishment. Stodelle's closest associate, Gail Corbin, continues this valuable aspect of the Humphrey tradition.

Stodelle was a prolific writer and educator in tandem with her dancing career. She authored two books, *The Dance Technique of Doris Humphrey and Its Creative Potential* (1978, 1995) and *Deep Song: The Dance Story of Martha Graham* (1984). She was dance critic for the *New Haven Register* for years and contributed regularly to other publications, including *Dance Magazine, Art Times,* and *Ballet Review.* She also served as adjunct professor in dance criticism and aesthetics at New York University from 1970 to 1991. She would drive in to the city early every Tuesday morning for her weekly lectures at NYU. On the occasions I accompanied her, she would recount tales of her time with Humphrey, Charles Weidman, and Limón, her regular partner. She also had a habit of making eye contact throughout a conversation that proved quite unnerving to the passenger seated next to her in a car moving at speed down the freeway. Nevertheless, the experiences were invaluable in providing insights into the individuals and the context of their work.

Having survived the journey into Manhattan, I spent my Tuesdays exploring the Humphrey Collection in the Library for the Performing Arts. Stodelle had become firm friends with Genevieve Oswald, then curator of the Jerome Robbins Dance Division, while researching her book on Graham. On my first visit to the library, Stodelle introduced me to Oswald, who then provided me with various treasures to get started, including several notebooks dated 1929, 1930, and 1935. I requested the same material on a subsequent visit from a different librarian. When presented with rolls of microfiche, I politely asked for the real notebooks and was informed, equally politely, that "nobody gets those." My previous visit took on greater significance, and I was deeply grateful for Oswald's generosity and trust in allowing me that direct contact with Humphrey. Researchers will appreciate the distinction between handling an original artifact and an arguably sterile reproductive copy.

For the next decade, I traveled regularly between London and Connecticut, assisting Stodelle whenever she came to Europe. I immersed myself in the solo and ensemble dances while performing with Stodelle and at the same time adding new Humphrey works through reconstructing the Labanotation scores. In time, I became increasingly concerned about my "traditional" reconstruction-based practice when I revisited familiar works, and I began looking for a fresh approach to the process of staging. One issue was whether the dances themselves had the potential to "speak" afresh to a contemporary audience; another was their capacity to have a life span similar to that of theatrical and musical works. As a Humphrey exponent, my position today is that they can and absolutely should. The question is how to achieve this longevity. The aim of this book is to explore this central question and its related issues, with a selection of Humphrey's best-known dances serving as illustrative case studies — *Water Study* (1928), *The Shakers* (1931), *With My Red Fires* (1936), *Passacaglia* (1938).

As a director, I aim to create a compelling theatrical experience by exploring what a work was in the past in order to discover what it could become in the present. A key factor is doing so within the stylistic philosophy that underpins the Humphrey tradition so that the works are recognizable as belonging to that tradition. Through analyses of recent staging processes, I articulate aspects that are more closely related to theater production than to dance reconstruction. An investigation of directorial practice uncovers parallels with interpretation and style that can be further adapted for dance. A related aspect is the difference between the director as one who reconstructs the past and the director as interpreter or even creative artist.

Alongside the specific focus on Humphrey, broader issues will appeal to a readership beyond dance history and reconstruction. In performative terms, the question of dance style is significant and has relevance and currency across the genre. "Style" as a term can have variable meanings. In the context of this discussion, style refers to the nature of the movement performed by the dancers. I argue that stylistically literate dancing is fundamental to a successful staging because the style of the dancing is a marker of the identity of the choreographer, not simply the work.[1]

Themes and ideas relating to the interpretation of history, authentic performance in music, and directorial strategies in theater practice will be of interest across disciplines. I identify historical paradigms advocated by R. G. Collingwood and Hayden White and apply these within a dance context. I also consider what constitutes a "work" and the means by which that work is conveyed. Production practices of theater directors familiar in the United States, including Peter Sellars and Robert Wilson, are discussed alongside UK-based directors Phyllida Lloyd, Katie Mitchell, and Deborah Warner. A comparative study of the staging of Shakespeare and Samuel Beckett illustrates that what is commonplace in one interpretive context is deemed controversial to the point of censorship in another.

It is important that today's dance exponents consider how the great choreographic works of the twentieth century are to survive, and survive in a form that is meaningful and relevant for dancers and audiences in the twenty-first century and beyond. There is a view that dance is ephemeral, "of the moment," and therefore not intended to exist beyond that "moment" of performance. This viewpoint may be appropriate for some but not for the choreographers who represent key developmental stages in modern dance history. Why should great dance works be considered less worthy of continuing existence than great plays? I ask this not simply as a Humphrey advocate but because I see and hear how audiences respond to her work today. Professional and student dancers alike feel similarly enriched by being inside these works because of the quality of the choreography and also because dancers must rise to meet the demands of the language, much as actors have to do with the languages of Shakespeare and Beckett.

I would challenge anyone who has seen a high-quality production of Humphrey's *Passacaglia* to suggest that it is not worthy of a similar longevity to works by Shakespeare, Chekhov, Brecht, Beckett, Miller, Mozart, Copland, or Ives. Dances by Graham, Weidman, Limón, Cunningham, Taylor, Cohan, and Sokolow carry similar weight. To those of us whose lives are lived within dance, whether as practitioners, writers, or spectators, these artists matter as key figures in our heritage. As they have given to us, so we as first-, second-, third-generation exponents have a responsibility to maintain these dance traditions as living, vibrant art forms that have meaning in contemporary society. Ways of sustaining the repertoire, however, are contingent on effective modes of presentation. We already have some methods of documenting dance works through notation systems. This book will refer specifically to Labanotation not in order to privilege it over other systems but because it is the one most often used with modern dance.

There are choreographers who are unconcerned about documenting their work for preservation or re-creation purposes. They create work for a moment in time and then move on. Other choreographers make a conscious choice to have their work documented through Labanotation, film, and choreographic notebooks. By so doing, the choreographer signals a desire for that work to exist beyond the ephemeral moment of its first performance. What happens, however, once the choreographer has gone and can no longer sustain the life or longevity of the work? The next stage might be for those dancers with a long-standing connection to the choreographer, regarded as "direct descendants," to take on the mantle of preservation. Such intervention is a commonplace occurrence across the art form.

The active direct descendants of Graham, for example, are an extraordinarily rich group that spans decades, from Kazuko Hirabyashi to Peggy Lyman, Therese Capucelli, Christine Dakin, and Janet Eilber. Artists such as these have the potential to sustain the Graham repertoire for some time to come. Beside them are dancers from the current generation who have recently

begun to emerge in directorial capacities, including Kim Jones for Arkè Compagnia d'Arte in Turin, Italy, and Sandra Kaufmann for Momenta Dance
Company in Chicago, both of whom danced under Capucelli, Dakin, or Eilber.
This emergence and crossover between generations is an important part of
any tradition's evolution but particularly so when much of the "documentary
evidence" lies within the ephemerality of human movement as opposed to the
tangible pages of a book or images on a screen.

Humphrey's direct descendants include dancers who worked with her
in the Humphrey-Weidman Company from the late 1920s into the 1940s.
Stodelle, Eleanor King, Letitia Ide, José Limón, Katherine Litz, Nona Schurmann, and Beatrice Seckler are notable amongst this group. The contribution of these dancers, along with Humphrey's foresight in having her dances
notated, has ensured that the Humphrey tradition, in the repertory and the
dance technique, has solid foundations. However, a "gap" appeared when the
Humphrey-Weidman Company disbanded in the late 1940s. Humphrey and
Weidman elected to work independently of each other, with Humphrey becoming artistic director of the José Limón Dance Company for the remainder
of her life. Limón's emergence as an independent creative force signaled a turning point in the Humphrey tradition. Prominent dancers from the 1950s such as
Betty Jones and Ruth Currier danced under Humphrey but also had Limón's
stylistic influence in their bodies. There was a perceptible change in the feeling
and quality of movement from the early Humphrey period of the 1930s to that
of late Humphrey/early Limón.

I became familiar with these stylistic nuances after dancing for many years
with Stodelle and studying with Currier. Both forms are underpinned by "fall
and recovery," the core principle of Humphrey's movement philosophy. In
a broad sense, "Humphrey-based" technique as taught by Stodelle is fluid,
lyrical, expansive, with a core emphasis on breath rhythm and "whole body"
movement through the pelvic connection. "Humphrey/Limón" technique as
taught by Currier was similarly fluid with the pelvic connection but less expansive and possessed a greater emphasis on intricate gesture and rhythmic
patterns, in keeping with my experiences with other Limón teachers, including
Yasko, Clay Taliaferro, and Daniel Lewis. The gap between those early generations and those of us who represent the current generation of Humphrey
exponents is considerably larger in comparison with other modern dance traditions. The consequence of the declining participation of direct descendants is
that the Humphrey tradition is the first to become wholly reliant on its current
generation.

Over time, numerous colleagues working both in and outside the Humphrey tradition have cited examples of reconstructed dances that lacked any

sense of fall and recovery; the works, in turn, were rendered facile. The desire to stage a dance, however well intentioned, has to be supplemented by stylistic knowledge. Staging from a score or video is going to be problematic if a director fails to incorporate appropriate stylistic markers for the work to make sense, first of all to the dancers and then, through their embodiment, to the audience.

North American universities play an important role in the field of dance reconstruction. Many institutions regularly stage reconstructions as a matter of course. One great value of the US higher education system is that the educating of tomorrow's dancer can be framed within explicit cultural historic terms through the experience of performing modern dance works. The combined educational and artistic benefit is that student dancers are equipped with the specific language of a choreographer's style and, at the same time, an appreciation of the work within its historical cultural context. The dance works, in turn, become part of the students' lived cultural heritage. Dance training within many universities is of a standard that student dancers can rise to meet the challenges of modern dance works. While a specific technical style may not be studied on a day-to-day basis, the dancing bodies are technically equipped to deal with stylistic demands, given the appropriate stylistic input within a rehearsal process.

Great Britain became the adopted home of American modern dance in the 1960s. Students in Great Britain have an ongoing appreciation of these dance styles today and a desire to engage with the repertoire. Not all institutions offer modern dance, but those that do, including my own, Middlesex University, along with Laban, the Rambert School, Arts Educational School, and Northern School of Contemporary Dance, are producing students capable of dancing the repertoire. I observe first-year students being inspired to emulate graduating dancers in the likes of *Passacaglia* and Cohan's *Stabat Mater*. In my university, final-year performance students can choose to work with either a professional choreographer on a newly created dance or a director on a repertoire work. In recent years, there has been a noticeable change in the number of students opting for the repertoire experience to the extent that at least two and sometimes three large ensemble dances are staged in-house every year. This trend indicates that today's student dancers are hungry to engage with work of substance and quality no matter when it was created.

The Humphrey tradition itself reached a significant juncture with the passing away of Stodelle at age ninety-five on January 5, 2008. The most active and prolific of her generation, she continued to teach and stage dances into her ninety-second year. Stodelle's contribution to the Humphrey tradition is immense. Her articulation of the technique in *The Dance Technique of Doris*

*Humphrey and Its Creative Potential* provides a detailed exposition of Humphrey's core principles and movement fundamentals along with illuminating insight into Stodelle's own dancing experience with Humphrey and Weidman. The ideas are in concrete form and have moved beyond a "handed-down" existence. The book is intended as a practical insight into Humphrey's philosophy rather than a step-by-step handbook. It is possible, however, to experience fall and recovery in its simplest form, initiated by the breath and pelvis. Give these actions and ideas to a well-trained dancer with an open mind and body, and the stylistic challenge of a Humphrey work starts to become attainable.

Stodelle was not alone in contributing invaluable re-creations of works.[2] She focused particularly on Humphrey's early dances, from her years with the Humphrey-Weidman Company. Her involvement with *Water Study* and *The Shakers* is discussed in this book, but there are others of equal importance. Her re-creation in 1973 of Humphrey's signature solo, *Two Ecstatic Themes* (1931), for the Limón Company was followed by *Air for the G String* (1928), *Quasi Waltz* (1929), *The Call/Breath of Fire* (1929/30), *Etude Patetico* (1928), and *Concerto in A Minor* (1928). She spent the last thirty years of her career staging these dances all over the world. The cessation of Stodelle's dancing activity was the true marker of the generational shift. Her legacy, however, is well established through the current generation of exponents led by Gail Corbin.[3] Stodelle established a connection with Oak Park, Illinois, in 1990, a birthplace Humphrey shared with fellow esteemed figures Frank Lloyd Wright and Ernest Hemingway. Stephanie Clemens leads three connecting organizations based in Oak Park: the Academy of Movement and Music, Momenta Dance Company, and the Doris Humphrey Society. The Academy and Momenta have established traditions of historical dance through Clemens's own background with Ruth St. Denis as a child and, later, Eleanor King and former Denishawn dancer Karoun Tootikian.[4] Momenta performed Humphrey works (*Soaring* and *Air for the G String*) in October 1988. Humphrey's son, Charles H. Woodford, attended the performance, curious about a dance company doing his mother's works in her birthplace. At the suggestion of Woodford, Clemens organized a group of Oak Parkers to form the Doris Humphrey Society in 1989 and invited Stodelle to teach a winter workshop the following year.[5] Stodelle returned to Oak Park annually, often with Corbin, to teach technique and, in time, stage works for Momenta.

Stodelle had the foresight to appreciate the value of documentation for the longer term. During the 1990s, filmed recordings of Stodelle staging five Humphrey dances were produced and commercially released by Dance Horizons through the combined vision and efforts of Woodford, Clemens, and videographer Amy Reusch. Stodelle, in her eighties, gamely undertook filming in the excessive Chicago summer heat (in a non-air-conditioned studio). Her enthusiasm for the project was such that she never flagged, meaning that no one else could either. The films include *Two Ecstatic Themes* with dancers Mira Pospisil, Gail Corbin, Nina Watt, and Sarita Smith Childs; *The Call/Breath of Fire* with Nina Watt; and *Air for the G String, Water Study,* and *The Shakers* with Momenta Dance Company. Stodelle's commentary throughout each rehearsal process provides the insider's insight into the intention behind the dances and the reasons for the movement.

Three recent events in Oak Park illustrate the ongoing development of the Humphrey tradition. The first was an extensive project to reconstruct and notate Humphrey's *Concerto in A Minor* to music by Edvard Grieg. The reconstruction of the choreography involved King in the early stages of the project in 1989 and culminated in a version completed by Stodelle in 1997. The resulting work added to Momenta's Humphrey repertoire, with performances receiving critical acclaim. Just as significant are the new Labanotation score notated by Jessica Lindbergh, now published and available for production, and a soon-to-be-completed DVD recording of Stodelle rehearsing the dance.[6]

The second event was the realizing of a long-held ambition by Clemens to have *Passacaglia* staged for Momenta in 2007, my production discussed in part 2 of this book. The 2007 season marked the first time the work was performed in Humphrey's hometown. Sharing the program with *Passacaglia* was the third event, a performance of *Sonata Pathetique* (1920), choreographed by St. Denis and Humphrey. Tootikian first reconstructed the dance for Momenta in 1989. Senior company members Patricia Ackerman and Gina Sigismondi restaged *Sonata Pathetique* in 2007, with additional coaching from Corbin. Both Ackerman and Sigismondi were part of the early Momenta performances of Humphrey and Denishawn works, and both had worked regularly with Stodelle. A cast of young teenagers from the Academy of Movement and Music performed the work. On a separate occasion, I observed the dancers give consummate performances in a classical ballet, complete with toe shoes. When they shifted genres, with hair down and shoes off, it seemed as if they had been unleashed. It was exhilarating to witness these young dancers move with such freedom and vigor — here indeed was the next generation in full flow. The quality of their dancing was due to the quality of their teaching and the rehearsal direction from Ackerman and Sigismondi. The example of this cast of high school teenagers exemplifies the point that well-trained dancers can embody the Humphrey principles with appropriate stylistic experience. The regular training at the Academy was classical ballet and Graham-based modern dance augmented by annual Humphrey workshops, now with Corbin and fellow Humphrey-Weidman and Limón exponents Deborah Carr and Jim May.

The instances described above are by no means isolated occurrences in the United States, and they illustrate that the Humphrey repertoire continues to be extended, that Humphrey works continue to be performed on a regular basis, and that there are young dancers for whom Doris Humphrey is a familiar cultural figure. Developments continue apace in Europe, the most encouraging sign being the reception of the dances whenever they are performed live, including my productions of *Water Study* in 2007 and *Passacaglia* in 2006 and 2008 for Arkè Compagnia d'Arte in Turin, Italy.

This book allows the reader insight into the selected dances from a dancing perspective. Each work is placed within its historical context accompanied by analysis of the work and discussion of the range of strategies developed in my recent contemporized stagings in the United States and Europe. I present arguments that demonstrate the need for a form of directorial practice in dance beyond reconstruction. These arguments are tested and analyzed through a series of production processes for each work. The practices I advocate are a departure from traditional methods of reconstruction and are intended to spark debate and fresh thinking. Current practice in dance reconstruction makes clear that works from the modern dance genre are being revived and that there is a genuine enthusiasm to continue to do so. What is not clear, however, is what will happen once the direct descendants are gone. The practices and principles outlined within this book offer a way forward.

# PART ONE

# CHASING THE EPHEMERAL

I f you are reading this book, then you either have heard of Doris Humphrey or have an interest in modern dance and the performing arts. Why is it important that we care about Humphrey and her work? There are some compelling reasons. First, she was one of the foremost pioneers of American modern dance. For that reason alone, preserving her legacy should be important to the American cultural psyche. There is Humphrey's repertoire of over eighty dances. Testament to her choreographic greatness are the number of dances still being performed today, including *Air for the G String* (1928), *Water Study* (1928), *Concerto in A Minor* (1928), *Quasi Waltz* (1929), *The Call/Breath of Fire* (1929/30), *The Shakers* (1931), *Two Ecstatic Themes* (1931), *New Dance* (1935), *With My Red Fires* (1936), *Passacaglia* (1938), *Day on Earth* (1947), *Fantasy in Fugue* (1952), *Ritmo Jondo* (1953), and *Dawn in New York* (1956). These dances continue to excite audiences. In addition, there is documentary literature, including Humphrey's seminal book on the craft of choreography, *The Art of Making Dances*; there are photographs and film footage of her dancing and of her dances; and her codified dance technique is being taught on an increasingly wider scale. All these elements contribute to and are part of the Humphrey tradition, so there is something tangible to work from. The dances themselves are perhaps most vulnerable because they need to be performed to remain alive and meaningful. The purpose of my work is to illuminate these dances for a contemporary audience because I believe not only that Humphrey's choreography has something meaningful to say today but also that her influence can be ongoing.

Humphrey was born in Oak Park, a suburb of Chicago, on October 17, 1895. She enjoyed an eclectic childhood exposure to dance and music that ranged from the traditions of classical ballet and piano lessons through tap dancing and vaudeville to expressive movement with the inspiring educator

15

Mary Wood Hinman. It was Hinman who encouraged Humphrey to go to Los Angeles at age eighteen to work with Ruth St. Denis and Ted Shawn. She quickly became a valued member of the Denishawn Company, dancing leading roles and teaching in the Denishawn School for ten years. As her choreographic experience grew, so did the desire to find a creative voice beyond Denishawn's exotic repertoire. This deep-seated need to pursue her own choreographic ideals led her to join forces with fellow "Denishawnites" Charles Weidman and Pauline Lawrence and to leave the company in 1928 to set up their own studio in New York City. The Humphrey-Weidman Company performed regularly in New York and toured the country extensively for many years. Notable engagements included concerts at the 92nd Street Y and summer residencies at the renowned Bennington School of the Dance in Vermont under Martha Hill's directorship and, later, Connecticut College.

On a more personal note, Humphrey met her husband, Leo Woodford, in 1931 on a cruise ship to the West Indies. She had been sent on vacation by her dancers to rest, and he was captain of the ship. They had one son, Charles Humphrey Woodford, who today runs Princeton Book Company, the prominent dance publishing house. In 1946 Humphrey became artistic director of the José Limón Dance Company until her early death in 1958 at the age of sixty-three. The drive to create dances that were indigenous to her American roots remained at the heart of her choreographic explorations throughout her life. She speaks of this desire in John Mueller's celebrated 1965 film *The Four Pioneers*:

> The body is extremely revealing. It tells us more than speech; more than almost any other kind of communication; what you are really feeling; what is going on in the inside of people. There are hundreds of things to dance about beginning with your own experience, what happens to you. There are also hundreds of things you shouldn't dance about. In general, it's a good idea to dance about something you understand. If we're going to be here in America and promoting the American dance, then we'd better try to work indigenously, that is to foster what we have.

Humphrey's "working indigenously," arguably, goes beyond "Americana," although such influences are evident in certain dances, including *The Shakers* and *Song of the West* (1940). My sense of Humphrey's meaning relates more to a complete freedom of creative expression that paralleled the notion of the "great American way," "everything is possible in the land of the free, home of the brave" sociocultural identity of the time.

Between 1928 and 1931 Humphrey continued her experimentations, defining her movement philosophy as "fall and recovery," the "giving into and rebound from gravity . . . the very core of all movement, in my opinion."[1] She further articulated her theories of movement as follows: "The desire to move stimulates organic matter to reach out from its centre of equilibrium"; "To fall is to yield; to recover is to re-affirm one's power over gravity and one-self"; "Falling and recovering is the very stuff of movement, the constant flux which is going on in every living body all the time. I . . . instinctively responded very strongly to the exciting danger of the fall, and the repose and peace of recovery."[2] The emergence of these principles came through Humphrey's creative response to movement exploration. Subsequent development, essentially to train her dancers to dance her choreography, resulted in the evolution of a more structured vocabulary. Important elements are the gravitational pull, lyricism, successional flow, opposition, the idea of taking movement to its very edge, the constant play between balance and imbalance, the use of breath in a "whole body" context in which the body's surfaces take on the physiological action of the lungs in terms of expansion and subsidence. A central characteristic of the Humphrey style is the role of the pelvis as the center of movement initiation, with its interconnecting relationship to the breath and abdominal muscles. Without this connection, the body is prone to move peripherally from the limbs. In turn, the principles of "wholeness" and "dancing from the inside out," the foundation of Humphrey's fall and recovery philosophy, are negated and the stylistic indicators lost.

To my mind, style is a crucial aspect in the staging of someone else's work. In 1996 the American writer and critic Marcia Siegel commented: "Labanotation has to be retranslated back to the bodies by someone who not only can read it but can teach the movement effectively."[3] Siegel made this comment in relation to performances given during the Humphrey centenary in 1995 that she felt were stylistically weak. She was right to raise this as a concern. It is questionable whether a director would be in a position to communicate the often-subtle dynamic and physiological nuances of a movement language without intrinsic knowledge of a style and its philosophy. Humphrey's dances survive not only because of her foresight in having her work notated but also because of the lifelong efforts of the early Humphrey-Weidman dancers, including Stodelle, Nona Schurman, and Beatrice Seckler, who passed on the stylistic means of "how" to dance the dances.[4] For a choreographer's work to be understood, the style must be clear, and it can be. Across the modern dance genre there remain "direct descendant" dancers who hand down the respective philosophies as well as current-generation exponents who are fluent in specific styles.

I was asked recently whether Humphrey's movement style is knowable. I had to consider why the question was being asked, because to me the answer is so obviously "yes." That the question was asked, however, necessitates a more well developed response. Earlier, style was defined as the nature of the movement performed. This is indeed the case, but the definition is broad in its parameters. One can cite works by Paul Taylor, Mark Morris, and Trisha Brown, to name but three alongside Humphrey that have lyrical, weighted, fluid dancing. The meaning I ascribe to style in relation to staging certainly embraces quality but goes deeper to include the physiological, dynamic, and philosophical markers that are specific to the individual choreographer. These markers are contained in the codified techniques for Humphrey, Graham, Cunningham, and Limón, so there are recognizable aspects to draw on. Other choreographers may not have dedicated "techniques," but the body undoubtedly has to organize itself and respond to Taylor's choreography in a way that is different from that of Morris or Brown. This is not "new" news. A point to consider, however, is that current staging of these dances outside the parent company is being undertaken by direct descendant dancers, and, in time, there will be no more direct descendants.

Dancing "in the style of" can be further defined as the ability to capture and harness the dynamic qualities necessary to produce or create a choreographer's philosophy in its moving form — in Humphrey's case, fall and recovery. What is it that the body has to do to achieve the "giving in to and rebound from gravity" that permeates her movement in whatever choreographic formation? The question itself suggests there is a finite response to be had, a collective understanding of fall and recovery. My experience suggests that this is indeed the case for stylistic exponents. Other traditions would make that same claim, with Graham, Cunningham, and Limón being the closest examples. The existence of a movement philosophy is significant because the "handing down" is rooted in ideas. The physical manifestation of these ideas may change over time as part of the natural evolution of the dancing body.[5] The ideas, however, will remain intact as ideas, and their continuing presence creates a foundation that can underpin a tradition, allowing for the coexistence of both roots and development.

Examples of such coexistence from the Humphrey tradition are movements considered core to an understanding of fall and recovery, such as swings, hinges, and successions. Central to all three and unchanged over time are the point of initiation through the pelvis, the correlation of the "out breath" with the fall and the "in breath" with the recovery, the element of weightedness, and the engagement of the whole body throughout the movement. These aspects could be defined as the roots of each movement. Developments have occurred in more than one context. One is the creative response to existing material. Humphrey did not confine her creativity to theater works alone. Her classes contained numerous "mini-dances" created around movement themes she was exploring at the time. Stodelle, Schurmann, and others would then create variations around the core movement themes in their own teaching, resulting in the swing or hinge having a different surround but still containing the core aspects of the movement. I learned a swing series from Stodelle that comprised the swings she learned from Humphrey with her own variations, to which I have subsequently added my own creative responses. Corbin likewise has her own set of creative responses to that same swing series.

There are numerous examples of core movement themes being extended in this way in the Humphrey tradition and others, and, again, it is not new. Robert Cohan did just so with Graham's technique in England over a period of twenty years through his work with London Contemporary Dance Theatre and the London Contemporary Dance School, led at the time by fellow Graham dancer Jane Dudley. Cohan presents a different example to Limón, who developed a related but distinctive named style, albeit based on Humphrey's principles. Cohan did not go as far as creating a named style, and there are clearly recognizable "Graham" exercises all the way through his class, including contractions, pleadings, and spirals in fourth position. The roots of Graham's style, therefore, are all present, but they feel ever so slightly different in comparison with the training base for the Graham company and the teaching at the Graham School in New York.[6] A different example again is Cunningham's technique as taught by Chris Komar and Catherine Kerr, both principal dancers with the Merce Cunningham Dance Company in the 1970s and 1980s and regarded as leading exponents. I took classes with both of them periodically, and there were discernible differences in the sensation of the movement despite both teaching virtually the same pattern of sequences. Both experiences were undoubtedly "Cunningham" classes, however, and it never occurred to me that they were anything but. All of these examples demonstrate that development can occur in varying degrees, while the core of each movement style remains intact. Invention is important in terms of the wider tradition because it creates the possibility of advancement and prevents movement becoming fixed.

A second developmental context is the way in which today's body responds in comparison with the dancing bodies of the 1930s. The natural evolution in bodily physique alongside the substantive changes in dance training over the past eighty years make clear that replicating "what was" is neither possible nor, in fact, necessary if the basic philosophy remains intact. Today's dancer is more accustomed to moving across styles, so he or she comes into a class or rehearsal process without fixed expectations. The dancers from Arkè Compagnia d'Arte in Italy are trained in Graham and Horton techniques, yet they adapted quickly to the Humphrey style because of their open approach. One aspect that needs to be made explicit is how to release and move from the pelvis, notably for dancers with extensive classical training who instinctively lift "up" out of the ground. The transition becomes more successful once they understand that their existing technique does not need to be discarded but used in a different way and a different direction.

Because of the inception of Labanotation and the vision of choreographers such as Humphrey and George Balanchine in agreeing to have their work notated in the very early days of the Dance Notation Bureau, documentary evidence exists that could have been lost but for the notating process. The Labanotation score incorporates a central staff that contains the bulk of symbol information plus indication of time frame, tempo, design of the work in space through a set of floor plans, and dynamic quality through the inclusion of Effort/Shape symbols from Labananalysis. Introductory notes and brief descriptors are also included throughout the score. In principle, this would suggest that a score contains the means by which a dance work can be produced. There is an issue, however, regarding the representation of stylistic, dramatic, and interpretive information, which is intrinsic to a production process.

In a broader context, it is perhaps unrealistic to expect a symbol-based system to have the properties capable of fully capturing the complex physiological and dynamic aspects that comprise a movement philosophy or style. The performance contract for a Humphrey work stipulates that stylistic coaches should be involved. *Two Ecstatic Themes* (1931) and *The Call/Breath of Fire* (1929/30) are two examples coached by Stodelle before her death in 2008. There are dances being staged, however, with insufficient coaching, as evidenced in 1995 during the Humphrey centenary celebrations in the United States. A recurring issue highlighted by knowledgeable commentators, including Siegel, Lynn Garafola, and Jane Sherman, was the poor quality of stylistic dancing in many of the reconstructions shown during this period.[7] I asked Garafola recently what it was about the dancing that brought forth such a negative response, and she stated emphatically that the bodies looked weak. Such performances contrasted sharply to those companies with a tradition of producing stylistically literate Humphrey works, including the Limón Company, Repertory Dance Theater, and dances staged by Deborah Carr, Ann Vachon, and Stodelle for the CORD special topics conference in New York City.[8] The issue is compounded perhaps by a contributing economic factor. Companies and universities on limited budgets may not have the means to engage stylistic coaches or directors. The consequences in artistic terms, however, are significant for the individual dances and for the (mis)representation of Humphrey's tradition.

Style is an integral aspect of the staging process because it encapsulates the choreographer's "signature" and identifies the work as belonging to that particular tradition. Muriel Topaz, former director of the Dance Notation Bureau, acknowledged back in 2000 that "almost every great choreographer has a movement profile, a vocabulary that is immediately recognizable," and, in the same discussion, warned that "the importance of coaching cannot be underestimated."[9] The thrust of her argument was that without direct access to a stylistic coach, a reconstructor had better find some way of communicating the stylistic needs of the dance beyond simply demonstrating the movement off the page. She talks of a combination of physical indication combined with explanatory coaching and shaping movement on the bodies of the dancers. This last idea in particular suggests a more considered and meaningful approach than sole reliance on a score.

## Reconstruction, Re-creation, Reinvention

Before considering new approaches, I want to look first at the range of directorial practice that currently exists for modern dance works. In defining what constitutes a reconstruction, Tom Brown commented that "the ideal reconstruction for some would be a macabre embalmed impersonation for others."[10] Mark Franko, in his discussion of Baroque dance, observed that reconstructions in the 1980s began to convey something closer to the "theatrical force of the original choreography" through the emergence of "a degree of literal accuracy with the requisite theatrical immediacy."[11] Franko's observations are relevant for modern dance because of his inference that the work itself can be more than a self-contained entity and can become part of a living tradition that continues to evolve. The idea of evolving work ties in with the "continuum" theory presented by Susan Manning. She describes the process that the scholar, in her example, will go through:

> The dance scholar has no choice except to pursue the elusive and uncertain text of performance. An event bound in time and space, a performance can be read only through its traces — on the page, in memory, on film, in the archive. Each of these traces marks, indeed distorts, the event of performance, and so the scholar pursues what remains elusive as if moving through an endless series of distorting reflections. But this process leaves its own sort of illumination, and that illumination is what the scholar records, in effect penning a journal of the process of enquiry.[12]

The approach laid out by Manning can similarly be attributed to the director, with the "illumination" aspect being especially relevant. Manning suggests that a reconstructor may favor one of the opposing ends of a single continuum, citing Millicent Hodson and Kenneth Archer's reconstruction of Nijinsky's *Le sacre du printemps* (1913) for the Joffrey Ballet in 1987 as an example of one end of this continuum. Hodson and Archer's process of reconstruction, for this work and subsequent productions, had a significant emphasis on documentary evidence and encompassed both scholarly and artistic intervention on their collaborative part. Their artistic goal is the preservation of masterworks, achieved through the restoration of "lost" work that has, in their judgment, historical relevance and contemporary resonance. The purpose of their artistic endeavor is to create a reasonable facsimile of the original.[13]

A further example from 1973 is Stodelle's re-creation of the Humphrey solo, *Two Ecstatic Themes* (1931).[14] Stodelle's intention was to bring back a dance that closely resembled "the original," which she defined as Humphrey's performances of the dance. The "re-creation" aspect of Stodelle's practice refers specifically to her process of bringing each dance together again from fragmentary evidence, much as described by Manning. In addition, there are elements within each dance that have been created by Stodelle herself because the evidence was incomplete. One example is the black-and-white silent film of Humphrey dancing *The Call/Breath of Fire* (1929/30).[15] There are moments when Humphrey dances in and out of the light, leaving some of the movement obscured. Stodelle "filled in" these moments—from memory as she watched Humphrey perform the dance many times, through what did exist of the dance before and after the gaps, and through her knowledge of the style.[16] She was with the Humphrey-Weidman Company from 1929 to 1935, the period during which Humphrey developed and articulated the philosophy of her movement style and that also coincided with the creation of all the dances subsequently re-created by Stodelle. Having this physical and dynamic knowledge enabled Stodelle to find a logical transition from one set of given facts to another: "If Doris was moving like so in this phrase and ended there six beats later, there are only so many possibilities for how she got there."[17] Incomplete evidence is likely to be a factor in many productions, and directors will inevitably incorporate aspects of themselves within a work, albeit as conduits, whether intentionally or not.

At the other end of Manning's continuum, though not necessarily opposing, she places reconstructions that involve significant interpretation. Here could sit Mino Nicholas's version of another Humphrey solo, *The Banshee* (1928), re-created initially by Eleanor King. The dance was originally intended for a woman costumed as an ethereal spirit, and Nicholas cast himself, in Kabuki makeup and wig.[18] Stodelle intentionally set out to re-create the dance as she remembered it from the numerous times she had seen Humphrey perform the work. Nicholas likewise embarked on a deliberate course, and the fact that he cast himself in the role is more indicative of a performer-oriented intention. Stodelle's approach is similar to that of Hodson and Archer in terms of reconstruction, although she herself preferred the term "re-creation."[19] Nicholas's work is more radical, and he uses a range of terms to describe his productions, including "transcribed," "revised," "re-creation," and "based on."[20]

Humphrey scholar Ann Dils refers to the notion of co-authorship in her analysis of Ray Cook's reconstruction of Humphrey's *Dawn in New York* (1956).[21] Cook's process with a number of Humphrey reconstructions has been far more comprehensive than mine because he was literally reconstructing "lost" work.[22] He used similar processes to Hodson and Archer as well as Stodelle, involving rebuilding from fragments of evidence that included partially completed sections of Labanotation, photographs, memories of original performers, and Humphrey's notes. There were also gaps in this body of evidence that required creative intervention on Cook's part in order to produce a cohesive whole, much in the same way that Stodelle had to act with *The Call/Breath of Fire*. The production work I have undertaken, in contrast, has begun from a body of evidence that is relatively complete in terms of vocabulary and structure, a starting point more in line with theater directors working from a script. A further consideration is how far my practice incorporates the element of interpretive intervention in comparison with those cited above. The degree of involvement may appear considerably less in practical terms, given the scale of material that had to be found or created. *Dawn in New York*, for example, was missing a number of short sections that comprised one-third of the work. Cook's reconstruction of *Fantasy in Fugue* (1952) was missing the entire second movement (of three); he subsequently rebuilt it from photographs and the memories of one of the original dancers. My recent production processes have not required this level of "detective work" because of the existing materials available. The director's task, however, is ensuring that the material Humphrey left can speak today so that it can make sense today. In that context, therefore, interpretive intervention is relevant, although the degree to which a director operates in such a capacity remains variable.

An intrinsic part of the process, as Hodson and Archer emphasize, is the role of the dancer.[23] Dils makes an important observation when she refers to the Humphrey tradition of dancers stretching to meet the needs of the choreography rather than the choreography giving way to contemporary limitations.[24] Topaz also implies this in a broader context, commenting that reconstructors and directors should not change material to make it comfortable.[25] I would take her point further and suggest that by using the particular choreographic needs of a work as a parameter or yardstick, a legitimate platform is created from which today's dancer and dancing body can respond. Dils also discusses the aspect of "period performance" and how this contributed to the success of Cook's production because of the clarity brought to the choreography through the dancing.[26] From this point and Cook's own analysis, it would seem that the term "period performance" equates with my notion of being stylistically informed and how crucial this is to a successful production. Yet while the philosophy that underpins the "style" remains, there will inevitably be an evolution in how the style is articulated, and this, in turn, can create new, invigorating possibilities for movement vocabulary.

Dils offers a further definition of reconstruction, citing Pauline Koner's *The Farewell* (1962) and José Limón's *A Choreographic Offering* (1964) as examples of "evolutionary reconstruction."[27] The works are similar in that both were conceived as tributes to "Humphrey as mentor" following her death in 1958. In addition, both incorporated movement vocabulary from Humphrey works, although Limón used excerpts from fourteen works, and Koner used only two. Here, Humphrey's choreography acted as a catalyst for the evolution of a new work. This form of creative production has parallels with my own, particularly to the interpretation of *The Shakers*, analyzed in part 2. There is a distinction, however, in terms of intention. Koner and Limón set out to create "new" works, whereas my approach with *The Shakers* was to discover what the particular vocabulary of Humphrey's work could say when considered from a different perspective.

In positioning my work within this range of practice, there are significant elements of the respective practices of Stodelle and Cook that differ from mine. A common aspect, however, is that the director approaches the work on even terms with the choreographer. This approach is underpinned by an empowerment to be creative where creativity is called upon. Working from within the Humphrey tradition engenders that empowerment. Our practices diverge in the context in which creativity exists. Both Stodelle and Cook begin from the premise of locating and producing Humphrey's work. I begin from the premise of exploring Humphrey's work to discover what more it can say.

Reconstruction as a form of staging is as valid a practice as ever. I still get excited when I receive a Labanotation score for the first time, anticipating what lies within its pages. Reconstruction is one option now, however, rather than the only option. The change in my approach started in 1995, when I staged *Passacaglia* for the Humphrey Centennial Celebrations in London. I became conscious that emergent processes had more in common with staging a play than reconstructing a dance. That realization led to a deeper investigation of "interpretation" that crossed theater, music, history, and literary criticism. I located a number of discrete ideas that, when considered together and transposed into a dance context, opened up new possibilities.

## History in the Making

When one is intent on exploring Humphrey's dances from a fresh perspective, it is important to do so from within the Humphrey tradition, to make historical, evidence-based connections. The ideas presented by R. G. Collingwood in his seminal work, *The Idea of History* (1946), helped me form these connections and, in broader terms, contributed to the development of a directorial stance firmly rooted in the present. On first encountering his ideas, I recognized parallel after parallel with the production process for *Passacaglia* in 1995. Collingwood sets out a number of approaches to the viewing perspective of history that are built around ideas such as the "living past," the "historical imagination," and the role of the historian as an active interpreter.[28] He observed: "Everyone brings his own mind to the study of history, and approaches it from the point of view which is characteristic of himself and his generation."[29] The "living past," therefore, is pursued from the present. This idea is in line with the position put forward by T. S. Eliot in his essay "Tradition and the Individual Talent": "The past should be altered by the present as much as the present is directed by the past."[30] More recently, Hayden White referred to history being "made sense of in the same way that the poet or novelist tries to make sense of it, that is, by endowing what originally appears to be problematical and mysterious with the aspect of a recognizable, because it is a familiar, form."[31] White acknowledges this aspect of his narration theory as "the problem of translating knowing into telling."[32] The process involved in "translating knowing into telling" is fundamentally what occurs in the performing arts within the context of directorial interpretation. The connection between White and Collingwood is through White's reference to the "recognizable form." The "recognizable" aspect could be read as "current" or "contemporary" and be placed alongside Collingwood's "living past" notion because the activity involves illuminating what we think happened in the past through the known experience of the present.

White and his contemporary Dominick LaCapra have distinct views from each other in many respects. Both, however, are intent on extending traditional boundaries of historical study by incorporating external disciplines, namely, from literature and philosophy. Neither refers to Collingwood at length, but a parallel exists because they are all going beyond traditional boundaries to seek fresh understanding of existing material. LaCapra states: "It is because of dissatisfaction with established procedures, procedures tying history too closely to narrowly documentary reconstruction of a precritically conceived past, that some historians have recently turned to other disciplines and newer interpretive approaches."[33] He stresses the value of traditional methodologies but emphasizes more the need to supplement what exists already.[34] If this notion is applied to a modern dance context, existing evidence could include a Labanotation score, early films and photographs, and text-based documentation.

Collingwood's "living past" implies that there can be continual evolution. He cites an aspect of Hegel's philosophy as an illustration: "History . . . travels in spirals, and apparent repetitions are always differentiated by having acquired something new."[35] This is comparable to Eliot's observation that "the arrival of a new work affects existing work. . . . [T]he whole existing order must be, if ever so slightly altered."[36] One interpretation of these ideas is that knowledge and understanding can increase without deliberate intervention. The "new" arrival, be it a planned or random occurrence, changes the existing context simply by its presence. These ideas taken together suggest a simultaneous shift and expansion. The fluidity inherent in this position is attractive because of the implication that knowledge — a work, a fact, whatever is being considered — is never entirely fixed.

Collingwood developed a model that is useful for looking at modern dance and the choreographic work as an entity in itself. He considers "what history is, what it is about, how it proceeds, and what it is for."[37] If Collingwood's "history" is defined as the choreographic work, the answer/s to what it "is" can be determined through an exploration of the remaining three questions. "What it is about" could refer to the spirit, the intention of a work (*whose* intention is another matter, however). Having engaged with the varying debates on issues of authenticity and authorial intention across the literary and performing arts in recent years, I conclude that "authentic" is not a useful term for a living and evolving art form.[38] Intention is more relevant, however. I am not of the view that an author's or artist's intention can be fully determined, but I do believe that traces exist and, further, that the search for these traces of intent is an illuminating part of the interpretive process. The act of searching relates to the next part of Collingwood's model, "how it proceeds," which is "by the interpretation of the evidence."[39] There is a direct parallel here because, within the Humphrey tradition and others in the modern dance genre, there is an existing body of evidence to explore. Collingwood's model concludes with "what is it for," summarized as follows: "The value of history . . . is that it teaches us what man has done and thus what man is."[40] I read this as saying that knowledge of and engagement with the past allow us to know where we have come from. This knowledge, in turn, allows us to know where we are in the present and how to approach the future. As a creative artist working from "within" a tradition, knowing where that work comes from is fundamental to being equipped to take it forward.

In applying Collingwood's model to a dance context, a key part of the directorial process involves interpreting evidence to search for traces of the choreographer's intention. Collingwood's perspective on viewing evidence has proved effective here. He suggests that it is the business of the historian to discover something through the interpretation of potential and actual evidence: "The potential evidence about a subject is all the extant statements about it. The actual evidence is that part of these statements which we decide to accept."[41]

This position continues to incorporate the active participation of the historian and introduces the idea of selection. He further defines evidence as being "a part or aspect of the historian's present world, and the goal of historical inquiry is to explain this present world by tracing its origins."[42] Here, Collingwood re-emphasizes the "living past" notion, in that the process he describes begins from the present, and his use of the term "tracing" suggests possibilities rather than absolutes.

I have added a further dimension to Collingwood's actual/potential viewing model to create two phases, with the element of choice distinctive in each. The first phase focuses on the search for traces relating to intention. Adopting Collingwood's stance, I have chosen to accept only evidence that comes directly from the choreographer; thus, I will draw upon a limited pool. This type of evidence (actual) would comprise any indication from Humphrey on how the dance evolved, both during and after its creation. The second phase encompasses a much wider consideration of primary and secondary evidence (potential). The element of choice is more far-reaching because the scale of material is greater, and this secondary phase would encompass use of a Labanotation score, for example.

To expand on this idea in relation to the first phase, the actual evidence for these dances is rooted in what Humphrey has said about the nature of the work, the theme, the choice of music, the characters (if these exist) — any indication from her of how this work came into being, and such indications do exist. Visual references can make a valuable contribution, if they can be directly attributed to the choreographer. A filmed version of the work directed by the choreographer could be termed a primary source, as can photographic evidence, although Humphrey was known to create poses that were not actually in the dance but would fit into a photographer's studio.[43] A further indicator is Humphrey herself, dancing during the period of time when the work was created, illustrative of dynamic and how she actually executed movement. One example from John Mueller's film *The Four Pioneers* (1965) is a short excerpt from *Duo Drama* (1935), in which Humphrey and Weidman execute a series of side leaps, falls, and tilts that are consistently weighted and have a sense of abandon and verve — a clear indicator of stylistic quality. There are further examples filmed at the Bennington Summer Schools and housed in the Humphrey Collection at the New York Public Library. *Doris Humphrey* (ca. 1938) includes footage of Humphrey demonstrating the circular fall, relevant for *Water Study*. The film also has two excerpts from *Passacaglia*. In one, Humphrey dances the "turn solo" and "bell" theme, and in the second she rehearses a group of women in excerpts from the work. *Young America Dances* (1939) shows brief fragments of Humphrey and Weidman dancing and of Humphrey teaching class. *Students and Teachers at Bennington* (ca. 1939) has footage of the Humphrey falls (side, back, and spiral) and again is relevant for *Water Study*. While film may not be as useful in determining intention, it would clearly have value here, as the footage that exists is sparse but clear.

It is unlikely that a consensus will ever be reached on issues of authenticity and intention — a healthy state, to my mind. In the 1990s, for example, a lively if vociferous debate erupted in the field of early music. Two distinct positions emerged, both of which can relate to dance. The debate revolved around the playing of original instruments or not, of playing from the perspective of the scholar — from the basis of textual historical evidence — or playing from the perspective of the performer, and the significance of seeking the composer's intention or not. The distinctions lay in what being authentic meant, the methods by which this was achieved, and the nature of the end product, the performance. Those who took the first position include Christopher Hogwood, David Munrow, Roger Norrington, and Trevor Pinnock. To this group, playing the original instruments was a crucial link to and part of the textual historical evidence, meaning that the route to the composer's "intention" lay through such engagement. Musicologists Richard Taruskin, Nicholas Temperley, and Will Crutchfield advocate the second position, favoring an approach to the music that is located in and through the performer and the performance given. They dismiss the need for specific instruments and the "instruction manual," believing that the composer's intention cannot be found and should not be sought.

Taruskin rejects the textual approach "because it places the chief emphasis on factors external to the music performed and can actually subvert any real interpretation."[44] Crutchfield shares his view: "The authenticity of a performance is to be understood in terms of the sources of the performance; and these lie within the person who is performing."[45] For this second group, the authenticity of a performance is determined not by the evocation of the author's intent but by the performer through the performance given. On the same side of the debate, Nicholas Kenyon comments: "Once composers have written their music, they 'let go' of it and it is up to posterity to do what it wants with it."[46] Pianist Wanda Landowska gives an example of this approach in her comments about playing Rameau. She asserts that if the composer were alive today, she would say to him: "You gave birth to it; it is beautiful. But now leave me alone with it. You have nothing more to say; go away!"[47] It is worth noting that Landowska was not quite as cavalier as her statement might suggest. She actively sought an affinity with the composer not through scholarly historical means but through the music: "By living intimately with the works of a composer I endeavour to penetrate his spirit, to move with an increasing ease in the world of his thoughts."[48] Arguably, Landowska's approach is as valid as any other because the degree of immersion in the music that she ascribes to is suggestive of a considered and meaningful study of and relationship with the work. She did not dismiss the composer from the process but exercised her choice as a creative artist in how his presence was incorporated. For Landowska, this came through *her* interpretation of the musical manuscript. The interpretive freedom advocated by Landowska, Taruskin, and others is further reflected in the relationship they feel they have with the composer and with the music, as equals.

## Theatrical Parallels

I referred earlier to the approach to *Passacaglia* changing from a reconstructive mode to an interpretive one in the 1995 production process. This was largely due to the discovery of a recording of the music by Leopold Stokowski and dealing with the very different "sound" his orchestration created in comparison with the more traditional, steady tempo of other organ and orchestral versions. I had not intentionally set out to do something different, but it became clear that I had to because of this new variable and, further, that these processes paralleled some forms of theater practice. Not only that, the experience of having to take a different approach made the dance come alive in new ways that, in turn, sent me off on another trail to consider "interpretation" in a much broader context. I undertook an analysis of two distinctive traditions of theater practice: Shakespearean production and the work of Samuel Beckett. The purpose was to observe directorial choices made within these diverse contexts and to determine whether these practices could be transposed to modern dance. I chose Shakespeare because of the range of variant interpretations his work has been subject to alongside its eclectic performance history and Beckett because of the rigid copyright procedures and restrictions imposed on the staging of his work. I had assumed early on that the precisely scripted dialogue and choreographic nature of Beckett's stage directions would create a play text similar to a Labanotation score. This assumption, happily for dance if not for Beckett, was not born out as my investigations went deeper.

The production of Shakespeare presents its own historical challenges for the director beyond the specter of the author. Peter Brook urges avoidance of the "definitive" mind-set: "Anybody's personal view of the play is bound to be less than the play itself." To emphasize the point further, he comments that the plays "are always more than the last interpretation trying to say the last word on something on which the last word can't be said."[49] Brook's inference is appealing, suggesting that, no matter what, the power of the work is greater than any human interference. Jonathan Miller makes a similar observation: "Each time a play is staged the production is inevitably a limited version of the range of possible interpretations."[50] In relation to his interpretation of *A Midsummer Night's Dream*, Miller asked: "What does a fairy look like?"[51] His question could equally describe the task facing any director working from a play text or score, that of creating a reality from an intangible ideal, with the ephemeral nature of the fairy serving as an allegory for the act of interpretation. Miller's question could be taken further in terms of how the ephemeral is determined and, when transposed to the play text, how the message and spirit of a play can be captured and made real. The "reality" created by the director contains the answer and, arguably, will have as many variations as there are productions.

Integral to the directorial process is the relationship between the elements of a work and how these are interpreted, including vocabulary, phrasing, rhythm, setting, narrative, design, and accompaniment. Adrian Noble notes that "there's a danger for us directors in being over-attracted to one element of the play, and thereby, through the lack of water, allowing another element of the play to wither and die."[52] American director Emily Mann talks about "keeping everything going, taking in everything, to preserve all the variety and yet keep a clear line going for the audience."[53] Noble, likewise, emphasizes the need for "creating a world that is logical," as does Nagle Jackson: "Above all the director is the audience's advocate. It is his responsibility to see that the story is told with clarity and interest, and without extraneous clutter."[54] When these comments are considered in relation to the direction of a dance work, there are no differences. The common intent is to create a work that engages an audience.

In terms of interpretation, director Robert Benedetti suggests that the directorial approach can be categorized, which, in turn, can have a bearing on how a work is interpreted. He provides a model that could also be applied to dance works, using a political metaphor to distinguish between approaches: conservative (fidelity), liberal (relevance), and radical (creative).[55] The first approach, for which one could also read "conserve" and "conservation," has a direct parallel in dance with reconstruction and re-creation. Benedetti describes the value of this approach in certain instances, citing medieval morality plays and outdoor Shakespeare productions. One can also determine resonances here with the debate in early music. The parallel is constant across the three art forms in that certain forms of production, such as the playing of original instruments, the re-creation of Humphrey's *Air for the G String*, the staging of mystery plays, and Chaucer's *Canterbury Tales*, have significance for audiences who respond to this type of performance.

The liberal point of view, according to Benedetti, "holds that the value of a play lies in the way it lives relevant to the present moment, and that a successful production results when the essential spirit of the play, transmitted by but not entirely bound in the text, is happily married to the specifics of a given cast, theatre and audience, even if this requires some adjustment in the play's form such as changes in period, language, or even structure."[56] He defines this further: "Whilst there is much which is 'creative' about this way of working, it also requires a dominant sense of responsibility to the original, which both inspires and limits the director's purely personal creative impulses," citing Brook's *A Midsummer Night's Dream* as an example.[57] The significant point is that the interpretation evolves from the work and is not something imposed through external factors. Brook himself warns against "using" a play and having a particular interpretation in mind, regardless of what the text actually contains: "The play is then no longer a vehicle for re-exploration. . . . [I]t becomes a vehicle for exploitation."[58]

Benedetti's radical position "eschews the forms of the past altogether and returns to the source of a play in order to generate new forms inspired by the original; thus the text may, for the radical director, be only a source of inspiration for a new intuitive creative process."[59] Here, one can compare directors like Robert Wilson and Robert Lepage with contemporary choreographer/directors such as Mats Ek, Matthew Bourne, and Mark Morris. Productions of *Giselle* (Ek), *Swan Lake* (Bourne), and *Dido and Aeneas* (Morris) can reside within the radical position because they are far removed from a more traditional reading of these works. Prior to these particular productions, one would not normally have expected male casting for the roles of Dido or the swans or the setting of *Giselle* in a modern-day asylum.

Benedetti's model was particularly useful in identifying the kinds of approaches that were emerging in my own practice. An initial expectation had been that productions would reside within his liberal approach due to the artistic parameters of working within Humphrey's tradition, with the radical end of the spectrum seeming too far removed. Paradoxically, it was the very act of working "within" the tradition that extended my creative boundaries. The interpretation of one work, *The Shakers*, could be defined as radical according to Benedetti's definition and was a seemingly natural consequence of exploring Humphrey's vocabulary in a contemporary context.

The Shakespearean play text compares well with the dance score because Labanotation could follow other notation systems, such as written text and music notation, and survive for centuries. In terms of insight into a work, my view had been that a play text or music score gave more to the director than a Labanotation score because the notation score contains some but not all of the essential information needed to bring a work to life. A consensus among practitioners favoring a performer-centered approach, however, suggests that a score or text should be regarded only as a part of the process. In his essay "The Authentic Shakespeare," Stephen Orgel makes two connecting points. First, when Shakespeare wrote a play, he "habitually began with more than he needed [in order] to offer the company a range of possibilities." Second, "the text is the basis of the performance, but the performance is an independent entity."[60] Orgel's observations imply a deliberate openness on Shakespeare's part. While it may not be the case with all playwrights, the performance history and traditions of Shakespeare's work have certainly encouraged interpretation. The interpretive stance is endorsed by a number of directors, including Miller, who regards the text as an "aid" to performance, and Giorgio Strehler, who comments that Shakespeare left a situation or relationship between characters vague because he meant to do so.[61] The interpreter, therefore, needs to remain open to the possibility that the creator did not intend to make everything abundantly clear and that some situations were left, perhaps, for the performers to explore. There are examples of such "possibility" within the Humphrey repertoire, including the roles of the Matriarch in *With My Red Fires* and the Eldress in *The Shakers*, where phrases are left open for improvisation despite movement being notated in the score. One example from *The Shakers* is the action written for the Eldress in the "Second Revelation," referred to in the score as "Recovery for the Eldress ad lib. A vague wavering motion leading into (bar) 31."[62] There are other such examples for this role and for the Matriarch in *With My Red Fires*, notably in sections of the work when the action attributed to this character acts as a focal point for the group.

Brook notes that Shakespeare was writing not in any personal way but of reality: "It's not Shakespeare's view of the world, it's something which actually resembles reality. A sign of that is that any single word, line, character or event has not only a large number of interpretations, but an unlimited number."[63] His comment suggests a continuing evolution in how the play text can be read, a position supported by Raymond Berry: "The production itself cannot be judged by its supposed fidelity to the Urtext of the myth, the words of the Folio. Rather, it must harness the myth's energies to a new pattern that holds meaning for us."[64] Berry draws a further parallel with Benedetti's liberal/ transposed model and White's "recognizable form." Miller defines a successful interpretation "by the extent to which the text now speaks with more or less coherent vitality."[65] Elizabeth LeComte talks of "the inherent lifelessness [of the text] without the intervention of an interpretive or outside consciousness."[66] These directors confirm my position for directing dance because the play text is viewed without restriction, allowing scope for maneuver and greater possibility for a fresh approach that can hold meaning for a contemporary audience.

Orgel's view on openness is further affirmed by Susan Bennett through this observation: "If authenticity and/or originality are impossible with the recognized theatrical script, those fetishized traces of the initial collaboration and improvisation now known as King Lear, it might be more productive to turn critical attention to some contemporary improvisation with and around those same textual traces."[67] Her remarks suggest that because Shakespeare came to his script through a collaborative process, it makes sense to continue this approach, as opposed to trying to re-create what cannot be re-created: "Authenticity, we know, is impossible: we cannot reproduce (since we do not know) the original conditions of Shakespeare's stage or text and all performances, by virtue of the genre itself, are necessarily different."[68] The late Sam Wanamaker and Mark Rylance would no doubt have taken issue with this position since the re-emergence of the Globe Theatre in London. For them, reproducing the original conditions of Shakespeare's stage was at the very heart of their artistic conviction, not unlike the early music position on original instruments. The issue of text, however, is separate because the location of a production does not necessarily determine the textual approach.

Cutting and amending a play text is a practice commonly associated with Shakespeare, perhaps more so than with other playwrights. The views cited here indicate a range of practice, illustrating that directors hold diverse ideas about what matters and, in turn, what best suits their own individual artistic endeavor. Trevor Nunn, for example, claims that "the cutting virtually is the production. What you decide to leave in is your version of the play."[69] Brook feels that some plays are tighter than others. He would never cut *A Midsummer Night's Dream* because to do so would diminish the play, though other plays could be cut with caution: "I think that this is really something for which there are no rules except the rules of sensitivity, that what in one line doesn't really matter in another line matters like hell."[70] Peter Hall prefers not to cut at all.[71] Michael Bogdanov will only do so if he feels it is essential, not just to shorten the evening for the audience.[72] Miller, conversely, cuts freely, as does Liviu Ciulei: "A line which holds up the action is in my way."[73] Ciulei is describing a production of *Hamlet* from which he cut over half an hour but also employed a text consultant to check the reshaped text. Coming from a different perspective but with a similar outcome, Strehler talks about not making "cuts" as such but of looking for a different way of representing the text.[74] This approach may involve omitting passages but with the omissions acknowledged for the audience. Robert Wilson takes "reshaping" even further by moving scenes, reassigning speeches, repeating words, and adding interludes because of the emphasis placed on the visual symbolism he is creating onstage.[75] One example is a production of *King Lear* in which he interwove three separate scenes involving each of the three sisters into one scene for all three. In so doing, he gave a new meaning to the relationships between these characters.

The idea of reshaping can have two meanings: first, that the text continues to have a coherent line through it, and second, that the ideas contained within the text are molded into a contemporary understanding. Lawrence Levine discusses this point in his essay "William Shakespeare and the American People." He concludes that such changes did not distort the text "but rather heightened the qualities in Shakespeare that American audiences are particularly drawn to."[76] Perhaps this is a further example of White's recognizable form. Levine's point not only addresses contemporary cultural relevance and understanding but also brings in the issue of something becoming acceptable through preference. Orgel cites Desdemona's "Willow Song" in *Othello*, which is invariably ascribed to Shakespeare, although there is strong evidence to indicate that he did not write it. As Orgel states, "Quite simply, it is Shakespeare's because it appears in a Shakespeare play and, more important, because we like it."[77]

The decision making on the shape of the play text may begin with the director, but for the work to retain vitality, it needs to be given the chance to evolve through the rehearsal process and through the performers. Such a process brings in the interrelated aspects of rhythm, tempo, and style, and here again are parallels for dance. Trevor Nunn and Robin Phillips cited productions where they had not trusted the rhythm of the text, and in retrospect both deemed this to have been a mistake.[78] Their conclusion infers the existence of a significant factor within the text. The most obvious example from Humphrey's work is *Water Study* because it has no musical accompaniment nor articulated counts. It does, however, have a very particular rhythm that, if not present, renders the dance facile. This "rhythm" goes beyond the dancers setting a tempo in performance. It is about the director locating and subsequently generating, through the dancers, the inherent physiological and dynamic impulses that together create the rhythm of the dance. Emily Mann talks about slowing down the tempo of a scene that alters the speech without changing the text, indicating that emphasis can be modified while content remains.[79] This aspect could be even more influential in dance because of the existence of multiple musical recordings and the fact that the rhythm, tempo, and style of the music can have a significant impact on the interpretation of the dance. One of the clearest examples from Humphrey's work is *Passacaglia* because the available options range from a steady organ arrangement to a far more colorful and romanticized orchestral score.

Rhythm and tempo can have a direct influence on style. If, for example, the speed is too slow or too fast, stylistic indicators may become incongruous or difficult to read. Shakespeare provides a useful reference point for dance in relation to language. There is a distinct style in relation to speaking a Shakespearean text that could equate with dancing in a particular choreographic style. Benedetti observed that "style is the medium through which the 'message' of action is conveyed, it endows that action with its specific quality and meaning," equally relevant in a movement context.[80] He comments further that the "aim in production is to manifest the particular reality of the play not only by telling the story but also by capturing the precise tone, texture, and meaning of the action as communicated by the play's style. Only then will we have produced an authentic manifestation of the essential life of the play."[81] This point could also be interpreted as capturing and articulating the ideas and spirit of the work in a language that is stylistically accurate.

Sir Peter Hall is noted for the significance he places on the speaking of the text.[82] For him, style is fundamental and encompasses understanding of the verse structure, the phrase rhythm, and the intonation. Kristin Linklater, former voice coach and colleague at the Royal Shakespeare Company, explains why: "If the plays are spoken and performed . . . and if the sounds of the words and rhythms of the language are felt, Shakespeare's voice will call to the voices of eloquence that live in everyone."[83] I interpret her remarks as saying that for the playwright's message to be understood, it needs to be conveyed in a specific way. Other Shakespearean directors may debate Linklater's point, but, for the form of modern dance I am concerned with, it is highly relevant because of the significance of style in relation to identifying a particular choreographer's work.

The location or setting of a play is a further element open to interpretation. Bill Alexander suggests that the play itself should determine its setting, an identifiable approach from my perspective because the work is at the forefront, supported by the director's imagination. Alexander discusses three basic categories for setting a play that could also work in a dance context. These categories are "Elizabethan," meaning as it was written; "transposed" to some other period in order "to create a complete social context to unleash the play"; and "eclectic," which ranges from "fairly neutral to very abstract and amazing and adventurous, but it is essentially a world of the stage rather than the world of a society."[84] Combining his categorization with the Benedetti model creates a breadth that, in turn, provides a useful framework for considering the extent to which co-authorship can exist in the interpretive process.

The definitions of the first category—"conservative" (Benedetti)/ "Elizabethan" (Alexander)—are similar in that the focus for both is on the text as it was written. The creative opportunities are limited, as would be the participation of the director as co-author. The definitions of the second category— "liberal" (Benedetti)/"transposed" (Alexander)—encompass creative change, and there is a marked shift in the relationship between director, work, and author. Alexander argues that a transposed work is set in a particular time and context so that the ideas contained within the play are coherent for a contemporary audience. An example is his production of *The Merry Wives of Windsor*, which he located in the 1950s because he identified that particular time as having a societal balance that was reflected in the play. Benedetti presents a similar viewpoint when he remarks that the director is engaged in translating the essential meaning of the play from one time to another or from one set of cultural or theatrical assumptions to another.[85] Miller makes the following observation about his own production of *The Taming of the Shrew*: "When I tried to modernise the play, it was not in the sense of setting it in the present but of looking much more carefully, through contemporary eyes, at what it was expressing in the past."[86] This does not preclude setting the production in a different time and may well mitigate such a decision, because "what it was in the past" may only be clear today by expressing it "in" the present. Benedetti further illustrates this point when he talks about modernizing "not merely to make the play easier or more entertaining for the modern audience, but rather to manifest as much of the play's power as possible."[87]

The third category — "radical" (Benedetti)/"eclectic" (Alexander) — is more divergent. Benedetti refers to "the source of the play generating new forms" and notes, further, that "the text may be a source of inspiration for a new intuitive creative process."[88] The degree of creative participation, therefore, extends beyond liberal parameters. Alexander's eclectic position, ranging from "fairly neutral to very abstract, amazing and adventurous," seemingly embraces a broader range of practice that would include Benedetti's radical and liberal interventions. Robert Lepage's 1995 production of *Elsinore* is an example that straddles both the radical and eclectic definitions. Lepage created, directed, and acted in this one-man show based on *Hamlet*, which toured internationally, including the Edinburgh International Festival. He describes his play as "assembling in a single person all the aspects of the universe of Elsinore."[89] He devised the new work through Shakespeare's text, both drawing on and accentuating specific themes, including the incestuous nature of the relationships between the characters. This process, in turn, guided the creation of the new text.[90] Conversely, Peter Brook's *A Midsummer Night's Dream* could also be categorized as eclectic but is defined as liberal in Benedetti's model, an illustration of the divergence between the two models.

Further examples of the range of interpretive intervention can be found in the work of Deborah Warner, discussed in more detail shortly, and Phyllida Lloyd. I observed Lloyd in rehearsal for her production of Verdi's *Requiem* at the London Coliseum in December 2000. Lloyd transformed a work traditionally presented in oratorio form in the concert hall into a full-scale theatrical event and did so by creating a narrative that had not previously existed. From the libretto used by Verdi, Lloyd's narrative developed through a series of collaborative and improvisation-based workshops devised with movement director Kate Flatt. While Lloyd created a new form of the work, she did not actually create a new work, as Verdi's *Requiem* was still there in its entirety. The result was a visual and dramatic interpretation that could not but influence the audience's perception, whether they were coming to the work for the first time or with seasoned experience. With a "new" narrative, some might consider Lloyd's approach radical. In relation to the Benedetti and Alexander models, however, the resulting production would be defined as liberal, because the "work" is still a formative part of the process, and transposed because of the setting and accompanying recognizable experience. Lloyd opted for the fundamental fear of death in its variant stages and the subsequent confrontation through the horror of a plane crash.

## Battling Beckett

The examples given above illustrate the freedom directors can have with certain genres of work. When starting to research theater practice, I mistakenly assumed that freedom of interpretation operated across the board. It soon became apparent that this was not the case. There is unquestionably a range of interpretive practice. More significantly, there is also a range of interpretive parameters enforced by estates and foundations holding the copyright to certain playwrights, including Beckett and Brecht. It is important to consider the staging of "restricted" texts, therefore, because of perceived similarities with dance reconstruction. Beckett proved to be an illuminating comparison. The explicit stage directions and level of detail in his play texts added a further parallel with the Labanotation score. In his landmark book, *The Empty Space*, Peter Brook defines the staging of a Beckett play as encompassing "intense work, rigorous discipline, absolute precision."[91] Billie Whitelaw, regarded by many as Beckett's "muse," commented during the original production of *Footfalls* in 1976: "I realised why for most of his plays, Beckett writes such incredibly detailed stage directions—with maps and diagrams, showing exactly how one should walk, how many paces to take this way or that. He did this in the hope that his intentions concerning the staging of a piece should be absolutely clear."[92]

Unlike the Shakespearean canon, Beckett's work is under the custodial aegis of an estate, a situation similar to the majority of modern dance choreographers, including Doris Humphrey. Estates play an important role, with custodians responsible for preserving an artistic legacy, allowing the work to live on beyond the artist. The Humphrey estate takes a liberal approach, acknowledging in the terms of the performance contract that directors can "keep the works alive" by creating a more contemporary feel in terms of production. This is not always the case, however, and preservation can evolve into stultifying protection. There may be justification in the eyes of estate custodians for such "protection." Equally, there is a potent argument for the relinquishing of rigid control and allowing the works to live on as organic entities.

Deborah Warner made such an argument following the furor surrounding her production of Beckett's *Footfalls* in 1994. This very public row ultimately resulted in the play being taken off and Warner receiving a lifetime ban by the Beckett estate because she had altered the text and stage directions. The text "alteration" referred to three lines transposed from one character to another. On hearing the estate's objections, Warner restored the lines before opening night. The ban, however, remained. When asked if she felt the ban was censorious, she replied, "Absolutely. My work was a serious, careful approach through text, and in the name of Beckett, not 'Deborah Warner messes with Beckett.'"[93] Warner's interpretation of *Footfalls* involved partially locating the action in the circle of the auditorium, with the audience in the stalls, and was a radical departure from the original staging. This change of perspective was further enhanced by the lighting design, which focused tightly on the central figure, played by Fiona Shaw. These aspects were integral to the meaning of the play as discovered by director and performer through the rehearsal process, the basis of which had been Beckett's text. The inspiration, therefore, came from the playwright via his text.

In tracking this event further, I uncovered evidence that made clear Warner did nothing that had not been done before with Beckett's work, and, further, she was not setting any precedents by changing Beckett's staging directions. Susan Letzler Cole observed Peter Sellars in rehearsal for *Ohio Impromptu* in 1986. She notes: "Although he makes no changes at all in the text of the play, the director violates almost all of the playwright's directions for set, lighting, costumes and physical placement of the actors in relation to each other."[94] While Warner's vision evolved through a collaborative rehearsal process, Sellars's was a conscious rejection of Beckett's directions from the outset and was presented to actors David Warrilow and Richard Thomas as such. Sellars's production took place during Beckett's lifetime, and while there was no estate to contend with, there was, of course, the playwright himself. This appeared to hold little sway with the director, who commented, "I've never stopped in my life to think, 'What will the author think?' I feel what I'm doing is the only authentic production."[95] An analysis of Sellars's staging in comparison with Beckett's directions illustrates the point that while the vision may change, the spirit of the work and its creator remains intact.

*Ohio Impromptu* is written for two characters, the Reader and the Listener, both of whom are seated at a table — rectangular and white in the text, square and brown in Sellars's production. The opening image is essentially the setting for the entire play. In the text, one figure is seated at the side of the table in profile, with the other figure sitting facing the audience at the back of the table. Sellars positioned both men in profile, side by side on a diagonal, the Reader to the left of the Listener. Cole notes: "They seem alternately and simultaneously a figure and his shadow as well as two distinct figures working in tandem."[96] This image is quite different from the one suggested by Beckett, but visually it is just as evocative. Sellars emphasized the relationship between the two figures with a deft play on audience manipulation. The play was performed twice. For the first run, the audience was taken into a dark, curtained-off space. The actors' voices were relayed from the performance space via a speaker system located behind and to the left of the audience, replicating the position of the Reader to the Listener. The audience was then brought into the performance space for the second run, having had this unwitting encounter with the text from the perspective of one of the play's protagonists. Sellars's intention was "to make them really hear the text before being distracted by seeing it."[97] A further device used by Sellars, borrowed from Japanese Noh theater, was the use of natural light. Beckett's direction states: "Light on table mid stage. Rest of stage in darkness."[98] Instead, Sellars chose a performing space with floor-to-ceiling windows specifically so that he could stage the play within natural light, knowing that the light would change through each performance and with the added uncertainty of weather conditions from performance to performance.

From this description it is clear that the Sellars production did not visually resemble the directions provided by the playwright. There remained a clear connection between the director and the playwright, however, through the creation of a startling and evocative theatrical experience, albeit very different. The question in relation to *Footfalls* is whether this was enough. The answer is twofold. In the playwright's lifetime it would appear to be so — Sellars's production caused no controversy, and its run was extended. After the playwright's death it would seem not, as Deborah Warner discovered to her and, arguably, the playwright's cost. Whitelaw writes: "Beckett didn't write this play [referring to *Footfalls*] for actors to 'experiment' with. The plays in themselves were experimental. He wanted them to be done as he wrote them."[99] In this instance, the intentions of the playwright are clear. Beckett stipulated in his will that the stage directions and text must be followed, and these instructions are part of a director's contract with the Beckett estate. Writing in support of Warner's production, theater critic Anna McMullan comments that while Beckett's extensive production notes would always exist and, therefore, could be consulted, there was also a place for perceiving new dimensions in his work, and directors should not be deterred from pursuing this, even if subsequent productions were deemed as failures.[100]

One of Warner's chief concerns was "to release the play for a new generation," reflective of Benedetti's liberal position. She observes: "The fact that the custodians of the estate preferred the play as it once was directed by Beckett himself means that the work is now effectively dead. Significantly so is the writer, and a dead man cannot arbitrate for future productions of his plays. I hope he'd be appalled by what happened. . . . [H]e was one of the great experimenters; so if one can't experiment to reinvent his work, he won't last the century, but be locked in an academic world."[101] Phyllida Lloyd echoes this view: "By placing a preservation order on a certain 'way' of producing a work, it may atrophy and refuse to speak to the audience of the moment."[102] This issue, relevant to any body of work governed by copyright, is illustrated further by Robert Butler in his review for the *Independent on Sunday* of Beckett's *Endgame*, directed by Katie Mitchell at the Donmar Warehouse, London: "It requires someone with Mitchell's scrupulous tenacity to rescue Beckett from his admirers. The text is replete with stage directions: three steps forward, two steps back, sniff, yawn, and so on. If that isn't inhibiting enough the Beckett industry threatens to submerge this wonderfully light footed playwright in a welter of reverential foot notes."[103]

Mitchell is a particularly good example because she is renowned for a directorial approach that is at once meticulous in terms of adherence to the text and visionary in what she is able to create.[104] There might seem to be a tension between these two positions, but it is the nature of Mitchell's approach to Beckett's text that creates space for this duality to operate. What does it mean to be meticulous in relation to the text? Defining "meticulous" as careful, detailed, and thorough rather than rigid or strict creates a relationship with the text that goes far deeper than an exact transposing of Beckett's lines and directions onto the stage. Mitchell's pre-production process involves getting inside the world of the play as she sees it. She achieves this through activities similar to those identified in early music and reconstruction in theater and dance. She is not, however, engaged in reconstruction but in interpretation, supported by methodologies that include researching the historical, social, political, and economic context in which a play both is written and takes place; learning about the art and architecture of the period in which the play is set; discovering as much as possible about the author; and taking trips with her designer to wherever a play is set to explore the environment. Mitchell's research process can take up to five months and is reminiscent of the processes Wanda Landowska, for example, undertook to seek affinity with a composer.

With regard to Beckett and her production of *Endgame*, Mitchell was able to locate the interpretive stimulation she needed from within the text as it stood by finding her way into the world of the play and the playwright through the research processes she employs. Warner's process is "through" the text as opposed to "within" it, drawing more heavily on the rehearsal experience and resulting interchange between director, actor, and text. The aspect of experimentation is key to Beckett and relates back to the Sellars production of *Ohio Impromptu* and the issue there of capturing the spirit of the playwright. As Sellars did, so, arguably, did Warner with *Footfalls*. For Warner herself, the ban was eventually lifted because of pressure from within the industry, but only on the proviso that she adhere absolutely to the text and given directions in any future productions. The media response to Warner's production was varied and heightened by the controversy. The play was both exulted and damned, but, most interestingly, those critics who wrote negatively about the production itself were supportive of the director's actions in principle. Theater critic Michael Billington in the *Guardian* observes: "I believe her production was misguided but should emphatically have been allowed to continue. And the Beckett estate, by its interference has unwittingly conceded that the author's later work is as circumstantially confined as its characters. Two wrongs don't make a right. What they suggest however is that the acid test of great drama is that it can survive limitless interpretation. Hamlet, Peer Gynt, Godot all pass; Footfalls doesn't."[105]

In the same article, Billington also notes that while there is room for interpretive maneuver in the likes of Chekhov, Shaw, and Shakespeare, Beckett should perhaps be a special case. Beckett, clearly, has a distinctive style, but that alone does not make him unique among playwrights. There is, however, the added complexity of the precise instructions left by the playwright on how his work should be treated. The fact that he left these instructions raises the question of whether the director has a moral obligation to adhere to the playwright's wishes. Billie Whitelaw's reaction to Warner's production was "sadly negative" and is relevant because the play was originally written and directed for her by Beckett.[106] Whitelaw's experience of this play and of Beckett's work in general always involved the participation of the playwright either as director or advisor. In one respect, this experience frames her position on the continuing production of his work because for her it had always been within a fixed set of parameters that can no longer be replicated because the playwright is dead. She and the Beckett estate are taking a position similar to that of the early music protagonists, who believed that a composer's intention could be found and should be demonstrated. Warner and Peter Sellars reside within the opposing position, where production and performance are based on interpretation. The directorial processes involved incorporate interpretive intervention through the nature of the relationship between director, work, and author and the degree of creativity encompassed in the directorial role. There is also a "middle ground" occupied by directors such as Mitchell who believe that the playwright's intention is significant but that its realization is through an interpretive process rather than a reconstructive one.

One interesting postscript indicates that the Beckett estate appeared to have a change of heart regarding its enforcement policy, illustrated by Charles Sturridge's production of *Ohio Impromptu* for television. The play aired on March 31, 2002, in Great Britain as part of the Beckett on Film series on Channel 4, with Jeremy Irons playing the roles of the Reader and the Listener simultaneously. The stage directions appear to have been followed as scripted, but with one fundamental difference or addition. Following the final speech, the figure of the Reader vanishes, seemingly into the ether, and the viewer is left with a startling final image that induces an instantaneous reassessment of the entire play. This image, and the resulting impact on the play itself, is created not by the author but by the director.

A more recent postscript relates to Warner's acclaimed production of *Happy Days* for the Royal National Theatre, London, on February 27, 2007, with Fiona Shaw playing Winnie. In a Platform event onstage, Warner recounted that she had not directed Beckett since the *Footfalls* debacle in 1994. Comments from both herself and Shaw made clear that it had been a deeply wounding episode. There was also a rueful reference to stage directions being followed in *Happy Days*. Both artists talked eloquently about their approaches to experimenting with the experimental in a confined context, but there was an undercurrent of regret. Warner did refer to elements of the play that she found open to interpretation. One example was the contrast in scale between Beckett's own production in 1976, seen by Warner in an intimate studio theater setting, and the expansive Lyttleton stage. The set design was an integral part of Warner's interpretation and was an extraordinarily evocative landscape — barren, vast, apocalyptic, and desperate. Warner had also been able to redefine the central character of Winnie through changing her age group from elderly to around fifty without any textual alteration. This change, in turn, affected Shaw's characterization. Shaw talked further about unpicking the directions in her mind, obeying the pauses and finding a freedom within the text. When asked if she would direct Beckett in the future, Warner replied that she had wanted to stage *Waiting for Godot* with Dame Maggie Smith and Shaw as Vladimir and Estragon, respectively, but the Beckett estate had refused permission. As Warner related this story, there was a collective sigh in the auditorium for what might have been with two of the most exceptional stage actresses of our time. The reaction was evidence perhaps that a theaterful of Beckett admirers were privileging the performer over the text, albeit in a hypothetical context.

Beckett's work is a particularly interesting example because of the precise documentation in the play texts coupled with the precise instructions he left for future productions. In one respect, Beckett made his intentions clear, and the estate is carrying out his wishes to the letter. Any director wishing to stage a Beckett play knows what is expected. The argument for supporting Warner's position, however, is equally compelling but for different reasons. Her predicament in 1994 engendered significant support, a support that continues today. Whichever side of the divide one favors, Beckett's work is not actually being disadvantaged. If one compares the diverse approaches of Mitchell and Warner, there is a shared care and integrity toward the work. One could lay this example alongside those from early music and identify similar parallels. The same is true for Benedetti's conservative, liberal, or radical model as it relates to productions by Brook, Miller, and Lepage and to dance reconstruction, re-creation, or interpretation by Cook, Stodelle, and myself.

The notion of a work represented in the first instance by a score or play text has currency across the performing arts. Earlier, the discussion indicated a general consensus from performer-centered practitioners that the realization of a work will also embody aspects the interpreter, director, or performer chooses to incorporate beyond the symbols or words on a page. Thus, the symbolized representation of a work serves as a vehicle through which it can be realized on the stage. The means of realization will differ, although not necessarily from genre to genre. The staging of an opera, for example, can incorporate many of the same directorial strategies employed in the staging of a Shakespeare play. One just has to look at the number of theater directors who regularly direct opera to see the range of practice at work in this crossover, including Peter Sellars, Jonathan Miller, Robert Wilson, and Phyllida Lloyd. What differs is how the score or play text itself is read and interpreted.

An associated issue to consider is "person transmission," a regular practice in dance, both classical ballet and modern dance, where past and current performers undertake staging works. Paul Taylor and the late Merce Cunningham routinely sent out their most experienced dancers to oversee stagings for other companies. Betty de Jong (Taylor) and Chris Komar (Cunningham) were rehearsal directors in addition to their extensive performing careers and thus were equipped with an overview and understanding of whole works. In considering "score versus person transmission," is one form better than the other? Not necessarily. There are certainly differences between the two and dangers inherent in both. There might be an argument for saying that a dance work is best staged by someone who has actually danced in it. Suppose, however, that individual has little idea about the parts of the work he or she did not perform? There might be another argument for saying that a Labanotation score should be regarded as "the work." Where does that leave the director's imagination and, indeed, the work itself in terms of any contemporized interpretation? And what about the positive aspects of both approaches? In the early years I spent with Stodelle, when she would recall the ideas and details Humphrey talked about in rehearsal, I had such a profound sense of touching history. It seeped into us and gave us a connection with the dances that can only come from someone who was "there." There is no other experience quite like that. There is, however, a different kind of experience, one that entails connecting with the creator by means other than being in the same room. Working from a document that is not fixed and finished allows a director to consider the available evidence and to make those connections, a process that can be both creative and imaginative.

A common thread across the performing arts is the relationship between the interpreter, the work, and the creator. Fundamental to this triangulation is that the relationship is balanced. Herein lies one difference between dance and the other art forms. In the process of reconstructing from a Labanotation score, it is the score that can become the privileged aspect of the triangle, with the remaining two aspects potentially having little influence. There are several ways this can play out. The first and most damaging is the situation where a score is reconstructed without stylistic knowledge or coaching. In this instance, the mechanics of symbol reading is at the forefront of the process, while an essential need of the work and, in turn, its creator is ignored. A second way is reconstruction from a score *with* stylistic knowledge and coaching. This form of production, as described earlier by Dils, resonates with the past but, importantly, has that direct connection with the creator through its means of expression, the dancing. A third way is the re-creation process as practiced by Stodelle and her successor, Gail Corbin. No score is involved because the dances are re-created through experience and memory, with stylistic knowledge implicit to the process because of the individuals involved.

There is a further way, incorporating an evenly balanced triangulation between interpreter, work, and creator. This triangulation is what differentiates between the director as interpreter and the reconstructor, because the latter is essentially working on behalf of the work and creator and, therefore, in a secondary role. The practice of reconstruction is not at issue, however, and developing these new directorial strategies has not been driven by a need to "replace." I offer, rather, a move beyond what we already know, a move that allows deeply valued dance works a broader existence that accommodates the ephemerality of the art form without losing the integrity of the individual work. Drawing on ideas and acknowledging points of identification with current practice in theater and music have indeed been useful. However, the layering of these ideas alongside those from Collingwood, White, and others has created a position that embodies historical credibility with interpretive freedom. The dance stories that follow in part 2 illustrate the possibilities.

# PART TWO

# Exploring the
# Creative Impulse

The diverse approaches taken with these four Humphrey dances illustrate the kinds of positions available to the contemporary director when dealing with the past. Ideas borrowed and adapted from other disciplines have provided a way forward in supplementing and extending existing practices. Collingwood's notion of the "living past" alongside White's "recognizable form" and Eliot's premise that "the past alters the present as much as the present directs the past" are central to an interpretive stance. The implication is that nothing is fixed or immovable, but at the same time there is a foundation to take into account and use as an underpinning. The implied emphasis on "historical imagination" provides a framework from which the contemporary interpreter can then operate.

The living past concept implies continuing evolution. Collingwood provides a useful illustration through the Hegelian spiral cited earlier: "history travelling in spirals, with apparent repetitions differentiated by having acquired something new."[1] The spiral and its acquisitions become clear through applying this idea to a single instance of a work's performance history: the center of the spiral is Humphrey's original production; dancers in the original production perform it many times with numerous cast changes; these direct descendant dancers stage the work for a subsequent generation of dancers who have had no exposure to the source, the choreographer, but who do possess an immersion in the style and philosophy; dancers from this generation pass it on again, in a time when dance technique and training have changed out of all recognition in the eighty-plus years since the spiral began. If nothing else about the dance is consciously altered, the passing of time creates an evolution. This same notion can be applied to a director's process, with past experiences of a work having an inevitable impact on any subsequent interpretation. Both examples indicate the capacity for change within the seemingly fixed entity of the work itself.

Adopting the Collingwood stance on evidence provides the freedom to look at a body of evidence from the present and, further, to consider it without restriction. Privileging evidence is an important aspect of Collingwood's "actual/ potential" viewing model. In choosing which parts of the evidence to accept, new frameworks of enquiry can be created from which to explore a dance. I chose to privilege evidence directly attributable to Humphrey as the starting point for each interpretation because the connection back to the source is central to my motivation. That connection is not limiting, in terms of imposing fixed parameters; rather, it creates a credible reference point from which to begin. Engaging with the evidence from a fluid standpoint allows for "possibility" rather than fixed "certainty." The presence of possibility in turn creates the potential for new interpretation, and herein lies the attraction of an idea such as the historical imagination. If one approaches a work with discovery at the forefront of the process, there is a strong likelihood that one will uncover something new and fresh. The "new discovery" may indeed transmit as far as the audience, the most extreme of my examples being *The Shakers/The Chosen*, but not necessarily, because the discovery aspect can relate as well to the directorial process, as illustrated through *Water Study*.

The selection of evidence can make sense of themes, ideas, and situations from the present, no matter what period setting a work might have. White's notion of the "recognizable, familiar form" is helpful because it can be applied as a yardstick of understanding throughout an interpretive process. The crafting of selected evidence and ideas creates the first instance of a recognizable form—for the director at least. From there, the "form" is explored, fleshed out, expanded upon, further defined until it is made sense of by the performers through the rehearsal process. The final instance is the production itself in its moment of performance for an audience.

A related idea is that of "reshaping" a work, a device applied to two of the four Humphrey works but from different standpoints in each case. The reshaping of *With My Red Fires* was driven by a sociocultural imperative alongside narrative exploration, whereas the reshaping of *The Shakers* came about through creative exploration of the choreographic structure and vocabulary. These examples illustrate that divergent approaches are possible for dance works. One can make the same claim in relation to an individual work, with each new interpretation offering the possibility for a different approach, much in the same manner as exists in theater practice. A sociocultural/narrative approach could work as well for *The Shakers* given the dramatic possibilities and contemporary cognizance of a religious sect, community, or cult. The same approach applied to *With My Red Fires* but with a single-sex couple in the lead roles instantly changes the meaning of the work. The permutations are not limitless, otherwise one would produce a "radical" creation each time, but they are broad enough to find new ways into the dance without disrupting the dance itself.

Manning's application of a continuum framework to analyze reconstructed dance works was discussed in part 1. Adopting this construct helped me identify the degree of interpretive and creative intervention that occurred across the four production processes. Similarly, applying the Benedetti radical/liberal/conservative model enabled me to place what I was doing with each work within a coherent context. I chose these particular dances because they represent, arguably, Humphrey's most formative decade and are still performed regularly today. There was no deliberate intent to create four distinctive positions along a continuum framework, but it is interesting to observe that there *are* four distinct positions and to consider why this might have happened. The continuum runs *Water Study*, *Passacaglia*, *With My Red Fires*, *The Shakers*. I expected "change" at the outset of each production process, and I assumed that the degree of change would differ from work to work, influenced by my creative tendencies toward abstraction and contemporization. I applied abstraction in each work relating to one specific element. Identifying that element and exploring its possibilities created a new understanding and interpretation of the work. In *Water Study*, the abstracted element was a specific movement, the forward successional curve; in *Passacaglia*, it was the sound of the Stokowski orchestration; in *With My Red Fires*, it was Humphrey's underlying themes of intolerance and bigotry; and in *The Shakers*, it was a particular phrase, the nine-count phrase.

Alongside discussion and analysis of each work, I offer recent production processes to illustrate the range of identified strategies in practice.

# WATER STUDY

*Choreography*: 1928
*Premiere*: October 28, 1928, Civic Repertory Theater, New York

*Water Study* opens with an ensemble of fourteen dancers clad in skin-toned unitards, arrayed across the stage in asymmetrical formation, bent low to the ground in profile. A series of ripples emerges through the backs of the dancers, who are in a tucked, kneeling position, and traverses the space, one picking up from the other until the outward surge gives way to a receding pull back to its point of origin.

This "first wave" builds subtly into a second, more expanded form, which advances and recedes. The third, fourth, and fifth forms come after, ever growing in speed, height, and intensity until the form dissolves and separates. From either side of the stage, dancers swing, run, leap, and fall in opposition, creating new forms that pull away, lifting far above the ground before falling, crashing in toward each other. The ensemble is drawn together to one side, then falls as one, back and forth across the stage. Bodies spill forward or arc high, suspended over the tumbling forms below. These "tumblesaults" give way to increasingly expansive and powerful surging runs up and down a diagonal pathway, climaxing in a burst that fragments the group, some racing out and around the stage, others being drawn into sweeping, descending falls, reminiscent of the drag of an undertow. Calm returns, but stillness is some way off.

Rocking, undulating shifts crisscross the space, in time returning the bodies to the low, tucked position of the opening sequence. There is a final flurry, a "spray" cascading across the group before the pull of the tide rolls across the

Figure 1. Opening. *Water Study* re-created by Ernestine Stodelle for Silo Concert Dancers, 1986. Photographer: Jennifer Lester.

Figure 2. "15 Rocking Waves." *Water Study* re-created by Ernestine Stodelle for Silo Concert Dancers, 1986. Photographer: Jennifer Lester.

stage one final time. Darkness comes, but the movement, it seems, will go on, and on, and on.

One of the great pleasures of working in dance is dealing with the elusive ephemerality of movement on a daily basis. The constant challenge of finding and re-finding technical mastery and dynamic quality so (seemingly) secure one day and (seemingly) gone the next is at once thrilling and daunting, a state of being no different for the director as for the dancer. I am reminded of early attempts at side swings and successions from *Water Study* after months away from the dance and how hopeless these feel for the first day or so until muscle memory kicks in. I learned early the wisdom of preparing in good time for a first rehearsal.

The production processes discussed elsewhere in this book all incorporate degrees of interpretive change. *Water Study* presents a different proposition. An ensemble dance for a cast of ten to fourteen, it has no musical accompaniment other than breath rhythms. The work offers little scope for interpretive intervention in terms of its vocabulary, structure, design, and form, and, frankly, no director worth his or her salt would consider tampering with it. Marcia Siegel describes *Water Study* as "perfect," "one of the most extraordinary works in American dance," and "still one of the most stunning achievements in abstract dance."[1] Deborah Jowitt, agreeing, observes that it "beautifully expresses the analogy between the human being and universal processes."[2] Despite Siegel's notion of abstract dance and Jowitt's metaphysical interpretation, the work does conjure up images of the movement of water and waves traversing through space, building in speed and intensity in a seamless flow of energy.

I first experienced the work as a dancer with Ernestine Stodelle and subsequently as her assistant in Europe. This combined exposure gave me a deep insight into the work. My own reconstructions never felt quite "right," however, and I couldn't discern why. This discussion details the exploration I undertook to find a new way into the dance without disrupting the dance itself.

## Performance History

As a Humphrey exponent, I regard *Water Study* as a cornerstone of Humphrey's tradition because it embodies the first representation of her movement philosophy.[3] Humphrey went on to formulate and articulate her philosophy over subsequent years, observing, "only much later did I find in Nietzsche a word expression of the meaning of these movements."[4] It was, in fact, in 1931, three years after choreographing *Water Study*, that she read *The Birth of Tragedy* (1872) and identified Nietzsche's Apollonian/Dionysian concept with her own theories of movement that she named "fall and recovery." Humphrey's movement philosophy encompasses the interconnecting aspects of breath rhythm, successional movement, gravitational pull, wholeness of movement, and moving from the inside out. She recognized the diametrically opposed urges toward danger and repose that Nietzsche ascribed to the two basic kinds of human beings, for "not only does the fall and recovery make movement living and vital, but it has psychological meaning as well. These emotional overtones were recognized very early by me and I instinctively responded to the exciting danger of the fall and the repose and peace of recovery."[5] Humphrey described the creation of this dance as "starting with human feeling, with body movement and its momentum in relation to the psyche and to gravity, and as it developed the movements took on the form and tempo of moving water."[6] Her intention was rooted in a broader need for experimentation. Her motivation was an exploration of natural movement and its relationship to natural forces, including the gravitational pull, rather than any conscious decision to create a dance "about" a specific theme.

A notebook of Humphrey's dated from this period contains the starting points for the work: "Nature moves in succession, usually in an unfolding succession to a climax and a more sudden succession to cessation or death."[7] Humphrey's emphasis on succession is key, because successional flow is a central aspect of the fall and recovery action. Her brief description also completely encapsulates the eventual structure of the dance itself as it grows from a state of stillness through a progressive series of rising crescendos to a point of climax that explodes into the sudden cessation she describes above. She concluded: "All natural movement must follow that law of nature — of which water is the best example to follow as it most nearly approximates the capacity of our rhythm and phrase length."[8] Rhythm, alongside successional flow, is at the root of the work. As Humphrey discussed in a program note from 1928, "probably the thing that distinguishes musical rhythm from other rhythm is the measured time beat, so this has been eliminated from the *Water Study* and the rhythm flows in natural phrases instead of cerebral measures. There is no count to hold the dancers together in the very slow opening rhythm, only the feel of the wavelength that curves the backs of the group."[9] There is, in actual fact, no "count" in the conventional sense at any point in the dance, one reason why dancing in or watching this work is so exhilarating.

*Water Study* was first performed at the Civic Repertory Theater in New York City on October 28, 1928, shortly after Humphrey and Weidman left Denishawn to set up as independent artists. Mary F. Watkins, dance critic at the *New York Herald Tribune*, found in the dance "the authentic feeling of the sea casting itself relentlessly, in torpid or in stormy mood, against the wall of some New England shore. Real genius has gone into the creating of this."[10] The work continued to receive acclaim in the coming years. In 1930 Watkins described *Water Study* as "inimitable," "calling forth the evening's loudest applause."[11] Margaret Gage in *Theatre Arts Monthly* wrote enthusiastically about Humphrey's work, describing *Water Study* and *Life of a Bee* as "typically modernistic, each expressing one central idea and unfolding it with clarity and completeness, yet with economy of detail."[12] In 1932 Watkins wrote of *Water Study*: "Perhaps the most remarkable of earlier group works, proved itself the peer of much that has come later."[13] During the Humphrey-Weidman Company's tour in 1935, Claudia Cassidy, critic for the *Chicago Journal of Commerce*, described *Water Study* as "strangely engaging," and Russell McLaughlin in Detroit thought *Water Study* "brilliant."[14]

Margaret Lloyd, longtime critic for the *Christian Science Monitor* and advocate for modern dance, talked about *Water Study* being "a novelty of its time and a delight to see."[15] The "novelty" aspect is not specified, but a strong possibility is the absence of music. Humphrey was not alone in exploring silence at that time, as she observed many years later in *The Art of Making Dances*, "for dance can dispense with sound almost entirely and be done in silence. This approach was particularly popular in the twenties and thirties, when many were intent on proving the thesis that dance was an independent art and could stand alone."[16] She continued:

> The dance without music—the absence of sound on a program which is otherwise ear-filling in musical opulence—has a contrary effect to that which might be expected. It does not seem empty, or as though the bottom has dropped out, but increases concentration and attention to movement to an astonishing degree. *Water Study* was composed for fourteen girls whose bodies rose and fell, rushed and leaped like various aspects of water, the only sound being the faint thudding of feet in running movements, reminiscent of surf. This was so striking that the Schuberts themselves—those canny showmen—put it intact into a revue called "Americana," where it was staged complete with blue cellophane floors, walls and front drop.[17]

A further "novelty" aspect was the cellophane "Americana" set conceived by Albert Johnson. The set pleased Humphrey because it made the dance look "very blue and watery."[18] Eleanor King, a member of the original cast, observed: "In our nude-colored leotards under blue lights . . . we danced with delight on that smooth, slightly crackling surface." King went on: "Not trusting a Broadway audience to sit still through something so new as a musicless dance,

Doris compromised to the extent that she had Pauline (Lawrence) stand in the wings to beat softly on an orchestra-sized gong, adding a muffled roar."[19]

It is not by historical chance that this work has survived where other ensemble works from that period have not. *Drama of Motion* (1930), *La Valse* (1930), *Dances of Women* (1931), all acclaimed at the time and in the Humphrey-Weidman repertoire for some years, were not subsequently brought back by Humphrey. *Water Study* and *The Shakers* are the most prominent ensemble survivors from her 1928 to 1931 period, and there are conclusive reasons why. Foremost was the popular appeal of both works throughout Humphrey's lifetime. The Broadway run of *Americana 1932*, for example, which included King and Stodelle, resulted in a four-month season of eight shows a week plus an out-of-town tryout in Philadelphia. Such regularity of performance was unusual in modern dance at the time, the norm being two or three performances every few months. The cumulative effect on movement memory was such that fine detail remained within the dancers' grasp decades after their initial exposure. King and Stodelle both contributed to the work's revival after Humphrey's death, but it was Stodelle's ongoing engagement that became especially important to the work's longevity. The publication of one Labanotation score in 1966 and a second in 1978 made regular reconstructions of the work possible within university modern dance programs in the United States and by professional companies, including the Limón Company and Repertory Dance Theatre.

The significance of the contribution by King and Stodelle to the continuing existence of *Water Study* should not be underestimated, yet it remains unacknowledged in virtually all existing literary references, including various analyses of the work. Stodelle was invited to restage the work at New York University in 1976, doing so in collaboration with King. In 1966 Odette Blum notated the work from a staging by Ruth Currier. Subsequent reconstructions from the Blum score, however, did not always incorporate clear stylistic dancing. Former Humphrey dancer Hyla Rubin wrote to King in 1974: "Recently I attended a revival of *Water Study* by the Ballet Company of Kennedy Center, Washington, D.C. Their ballet technique was insufficient for this work. Imagine, they couldn't do successions!"[20] It is all too easy to imagine. King's involvement with the work ceased at the end of that initial production in 1976, although she and Stodelle collaborated again on *The Shakers* in 1985. Stodelle went on to stage the work all over the world for professional companies and student dancers. In 1978 she was invited to stage her version in New York for a celebratory performance to mark the publication of the first volume of Humphrey's dances by the Dance Notation Bureau. At the end of the evening, she was presented onstage with the aforementioned volume containing the notation for Currier's version. Irony aside, DNB director Muriel Topaz had already commissioned a second score of Stodelle's version.[21] The issue goes beyond the existence of scores, however, and lies more in Rubin's observation on technique and style. Returning to Siegel's assertion that the dance is "perfect," I would agree but with a very large proviso, because the "perfection" Humphrey offers is utterly dependent on the stylistic quality of the dancing.

The existence of two Labanotation scores provides an example of conflicting evidence. The notators, Odette Blum for Currier's version (1966) and Karen Barracuda for Stodelle's (1978), include a significant amount of detail in terms of Effort writing on the score and introductory notes on style. There is also a greater proportion of Effort writing in these scores in comparison with other dances, which is appropriate given the "abstract" nature of this particular vocabulary. The question, however, is whether the level of detail is sufficient to give a complete enough indication of the stylistic demands. Blum's score, for example, does not include specific reference by word or symbol to fall and recovery, wholeness of movement, or the pelvic connection that is integral to every action. Her score does indicate pelvic movement but not as an initiating factor. Specific reference to and indication of these three key stylistic elements are essential in terms of conveying stylistic understanding. My reading of the accompanying notes in both scores is done from the perspective of knowing the work and the style intimately; hence, translating the meaning is unproblematic. For a reconstructor coming to this score from a different background, the question is whether these words and symbols can convey the root and foundation of the movement vocabulary and, thus, the work itself. While the notation for Blum's score was revised in 1998, the Dance Notation Bureau confirmed that the notes on style remained unchanged.

The structure of both scores is indicated in figure 3. Stodelle's version is in five sections, labeled A through E; the corresponding phrase numbers are used from the Blum score. Titles are those referred to by Stodelle and Blum. A comparative analysis of these two scores has proved intriguing. The introductory notes to the Blum score indicate that Stodelle contributed an alternate version, beginning with the fifth diagonal run, phrase 34, and continuing to phrase 45.[22] Sheila Marion suggests likewise in her analysis of the work from 1992: "The two versions vary principally in the arm movement for the final diagonal cross and the placement of the spiral," implying that the differences are even more minimal.[23] My observations are different. I identified sixteen significant differences in vocabulary, structure, and timing from the opening phrase running throughout the entire work.[24]

Performance notes by Stodelle and Gail Corbin are included in the Barracuda score.[25] Barracuda also performed in the 1976 staging at New York Uni-

| Stodelle / Barracuda | | Currier / Blum | |
|---|---|---|---|
| A | First 5 Waves | 1–9 | 5 Waves |
| B | Crashing breakers on rocks | 10–24 | — |
| C | Tumblesaults (waves rumbling out to sea) | 25 | — |
| D i) | Five big rushing waves | 26–35 | 5 Diagonals |
| D ii) | Splash/whirlpool with undertow | 36 | Splash/whirlpool |
| E i) | Calm returns | 37–61 | Calm undulating sea returns |
| E ii) | Spray/Final roller | 62–64 | Spray/be calm |

Figure 3. Score structures for *Water Study*: the Ernestine Stodelle version (choreographer, Doris Humphrey; notator, Karen Barracuda), 1978–80, and the Ruth Currier version (choreographer, Doris Humphrey; notator, Odette Blum), 1966; both courtesy of the Dance Notation Bureau.

versity. I had not seen this score previously, and I was struck by how closely the content resembled the detailed rehearsal notes I compiled over the years while dancing in and directing the work with Stodelle. Blum's score has always been something of a quandary because, as it reads off the page, the movement does not have the sense of flow I associated as belonging to the work. I have since had access to a second score, which has indicated one reason why this may be so. Barracuda opts for a single directional symbol with the accompanying degree of flexion, whereas Blum favors split symbols (one symbol containing two or three levels of indicators) as well as the degree of flexion, which automatically increases the amount of information representing a single movement (see figure 4).

Symbol use and stylistic information are possible reasons for my struggle with the Blum score. There is a further issue, however, relating more to Currier's version than to the score itself. Currier had a close artistic association with Humphrey in the final years of her life and was a highly credible interpreter of Humphrey's work. José Limón, with whom Currier danced for ten years, deeply influenced her dancing. From a stylistic perspective, therefore, Currier's way of moving was a combination of "late Humphrey" and "early Limón," in comparison with Stodelle's "early Humphrey" experience. Currier's interpretation of a Humphrey work, therefore, would be stylistically influenced by her own dancing experience — a further reason why the Blum score does not have the qualities and flow a Stodelle-trained Humphrey dancer could identify with in bodily terms.

Aside from the stylistic issue, my analysis also discovered fundamental differences in structure and movement vocabulary. Humphrey was known to make changes to works over time, *The Shakers* and *Passacaglia* being further examples. The two versions of *Water Study* more than likely follow that same scenario. Of the two, my preference is for Stodelle's version because it speaks in a

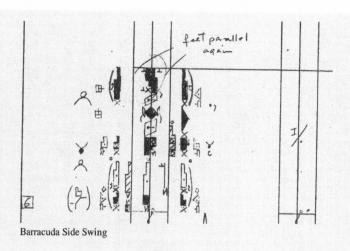

Barracuda Side Swing

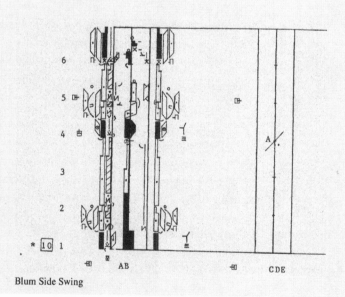

Blum Side Swing

Figure 4. Symbol comparison of Barracuda's (*above*) and Blum's (*below*) scores for *Water Study*.
Reprinted courtesy of the Dance Notation Bureau.

more stylistic and dynamic way than Currier's version. A key aspect is the sense of expanse that is generated with the accompanying dynamic and physiological impulses. An example is the floor pattern for the "Five Big Rushing Waves" section. Currier's version has a continual change of direction, in contrast to the single diagonal path employed by Stodelle. The spatial repetition in Stodelle's version allows the movement to build and intensify, organically and visually, before the climactic breakout into the "Whirlpool" section. Currier's pattern likewise generates energy through momentum and repetition, but not with the same visual cohesiveness because of the disparate nature of the spatial pattern. A similar comparison will be discussed in the chapter on *The Shakers*. There is a distinction between the two cases, however. The two versions of *The Shakers* look decidedly "different" in places because of the degree of contrast in the dynamics employed in key sections. The two versions of *Water Study* could, with the appropriate stylistic coaching, create a similar illusion because the central dynamic aspects of weight and flow can be constant in both, despite other marked differences.

## Identifying and Exploring the Evidence

The notion of score versus person transmission was discussed in part I. My early stagings of *Water Study* followed the traditional pattern of handing down the dance based on past performance experience and thus would be described as "person transmission." The process, therefore, was located in the past, in "what I did." Passing on the ideas given to us by Stodelle was important and remains so. Over time, however, I became conscious that something was lacking in the process. The idea of engaging with the past from the present allowed a different kind of directorial stance to evolve, one that could incorporate factors beyond past experience. A distinguishing difference between a reconstructive and an interpretive process is the treatment of evidence. An interpretive process provides broader scope to consider the actual versus the potential possibilities based on the evidence and then decide what to incorporate. The decision making, therefore, resides both in the present and with the director. The evidence base for *Water Study* starts with Humphrey's ideas and notes, the actual evidence for the work. The potential evidence includes commentary from original cast members and critics writing at the time; contemporary writing, including a number of analyses; and the Labanotation scores.[26] I chose to accept and incorporate evidence from three sources: Humphrey's ideas about the dance; the experiences of original cast members; and, coming out of this, Stodelle's version of the dance.

Humphrey provides a key set of ideas in an extract from her notebook, cited earlier, that encapsulates the structure of the dance: "*Nature moves in succession* [1], usually in an *unfolding succession* [2] to a *climax* [3] and a more *sudden succession* [4] to *cessation* [5] or *death* [6]" (my numbering and emphasis).[27] The first idea, "nature moves in succession," correlates with the opening section, "The First 5 Waves," as it builds from a point of stillness; the "unfolding succession" could describe the "Breakers" and "Tumblesaults," as the choreography becomes more expansive in both time and space; the "climax" comes in the "Five Big Rushing Waves" as the movement reaches its peak; the "sudden succession" is the "Splash/Whirlpool" as the "whole" fragments; the "cessation" is seen in the "Calm" and "Spray," as the power of the movement dynamic recedes; and "death" is the "Roller," the final progression to a final stillness.

I considered Humphrey's ideas collectively because they interlink through the common thread of "succession." A different choice, arguably, could produce a different interpretation. Succession as a concept is suggestive of one thing after another, connection, nothing happening in isolation, a natural progression, growing and diminishing, advancing and receding. King commented: "In the succession patterns which determine the flow, every inch of the exhilarated body moves, as the repeated successions pass from the toes through the knees, hips and spine to crown of the head."[28] Succession is described by King in experiential bodily terms, but at the same time it informs spatial terms, as the movement flows across the space, providing connectivity within the individual body and, simultaneously, from one body to the next.

The idea of succession in *Water Study* cannot be considered in isolation, however, and needs a further connection to "nature" and "the natural." Lloyd observed: "In her desire to get to the living source, Doris turned to nature rhythms as she turned to natural movement."[29] Here are two discrete yet interlinking ideas. Nature rhythms are ever present and unchanged by time—the wind blows today as it did in 1928, as the rain falls, as tides ebb and flow. It is not hard to identify the rhythms created by each of these natural happenings. Nor is it hard to discern that these rhythms are not constant but ever changing—"successional," one might say. Through the rhythms in nature comes movement in nature, the rise and fall of a rhythm creating the movement. As a breeze picks up, for example, the movement of leaves or branches increases correspondingly. That Humphrey choreographed *Water Study* right at the time she was engaged in a detailed exploration of natural movement based on the rise and fall of the breath and the gravitational pull is no coincidence but a natural consequence.

There are influences of nature and the natural in Humphrey's creative process in terms of movement, rhythm, and time. She talked about "starting with human feeling, with body movement and its momentum in relation to the psyche and to gravity, and as it developed the movements took on the form and tempo of moving water."[30] Interesting is her reference to "human feeling" and the "psyche," aspects of human nature rather than the natural world. Is there any difference, however, between the rise and fall of human emotion? One could argue that succession is equally prevalent in a human context. The absence of a structured time frame creates a freedom for the dancer that has a logical connection to the organic flow of Humphrey's choreography in corporeal and sequential terms. She not only created the natural in movement terms, but she allowed it to exist in a natural time span. In her program note, she referred to "the rhythm flow[ing] in natural phrases instead of cerebral measures" and "the feel of the wavelength that curves the backs of the group."[31] The sense or idea of freedom exists in a number of contexts. The human spirit, by and large, is free; nature, similarly, is unrestricted. The liberatory aspects of *Water Study* exist in terms of time and space, one interlinking with the other. The implication of "rhythm flowing in natural phrases" suggests an open time frame but not completely without parameters, since Humphrey's reference to "phrases" implies the existence of a formal structure of sorts. In fact, the actual phrase structure of the dance is very clearly defined, as illustrated earlier. The amount of space the dance can cover links directly with the amount of time it takes for the movement to unfold, examples of which I discuss shortly.

Having identified and selected evidence, Humphrey's ideas formed a framework for my own exploration. Through exploring the ideas of succession and successional movement, one particular facet emerged: the forward successional curve. This movement occurs repeatedly and in varying guises throughout the dance. The interpretation of the movement and its variant forms created a new standpoint from which to approach the dance, from within the dance itself and located in the present.

## Interpreting from the Present

Of the four directorial processes detailed in this book, *Water Study* is the only one in which the Labanotation score has not featured, because my own exposure came through Stodelle. Even though a score was not involved, past productions would be categorized as reconstructions because of the reliance on and adherence to my performance experience over a number of years. In relation to the Benedetti model, these early productions would fall into the conservative category because the approach was reliant on being faithful to the "original" as defined by my own performance experience. My current interpretation, however, lies firmly in Benedetti's liberal category for two reasons.

First, the viewing perspectives adopted from Collingwood allowed the existing evidence to be considered in a new way that, in turn, changed my relationship with the work. Through "choosing" which parts of the evidence to accept, I created a framework of enquiry to explore the dance afresh and away from the clutter of the past. Second, the interpretation focused on one aspect of the work that was not specifically Humphrey's focus. This aspect was the forward successional curve. Basing the exploration on the physiological and dynamic aspects of this movement concept and its variant forms allowed me to develop a new perspective from which to approach the work as a whole. Adopting this more open approach enabled interpretive exploration and at the same time removed the past encumbrance of "doing what Ernestine did." I had long felt something was lacking in my early productions. The new approach worked because it was allowed to evolve from the present. A significant factor was the shift in my position from reconstructor to interpreter in relation to the work and the choreographer.

In tracking the curve's progression throughout the dance, the first development comes in "The First 5 Waves." This opening section is an important example of movement design because of the physiological connections between the shapes created here and how they recur in developed forms later in the work. The constant running throughout is the forward successional curve, partially executed in the First Wave and then more completely from the Second Wave, with its greater height and volume, which produce both individual and group effects in the choreography. As the dance progresses, so too does the curve. I would suggest that it is the principal movement motif in the work because the development of the curve closely maps the development of the dance itself, certainly in Stodelle's version. Siegel observed something similar in her analysis of Stodelle's version from 1976. She described the dance "as being made of two kinds of circles. One surrounds the dancer like a wheel in front, below, behind and above. . . . The other circle encompasses all the space horizontally around the body."[32] The perspective of the dancer is different from that of the viewer, but I can see why Siegel would make such an observation. The emphasis Siegel placed on the circle parallels with the emphasis that exists experientially in the forward successional curve.

The curve continues to develop further in the "Breakers" phrase (section B) in two connecting side swings. Again, the sensation running up the front surface of the body is profound in terms of the sense of volume the body is creating. The curve itself expands organically through maintaining the shape of the design established on the floor and interlinking this with the physiological act of suspension, changes in level and support, and a marginal increase in speed. From the two side swings there is a progressive development through a central succession (B11), the "Tumblesaults" (C25), the "Five Big Rushing Waves" (Di), which then begins to subside into the "Undertow" (Dii), the undulating rock/hinge forward and back (Ei58) before the "Roller" (Eii64), which travels through the shapes of the First and Second Waves before moving on to its horizontal conclusion.

## "The First 5 Waves": Nature Moves in Succession

One of the exhilarating aspects of Humphrey's style is that it can appear effortless, an effect that belies what is happening in bodily terms to create that "look." *Water Study* is a revealing example because of its clarity and economy of movement vocabulary. On an individual and collective basis, dancers need a mature grasp of Humphrey's principles of successional movement in various forms. The opening section, "The First 5 Waves," is extreme in terms of how the body has to connect and maintain power and strength in the abdominals and quadriceps while creating the illusion of a perfect, natural form. This section is most challenging for the dancers as individuals who must also be part of a whole. The challenges are physical, dynamic, rhythmic, kinesthetic, and visual, with the visual requiring considerable skill and dexterity, depending on the dancer's position within the group.

The movement vocabulary for "The First 5 Waves" comprises a series of variations that create an image of waves growing in height and intensity from a state of calm. Beginning from a downstage left position, the emergence of the First Wave is subtle to the point that the audience may not even be aware that the dance has begun until the wave has progressed some way across the stage. The movement for the First Wave begins from a low, kneeling, tucked position. The pelvis lifts up over the heels on an in-breath, with the "breath" drawn up into the back of the pelvis. A successional curve is initiated in the torso, with the palms maintaining contact with the floor and the elbows lifting just off. The feeling is one of suspension, of a long curve coming up out of the ground through the tailbone and spine that proceeds back down into the ground through the crown of the head to move onward through space. For the dancer, there is a complete kinesthetic immersion from this first movement, with the sensory surfaces of the body alive to the energies that are being generated in both spatial and temporal dimensions. The key technical aspect is the pelvic lift over the heels, as it requires considerable control in the quadriceps and abdominals. Without the requisite muscle strength, the body weight will shift forward instinctively onto the knees, distorting the line of the curve. For the dancers, the scale of demand depends on positioning within the group. Those who are stage left and involved in the early part of the wave must hold

Figure 5. "The First Wave." Arkè Compagnia d'Arte, Turin, Italy, 2007. Photographer: Alberto Sachero.

Figure 6. "The Second Wave." Arkè Compagnia d'Arte, Turin, Italy, 2007. Photographer: Alberto Sachero.

an arduous body position for up to two minutes as the wave rolls out and then recedes back through the space. Two minutes may not sound long, but it is in this particular physiological context. For those at the far end of the wave, stage right, visual and rhythmic aspects are more pronounced in order to sustain rhythm and flow as the wave progresses across the space.

The pelvic in-breath is the point of initiation for the remaining four waves, with volume, expanse, and speed building as each wave unfolds. The physical act of executing this sequence of movement gives the dancer a clear insight into the technical and dynamic aspects of the whole work. A strategy in early rehearsals is to run this sequence in unison and without the full time span. The dancers can feel the movements sequentially and get a sense of the development before the more arduous element of dancing in canon is introduced. In the broader context of the dance itself, experience of and familiarity with this specific vocabulary prepares the dancer for the major movement motifs to come. In turn, awareness of physiological flow alongside dynamic and spatial flow becomes embedded. To illustrate, the pelvic-initiated curve in the First Wave is developed into a higher, more expansive curve in the Second Wave. Here, the fingertips lift just off the floor as the elbows billow out to enhance the shape. As the back surface of the body is drawn up into this shape, there is a sense of buoyancy in the hollow created by the front surface — denoted by the quadriceps, abdomen, chest, and underside of the arms. This hollow is not an empty space but has substance and volume. The Third Wave sees a higher curve, arms extending, one in front, one behind, with the weight shifting forward through the pelvis and right knee. The buoyant sensation increases and does much to instill a sense of the organic for the dancer, of being part of and immersed in a force that is alive and ever moving. The natural gravitational pull of the undertow becomes more pronounced as the wave recedes, one body picking up the resistance of the pull after another, dovetailing to create a continuous fluid image.

Humphrey, never one for repeating needlessly, introduces a "surprise" to augment the uniform canon as the Third Wave rolls outward. The last two dancers shoot forward together to lie prone, arms fully extended, then circling around, fingertips drumming on the floor, creating the image and sound of a wave breaking on the shore. The main movement motif from the Third Wave is developed further in the Fourth and Fifth Waves. The dancers now move through the canon in four small groupings as the curve grows further in height and volume. First, the successional curve is initiated by a single arm swing, up and over, taking the bodies of the first group into a higher curve as the second group billows out in the Third Wave movement. The third group reprises the action of the first group, with the final group repeating the "dive and splash" conclusion of the previous wave. The Fifth Wave succession has a double arm

Figure 7. "The Third Wave." Arkè Compagnia d'Arte, Turin, Italy, 2007. Photographer: Alberto Sachero.

swing for the first and third groups, with both the second and fourth groups diving forward to stillness. The opening section progresses from calm ripples, barely discernible, much as one might observe looking out to sea. The ripples build gradually into fully formed waves, and as they do so, there is a sense of the waves coming closer toward the shore—nature moving in succession.

## "Breakers" and "Tumblesaults": Unfolding Succession

The transition into the "Breakers" section signals a change in the tide—perhaps, even, a different tide. As suggested, Humphrey did not set out to create a literal interpretation of the sea at a particular point in time, and the structure of the dance allows us to see a successional or episodic form. The end of the Fifth Wave is a fleeting tableau of two waves peaking and falling. From here, there is a separation as the dancers are drawn upward from the floor and outward into two linear formations on either side of the stage. Stodelle referred to this section in rehearsal as waves crashing and breaking against rocks. Dancers are in unison on their respective sides and in opposition to the other group, allowing the "waves" to pull away and toward each other. The main movement motif commences with two weighted side swings, away from and into center. On each "up" swing/suspension, the arms and upper body are in a variation of the forward successional curve. The body creates the same sense of expanse within the space/shape in front of the torso. In "The First 5 Waves," the initiation point for the curve is a sustained pull up out of the ground. Here, the upward pull has increased in speed and is a consequence of the falling action of the swing. The second swing into center suspends prior to a fall into a central succession in a parallel fourth position. As the pelvis/breath falls, the arms and upper body follow in a corresponding drop. The succession rolls down, then unfolds back out and climbs up to a suspension point.

The audience, which views the dancers in profile, sees the form of two waves building to a peak before breaking and rushing in to center to "crash on the rocks" as the dancers run and burst upward into two leaps, the first with a successional curve in the upper body and arms, the second an upward high release that has the feeling of a spray cascading out of the palms and fingertips. The leaps are timed just before the running dancers crash into each other and culminate with a successional side fall to the floor. The dancers are then drawn up, as if by the pull of the undertow, and run outward to fall into the next breaking wave. Humphrey structured this section for two groups of dancers on each side, alternately rushing and falling, creating an image of constant breaking waves.

The idea of unfolding succession can be seen in the structure of the "Breakers" section, first as the alternate groupings are established and then in a varia-

Figure 8. The "Breakers" fall. Staging by Lesley Main for Middlesex University, 1989.

tion of the leaping/falling action that draws the group together into two lines on stage left. At this point, as the "Tumblesaults" begin, the whole group falls into a central succession in unison and in the same direction for the first time. Humphrey breaks the symmetry by having the front line drop to one knee for the succession. The change in level gives added expanse to the form of the "wave," still seen by the audience in profile. The dancers again fall out of the peak of the wave, this time running right across the stage until the front-line dancers drop down into a forward "tumblesault." The back-line dancers pull up sharply on one leg into a forward successional curve, much as the first "Breakers" leap, and hover above the "tumblesaulter" in front before landing in a deep lunge as the tumblesault spills forward. The undertow pull draws the wave back across the stage for a second, more expansive reprise that increases in speed.

## "Five Big Rushing Waves": Climax

One can attribute the idea of "climax" to this section, even though it is not the end of the dance, because the movement reaches its peak. The lined formation of the "Tumblesaults" dissolves into a cluster. Each wave begins with a deep forward successional fall and suspension, which is a development of the side swing movement in the "Breakers" and a further representation of the forward successional curve. From the peak, the body falls into a run. The upper body twists so that one arm is forward and the other back, elbows held into the sides, hands/palms open. The waves run on a constant diagonal path, downstage right to upstage left, with increasing speed, intensity, and turbulence. The feeling of being "inside" the body of the wave is different from the waves that have come before. There is a more profound sense of immersion as the bodies come together in a completely unified organism for the first time. Stodelle described the running as "surging" and "pounding." One can feel and hear the change in intensity.

When I direct the dance, the image I use for this section is drawn from the type of waves found off the North Shore in Hawaii favored by the "big wave" surfing community. These waves are the most extraordinary bodies of water, so immense, powerful, and potentially deadly as they reach a peak. The immensity can seem benign at first, belying the true nature of the waves as they unfold. The extreme contrast inherent in these waves parallels the extreme ends of Humphrey's fall and recovery theory, the Apollonian/Dionysian "arc between two deaths." Apollo and Dionysus represent conflicting but intertwining impulses of human nature: the Apollonian drive to achieve perfection and stability and the Dionysian desire to experience the ecstasy of abandon. Humphrey described these states as "different names for the will to balance and the will to grow," implying that one must reach out beyond one's known/safe experience in order to advance.[33] Stodelle described this growth as "a daring act of exploration leading to self-knowledge or disaster."[34] *Water Study* is full of potential disasters for the dancer, one of the reasons why it is so exhilarating to perform. As the dance reaches this climax, the timing of the fall is that "daring act of exploration." There is no cue, and there is no count. The dancers must repeatedly fall together as one, trusting their collective intuition.

## "Splash/Whirlpool": Sudden Succession

The sudden succession comes out of the Fifth Wave. The chest/arms are lifted for the final run with the hands performing a vigorous "sudsing" action (a term used by Stodelle), akin to "white horses" on a breaking wave, the right hand held slightly higher than the left. As the peak of the wave is reached, five dancers link hands and stream out of the group, running on a curved pathway down, around, and upstage, spreading out along a vertical curve. In turn, beginning with the leader of the group, each takes a "splash" curving action that decreases in height as it travels down the group, concluding with a full spiral fall by the final "whirlpool" dancer. The runners' sudden exit initiates a series of descending and decelerating sideways pulls in the remaining dancers, first left, then right, culminating in a sweeping side fall to the left. The pull is continued back over to the right side, with a shift of weight initiated through the pelvis, upper body curved forward and close to the floor — the feeling is akin to the pull of the undertow. The final part of this successional pull comes through the left arm

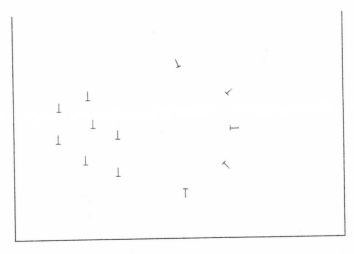

Figure 9. "Splash/Whirlpool" floor plan

as it ripples along the side of the body. This action is timed to subside with the spiral fall of the whirlpool. The breakout by the runners is unexpected; hence, the idea of "sudden" makes sense. What follows is a rapid succession downward to a point of stillness, reached in a matter of seconds. The tableau created is reminiscent of the end of the Fifth Wave, with its fleeting image of a still form.

## "Calm" and "Spray": Cessation

Out of the stillness comes a cessation, an "ending" rather than an "end," suggesting there is still some way to travel. A series of weighted pulling ripples, danced in unison, depicts calm returning after a pounding, relentless storm. The movement falls through a deep plié in second position that rebounds up on one leg as the body shifts to the side, arms extending outward, palms open. The fall is then repeated in opposition, fifteen times in all as the dancers traverse the stage, returning from where they came. The moving image is undulating; shifting, rising, and falling on the breath, bodies crossing in space, open to the audience for the first time — for reasons of movement design, arguably, rather than any intent to "address the audience" (see figure 2). It is noteworthy, however, that "the dancer" as identifiable individual has no place in this dance because of the emphasis on form. A constant rhythm is maintained that continues as the movement descends onto one knee on the fifteenth fall, bodies still open to the audience, then pulling round into profile, into the forward successional curve once more. Rocking hinges and curves maintain the rhythm and pull of the undertow, finishing in a final, deeper hinge that releases down into the opening tucked curve position.

The "Spray" is a final flurry and release and a delight to dance. From stage right, in canon, the body is propelled suddenly upward through the hips, through the forward successional curve. The left arm is flung high in the air, then the body arcs back to the floor, landing on the falling arm, one "splash" cascading up after another. The canon then reverses back across the stage, this time with a heavy pull around through the outstretched arm, one pull picking up from the next to create a sweeping successional action across the stage. The pull releases swiftly into the body, through the left elbow, as the opening curve is resumed.

## "Roller": Death

The movement of the "Roller" passes through the First Wave and then the Second Wave before the forward successional curve extends outward into a lunge. As the weight shifts forward, the peak of the wave is reached before a sustained descent into horizontal stillness. As each dancer reaches the peak, the next one begins. The result is a sedate, expansive image flowing across the stage, "rumbling out to sea," as Stodelle used to say. The last dancer in the canon completes the descent of the "Roller" off-stage. The image that is left is of ongoing motion, of a continuing succession of movement even though one cannot physically see it any longer.

The correlation between death and *Water Study* had not occurred to me before I considered Humphrey's ideas more deeply in interpretive terms. There is, of course, no literal death, but there is a link to Humphrey's idea of death as it related to her movement philosophy. She identified the "arc between two deaths" from Nietzschean philosophy, which she subsequently defined as "dynamic death" and "static death." Stodelle defined these states as the "precarious state of off-balance emotion" and the "symmetrical balance of locked-in perfection."[35] Having already considered the Apollonian/Dionysian correlation earlier in the work, the final position in *Water Study* is a clear example of static death because there is nowhere else to go beyond the prone horizontal place each body reaches at the end.

Identifying the forward successional curve and then charting its development throughout was the crucial factor that allowed me to engage with the dance from the present. Without changing a single movement or direction or idea, I was able to work with the dance in a way that made sense in the present and, more importantly, produced a version that came close to my past kinesthetic and emotional experiences of performing the dance. My first exploration focused particularly on the forward successional curve. Subsequent to this, the addition of Humphrey's ideas allowed me to think about the dance in a different way again. This example shows the extent of "possibility" one can find in evidence and, further, that having such possibility can generate fresh thinking and keep the process and the work alive.

## Catching the Undertow: The Dancing of *Water Study*

To dance *Water Study* requires a particular degree of stylistic understanding because it is distinct from the rest of the Humphrey repertoire. King described the dance as "the most satisfying of all Humphrey's works to perform [because it was] a masterpiece of flowing motion."[36] The distinction lies as much in the physicality required to dance the vocabulary, because it is significantly more demanding in terms of raw power and strength than dancing any other work from the Humphrey repertoire, except, perhaps, her signature solo work, *Two Ecstatic Themes* (1931). Humphrey wrote to King in 1932 while the latter was recovering from an injury: "I need you, as one of the best dancers to do the

*Water Study* because it is a difficult dance and because it is the one number that represents the group. Almost anyone can do the speakeasy scene [a dramatic interlude] . . . also the rest of the show [*Americana 1932*]. . . . So I feel you should work on the knee gradually until you can do the *Water Study*."[37] Alongside the inference that the dance was an important example of her work, Humphrey's comment also acknowledged the demands involved and that this was a work for an experienced dancer. A question to consider was the implication of interpreting the "natural" in a contemporary staging. How, for example, does natural movement originating in the 1920s "work" on twenty-first-century bodies? I would suggest that it works precisely because of the natural aspect of the movement. Of course, bodies moved differently back then. The beauty and simplicity of Humphrey's philosophy, however, mean that today's dancer can figure out the physiological connection involved in falling from the out-breath and pelvis much as did King and Stodelle.

Appropriate physical preparation is essential to achieving a fully realized production of this work because of the rigor involved throughout. Stodelle's practice for all the works she staged included a daily technique class. She insisted upon this for whatever level of company she was working with, professional or collegiate. The class would comprise exercises that worked specific muscle groups without inducing overload. The choreography is particularly demanding on the abdominals and quadriceps and in the physical transitions the body must go through as it moves upward from the floor to standing and aerial work. There is a certain "boot camp" aspect about learning to perform this dance. In much the same way an athlete will prepare for a specific discipline — speed work for sprinters, upper body work for throwers — there is a conditioning process that dancers go through for *Water Study*. Dancers acquire strength, physiological awareness, quality, and familiarity with the movement vocabulary in the technique class, leaving rehearsal time for other essential elements such as ensemble timing. A number of exercises described in Stodelle's book *The Dance Technique of Doris Humphrey* are examples of those used in a *Water Study* technique class, including successions, swings, and falls.[38] I have adopted this same practice for other dances, and while there are no set classes as such, there are physiological and dynamic themes one can incorporate that are appropriate for a particular work. An emphasis on lyrical, expansive movement and technically challenging legwork for *Passacaglia* is one example, and grounded percussive asymmetrical movement for *With My Red Fires* is another.

*W*ater Study was staged in 2007 for Arkè Compagnia d'Arte, a modern dance company based in Turin, Italy. The Arkè dancers had studied Humphrey-based technique with me for a number of years and had previously performed *Pas-*

*sacaglia.* To help the dancers embody the changes in movement quality from the *Passacaglia* vocabulary into *Water Study*, we worked on movement exercises that emphasized weightedness and strengthened the quadriceps prior to the rehearsal period. Adapted phrases from the dance allowed the dancers to focus on ideas such as the pull of the curve in the spine and the "space" in the forward successional curve. By setting up physical conditioning alongside key movement ideas ahead of time, the dancers came into the main rehearsal period physically equipped to deal with the technical demands and with an understanding of the choreographic intention and various forms of successional movement. Not every company can structure rehearsal time in this two-stage way, of course, but there was a decided advantage in being able to do so.

An important reason for dealing with the physical demands of the dance ahead of time is that it allows the rehearsal period to focus on the other equally complex demand—ensemble timing, which the dancers won't find until they have the physical capacity to sustain the movement. Rhythm and ensemble timing are integral aspects of this work, interlinking but also with discrete purposes. Rhythm, in a *Water Study* context, refers to the underlying foundation of the work as a whole. Ensemble timing refers to the means by which this is achieved and sustained. The key to *Water Study* is locating the rhythm; the challenge is being able to articulate that rhythm to a group of individuals and form a cohesive whole through them.

One aspect that became apparent through my own performing experience was a sense of moving on collective intuition. This sensation can be liberating because of the absence of formalized counts. In modern dance, recent and current generations have been so used to having every exercise and movement phrase counted out to the last beat that the absence of counts can be quite traumatic in comparison with members of an earlier generation who had the converse experience. Stodelle recounted: "At times Doris never counted anything, we just got on with it and followed the phrase," although Humphrey did expect her dancers to maintain whatever rhythm(s) she chose to set.[39] The issue of counts in *Water Study* came up when Stodelle directed the work at the London Contemporary Dance School in 1985. The most often asked questions were "How many counts for the runs?" and "Which foot do I finish on?," to which the answers were "Just run till you get there" and "It doesn't matter." Stodelle genuinely could not understand why the students needed such detail when to her those details were irrelevant to mastering the work. The students in turn found it difficult to let themselves go into the realm of the "uncountable."

Dancers can attain the sensation of being liberated once the rhythm has been found. There are five rhythms running through the work consecutively, correlating with the five choreographic sections as described by Stodelle.

Within this structure there are minor subsections with accompanying rhythmic patterns. Having already stated the importance of locating the rhythm, I would go further and say that the key factor is locating and securing the rhythm of the "Breakers." "Of" is used deliberately here as opposed to "for" because the movement vocabulary has a natural time span if weight and flow are allowed to exist freely. Conversely, the movement does not work if a time frame is imposed. Further, as Rubin observed in her letter to King, timing becomes problematic if dancers lack the physical strength to execute the legwork at a slow enough pace or attain sufficient depth of plié for the fall in the central succession. In turn, the recovery is affected, as are the height and power of suspension at the top of the "wave" that precedes the fall, run, and leap into center. The solution lies in allowing a collective natural time span to evolve through the rehearsal process. Once the movement phrase becomes familiar to the individual, attention can focus on developing the kinesthetic awareness of the group.

Locating and articulating the rhythm is a directorial responsibility. Securing the rhythm belongs to the group, and this is where ensemble timing comes into play. Part of the director's task in articulating the rhythm is to create the context in which it can be found. One strategy is having no musical accompaniment in class except the breath rhythm to enhance the sense of unison timing. Another is to position dancers in the spatial configuration of the first and final sections of the work to heighten kinesthetic awareness of the ensemble as a whole entity. "Moving on collective intuition" was referred to earlier as the sensation of dancing in the work. It is also something that needs to build and develop as the work itself progresses. Of course, the dancers will come to a performance equipped with all the intrinsic knowledge needed to create the dance afresh. However, even collective intuition needs a starting point. There is no music; thus, there is nothing fixed for the dancers to cue off at the start except each other. The opening lighting state is dimmed, with the body in a low, tucked position on the knees with the head down. Such a position does not lend itself to having a clear view of the dancer next in line or ten feet away, upstage right. There are a number of things the individual dancer can do to feel the rhythm as it passes through the group, including subtle adjustment of the head and neck to improve the sight line without losing the curved line of the spine. One can then take the cue from whichever dancer is in view and breathe through the rhythm with the intervening bodies. Aside from the practicalities, the focus required in itself creates a "collective intuition."

When Arkè first performed the dance in Turin in 2007, it had a mesmerizing effect on the audience. The auditorium was completely silent throughout and remained so for some while after the dance had concluded before the audience showed an unreserved appreciation. Subsequent performances were similar—a clear indication that the hypnotic power of the work can speak to-day as resolutely as it has always done. One reason for an audience being drawn in to the dance is the presence of silence. The lack of musical accompaniment was striking at the time of creation and remains so today but perhaps for different reasons. In 1928 dances in silence were unusual, so there was an element of novelty. Contemporary life, conversely, can be full of constant sound and unrelenting visual stimulation. One can see the appeal of being drawn into a still, silent place.

A further issue relating to audience reception is the history and position of contemporary dance in Italy in comparison with Great Britain and the United States. Italian dance history resides predominantly in the "opera house with resident ballet company" culture and, more recently, in commercialized dance. The modern dance evolution in Europe in the 1930s did not cross the Italian border, and, following the Second World War, there was indeed a reticence to embrace anything American. While the current trend in British dance has moved away from modern dance traditions (for the moment), there is a growing appreciation and demand for those same traditions in Italy. In witnessing audience responses over the last several years to both Humphrey's and Graham's work, it is clear that these modern dances are appreciated because there is an appreciation of "tradition" inherent in Italian cultural consciousness. When Arkè performs Humphrey and Graham repertoire, the performances are prefaced by press and media coverage that leads with the historical significance of the dances. The draw for the audience is the link with tradition. Kim Jones (former Graham Company member) and I have given public lectures ahead of performances because of the interest in the history and traditions behind the dances. Arkè as a company has taken a similar position to Momenta in Chicago and Repertory Dance Theater in Utah in that there is a long-term commitment to staging the Humphrey repertoire that also involves educating the audience to receive the dances. For the directors, it is not enough simply to have a work staged or take the necessary steps to ensure the dancers can dance the choreography. A context must be put in place so that the works can be appreciated. In turn, audiences are demonstrating their appreciation by returning to see the works over and over.

The form of approach detailed here is as relevant for a reconstruction process as for the more radical interpretive processes to be discussed later in this book. In fact, some may consider my "new interpretation" of *Water Study* as a reconstruction because it "looks like" *Water Study* has always done, much in the same way as the versions by Stodelle and Currier. Does it matter? No. What matters is that the dance is meaningful for its audience and is regarded as Doris

Humphrey's *Water Study*. The "new interpretive" aspect relates to process, not performance. The processes involved in staging a work should be invisible in performance. The processes themselves, however, are a vital part of the directorial engagement with the work, and it is within the context of the process that one can distinguish between a reconstructive or interpretive approach. In the wider context of the advancement of our modern dance traditions, it is perhaps dangerous to rely complacently on existing staging mechanisms of the past. The upcoming discussions will consider this argument and its implications in depth.

# PASSACAGLIA

*Choreography*: 1938
*Music*: J. S. Bach, Passacaglia and Fugue in C Minor
*Premiere*: August 5, 1938, Armory, Bennington, Vermont

*Passacaglia* is cast for a group of eighteen, including two "leaders," originally danced by Humphrey and Weidman. The opening tableau shows the
entire group arrayed on a configuration of rising platforms positioned center stage, facing away from the audience with arms held aloft in a striking
diamond-shaped pose. As the lighting builds and Bach's music seeps into the
gathering, a collective stillness pervades the arena until one figure and then
a second turn toward the audience. They emerge into the space and trace a
circular pathway from one side of the group to the other, their arrival causing
the whole ensemble to turn as one in a slow, dignified manner. A second pair
of dancers joins the first as they open up the space further, this time on diagonal pathways, until the leaders take over, addressing the audience head-on in
a series of rising, expansive gestures that reach out invitingly. There follows an
exposition of ensemble choreography that takes the audience through all manner of small groupings and configurations that constantly move in and out of
the main ensemble, on and off the platforms. The leaders lead without domi-
nation, the ensemble dancers all have individual significance within the whole.
The movement vocabulary encapsulates the ever-changing dynamics of Bach's
music, at one moment, intricate rhythmic gestures followed by expansive off-
balance swinging turns. The group wends its way together through a dynamic
procession in which each individual member participates in trios, quartets, and
quintets and in the magnificent ensemble displays that climax both parts of the

79

dance. The mood is never introspective and maintains an open, engaging tone to the end.

On August 1, 1995, the Royal Festival Hall in London reverberated to the sound of Bach's Passacaglia and Fugue in C Minor—not in the renowned concert hall, as one might imagine, but in a performance space open to the public on three sides. A multitude of young dancers, elegantly clad in two-color silks, swept through the spacious, high-ceilinged ballroom, making expansive spatial patterns and configurations with exuberant intent. The occasion was the inaugural event of the Doris Humphrey Centennial Celebrations in Great Britain.[1] It was also the work's first performance in Britain and a culmination of a decade's work in establishing the technique in British dancing bodies.

Thirteen years on, in November 2008, the dance resounds again. This time the location is Oak Park, Illinois, the birthplace of Humphrey and home state of presidential candidate Barack Obama. That the performances took place on the two weekends either side of the election was coincidental. Of note, however, was the sense of hope the dancers took into the first performances and the celebratory nature that infused the second. It is no coincidence that the message in this dance mirrors the ideals expressed by Obama and eagerly taken up by a nation hungry for change. Nor is it coincidental that war figures prominently in both periods. Humphrey did not set out to create a dance "about" war, but she was keenly aware of the rise of fascism in Europe and the dangers it presented to humanity. The message of idealism, of sensitivity, of acceptance and inclusion of all is unchanging. It is no surprise, therefore, that *Passacaglia* speaks as resolutely today as it first did in 1938.

The Chicago production was first staged a year earlier, in the fall of 2007, for Momenta Dance Company, resident company in Oak Park. Having staged the dance throughout my career, I have found that there have been key periods and productions that represent a shift in the nature of my engagement with the work. The first, in 1981, would be defined as a reconstruction because it was based firmly on a Labanotation score. The second came in 1995 for the Humphrey Centennial and was influenced by factors beyond the score, including musical interpretation and interpretive strategies adopted from theater practice. The staging process in 2007 was the third of these key periods and represented a deeper consideration of the interpretive choices made in 1995. The following discussion will explore what changed in those later periods to move the directorial position beyond that of traditional "dance reconstructor" to embody characteristics and practices from outside the genre. The shifts illustrate the changing nature of directorial engagement and, significantly,

Figure 10. Passacaglia 3 (*above*) and Fugue 1 (*below*), Momenta, Oak Park, Illinois, 2007. Photographer: Lisa Green (Steve Green Photography, www.sgreenphoto.com).

the capacity within a work for interpretive change without disruption to the work itself.

## Performance History

Humphrey wrote to her dancers following a nationwide tour in 1939: "I think *Passacaglia* is my most mature dance, with the finest choreography so far."[2] Dance critics and scholars have consistently agreed that *Passacaglia* (1938) does indeed embody the mature development of Humphrey's choreographic philosophy.[3] The precursor to *Passacaglia* in both chronological and creative terms was the *New Dance Trilogy*. The three dances that comprise the *Trilogy* were performed as independent works but with interconnecting themes. On completion of the third and darkest work, *With My Red Fires*, Humphrey sequenced the dances as follows: *Theater Piece* (January 1936), a cynical observation of modern commercial life; *With My Red Fires* (August 1936), a study of possessive and destructive matriarchal love and manipulation of the mass of dancers who represent society; and *New Dance* (1935), a positive affirmation of humankind existing in harmony. The *Trilogy* collectively conveyed humanistic idealism rising above destructive elements, a theme to which Humphrey returned regularly. *New Dance* addressed themes that recurred again in *Passacaglia*. Dance critics, including Selma Jeanne Cohen and Marcia Siegel, agree that the later work is a more mature representation of the ideals first expressed in *New Dance*.[4] Humphrey shows her greater sophistication in the movement vocabulary, quality, and dynamic embodied in *Passacaglia*. The movement is more deeply grounded and richer; it feels more expansive in spatial and physiological terms. I concluded, after having directed both works, that music is the defining factor that distinguishes one from the other. The two scores exhibit large contrasts in both style and sound. The exhilaration and energy generated by Wallingford Reigger's composition for *New Dance* resonates also in the Bach score but in a more resolute manner.

Humphrey's choice of Bach was regarded as radical at the time. Bach, as with Beethoven, was considered out-of-bounds for dance, which further underlines Humphrey's progressiveness as a choreographer. Humphrey had an affinity for Bach throughout her career.[5] Unlike her other Bach dances, she took on a work of enormous musical complexity with *Passacaglia*. Humphrey used the 1922 orchestral recording by Leopold Stokowski while choreographing the work. Performances by the Humphrey-Weidman Company were accompanied by piano, although she later used the orchestral recording in rehearsal in 1955 with the Juilliard Dance Theater and for a performance at Connecticut College in 1957. Humphrey's program note describes the work and lets us glimpse her thoughts on the music and its influence on her creativity: "An abstraction with dramatic overtones. The minor melody, according to the traditional Passacaglia form, insistently repeated from beginning to end, seems to say 'How can a man be saved and be content in a world of infinite despair?' And in the magnificent fugue which concludes the dance the answer seems to mean — 'Be saved by love and courage.' . . . [The dance was inspired by] the need for love, tolerance and nobility in a world given more and more to the denial of these things."[6]

While *Passacaglia* came to be regarded as a magnificent work, critics at the time were mixed in their responses. Walter Terry, writing in the *Boston Herald* on November 28, 1938, thought it pleasing, theatrical, but undemanding, missing Humphrey's deeper meaning. *Dance Observer* took a more disapproving stance, noting: "The abstract patterns were of questionable significance for an audience concerned with what dance had to say to them."[7] In the same vein, Margery Dana of the *Daily Worker* commented on December 5, 1938, on Humphrey's lack of overt political meaning, labeling the work "insignificant" and failing to appreciate Humphrey's subtle critique on the rise of fascism. Former company dancer Eleanor King remembers Humphrey being unmercifully criticized for going "Bach-ward" and would have liked to have seen the dance without music.[8] John Martin, dance critic for the *New York Times* and influential theorist and advocate of modern dance, admired the choreography but could not reconcile himself with Humphrey's choice of music.

Martin's stubborn resistance, documented over thirteen years, spurred Humphrey to write a spirited defense of her use of Bach in 1943 that the *New York Times* published. The great value of this essentially good-natured exchange lies in the surviving account of Humphrey's position. The letter, subsequently published unabridged in Cohen's book *Doris Humphrey: An Artist First*, contains insights into the choreographer's thought processes and approach to a number of works. Her remarks in the following passage add a further dimension to the original program notes for *Passacaglia* and show how her responses to the work may have evolved over time: "I picked Bach for music because I still think he has the greatest of all genius for these very qualities of variety held in unity, of grandeur of the human spirit, of grace for fallen man; not only this, but I sincerely believe the music has movement in it, based on dances of forgotten men and women who are the authors of much of the music of this or any other age."[9]

Stokowski was renowned for his transcriptions of Bach's music, having tackled almost forty compositions over his career.[10] For a time he was discredited by musicologists because of the idiosyncratic nature of his arrangements. The debates in musicology on the interpretation and performance of Bach subsequently broadened beyond the traditionally acceptable "geometric" style to encompass the performer-centered "vitalist" style.[11] Stokowski's approach, representative of the latter position, in due course became less controversial. In notes accompanying the 1973 recording of *Bach Transcriptions*, the conductor observes: "Bach himself was the greatest transcriber of another's music, particularly Vivaldi, who was a totally different kind of composer. So the freedom of his thought encourages me to be a little free sometimes. I'm sure he wouldn't mind me orchestrating his keyboard pieces. He might not like the way I did it, but he wouldn't mind the principle."[12]

Stokowski's own description of the piece invites parallels with later observations by various dance commentators on Humphrey's choreography.[13] "The *Passacaglia and Fugue in C Minor* begins quietly and gradually mounts up to a lofty height of noble emotion — creating in us a state of exaltation in which we inwardly perceive a glorious vision. It is in music what a great Gothic cathedral is in architecture — the same vast conception — the same soaring mysticism given eternal form. It is one of the most divinely contrapuntal works ever conceived."[14] Compare this language with that of dance critic Margaret Lloyd, for example, writing after the first performances of the dance: "Doris made a serene and *noble* work of it. . . . [S]he simply needed music of a *lofty* serenity for what she wanted to express."[15] Stodelle describes *Passacaglia* as "resembling the *architecture* of a resplendent *cathedral*," containing "*lofty* philosophical concepts."[16] In fact, the "lofty," "noble," and "cathedral" descriptors appear in many accounts of this dance, including Humphrey's own program note from 1938.[17] Although the exact date of Stokowski's remarks is unknown, his orchestration dates from 1922 and existed before the dance was created. Thus, his thoughts on the work may have predated and perhaps even influenced Humphrey in her own thinking. She corresponded with Stokowski at various times in the late 1930s and early 1940s and in fact worked on an opera with him as early as 1930. Humphrey invited him to conduct *Passacaglia* in performance in 1940, but he was unable to do so because of prior commitments.[18]

Over time, the debate about Humphrey's choice of music for *Passacaglia* subsided. Contemporary commentators now recognize the significance of both the music and the recording used in the production of this work. Stephanie Jordan, the British dance scholar and writer, argues convincingly that directors need to acknowledge the music. In her analysis of *Passacaglia*, she suggests that the work finds its origins in two periods, "a 1938 piece remembered by its choreographer in the 1950s."[19] The later version became the basis for subsequent productions through Lucy Venable's Labanotation score from 1955. Jordan's analysis cites comments from original cast members Beatrice Seckler, Nona Schurman, and Charles Weidman, all of whom suggest that the later version was not the work as they knew it. Humphrey did make structural changes to works she revived and quite radical changes to *Water Study* and *The Shakers*, as two examples. The structure of *Passacaglia*, however, remained essentially intact because of the close relationship between musical structure and Humphrey's choreographic structure.

I recall being completely captivated by the power of the dance when I first saw Venable's 1965 production for the American Dance Theater, recorded for John Mueller's film *The Four Pioneers*. Venable can be regarded as an authority on *Passacaglia* because of her interconnecting experiences as performer, notator, and reconstructor. Humphrey cast her in the leading role for the 1955 Juilliard production. Doing so acknowledged Venable's skill as both performer and stylistic exponent. In addition, the actual experience of dancing this particular role under Humphrey's direction gave Venable as close an insight into the work as there could be. The two soloist roles incorporate so much of the movement vocabulary and dynamics of the work that dancing either one is a more all-encompassing experience than dancing a role in the ensemble. Venable's performance experience certainly contributed to her notation of the work, providing an "inside" perspective.[20] In turn, notating a work of such scale and detail would inevitably inform her reconstruction process for the 1965 film.

A further, related aspect of Venable's film is the performance of the female soloist, Lola Huth, noted here because both the film and the score were integral to my first production. Of further note is that Venable and Huth performed in the work when Humphrey staged it for the Juilliard Dance Theater in 1955, Venable as the female soloist opposite José Limón and Huth as one of the leading ensemble dancers. From my perspective, this gives added credence to what they have to "say" about the dance. Huth was an exceptional dancer whose early training was in Utah with Virginia Tanner. Tanner had studied with Humphrey at Perry Mansfield College and in New York City. Like Stodelle, she developed her own training system for children built on Humphrey's ideas. She also cofounded Repertory Dance Theater, one of the most stylistically literate of the companies today that present Humphrey's work. A photograph of Huth dancing at age fifteen indicates the off-balance daring that she also demonstrated, to a greater degree, in the 1965 film.[21] One can understand why Humphrey cast her in the 1955 Juilliard production while Huth was still in her late teens. Although the film version as a whole encapsulates the sense of expanse, it is Huth's individual articulation of this expansiveness that draws attention.

Huth performed with Juilliard Dance Theater and the Limón Company in the late 1950s when Humphrey directed both companies and danced one of the leading ensemble roles in the 1955 Juilliard production.[22] As with Venable, the fact that Humphrey cast her as such indicates Huth's capabilities — or certainly her potential, as there was a gap of ten years between the two productions. Of the two soloists, it is her performance that has stood out for me over time. Chester Wolenski was also in Humphrey's Juilliard production in a minor role and was a member of the Limón Company. Despite his commanding presence, his dancing at key moments has a controlled tension that seems to belie the expansive and exuberant aspects of this work that are so apparent in Huth's performance.[23] Her dancing epitomizes what, arguably, the work is about because of the way she encapsulates the sense of "breath" and because of the sheer range of dynamic articulation her performance contains. Huth's performance embodies Humphrey's principles because she is dancing with total control and complete abandon. A particular illustration is her execution of the renowned "Turns" variation and the bell turns at the climax of both parts of the dance. Huth produces a daring level of suspended off-balance achieved through the depth of side tilt in the upper body and, significantly, by dropping the weight of her head into the tilt. This has the dual effect of increasing the amount of weight going into the fall and the level of risk.

Venable's Labanotation score has been one of the most popular and widely used in the United States since its publication. The score also includes alternate phrases contributed by José Limón, principally for his own role as the male soloist in Fugue 5 and Fugue 7. There is no other score as such, but there has been another version of the work based on Limón's own interpretation that he staged at the American Dance Festival in 1960. An interesting comparison is that he appears to have added not movement vocabulary but images that redefine Humphrey's own ideas about the work. Limón emphasized two principal images: "bells tolling" as a progressive theme throughout the work, and a "gift" being given outwardly, which again recurs progressively. While there are at least two instances of the former (the "Bell Theme" variation [Passacaglia 13] and the "bell turns" in both sections), neither Humphrey's own account nor Venable's score identifies this or the image of the gift as major themes. It would seem, therefore, that Limón allowed his own creativity, coupled with his extensive experience of performing the work, to take the dance somewhere new, and with Humphrey's approval.[24] Given the earlier observation by Jordan regarding Humphrey's two versions of this work, Limón's interpretation adds a third, based as it must inevitably be on his own performance experiences from 1938 as part of the ensemble and subsequently as male soloist.

Susannah Payton-Newman learned Limón's version from him at the American Dance Festival in 1960. In comparing his version with Venable's film, she observes that Limón's was more heavily accented and that Venable's was "lighter and smoother" than the version she performed. She concludes: "Interpretations will vary according to the particular character and physicality of the choreographer. Doris Humphrey was delicate and light in frame, while José Limón was large and dramatic."[25] I agree with this view and would also cite the contrast between the Huth/Wolenski performances in 1965 as a similar example. To add a further dimension, former Limón dancer Doug Varone describes his experience of performing the work six years after Limón's death under the direction of Carla Maxwell, the company's current artistic director:

> I was attracted to how architecturally defined the Humphrey work was, and how its formal structure used bodies in space to create the emotional balance of a society. She ingeniously manipulated patterns geometrically through space to build and rebuild relationships, creating this utopian ideal that is the subtext of the work. Humphrey was a genuine abstract artist. She understood how to make the simplest walking pattern speak volumes in intent. A unifying theme of her work seemed to be the harmonious development of people within a society, and her dances were and remain extraordinary essays of humanity and community.[26]

His recollections are in line with Humphrey's version of the dance, with the emphases on "architectural," "formal structure," "harmonious society." Varone's observations imply a more abstract experience than the one described by Payton-Newman with its specific images. Carla Maxwell is noted for her sensitivity to the production of Humphrey's work alongside the Limón repertory.[27] The Varone example is interesting because it indicates a further stage of development of Limón's interpretation, this time by a female artist. Maxwell, in turn, took the interpretation back, not to the "original" dance but perhaps toward the original impulses of the dance. From these experiences and my own with *Passacaglia*, it is clear how much one seemingly fixed entity can change, even if change is unintentional. All the more reason perhaps to accept the notion that a single version of a work, and particularly a dance work, is not going to exist.

## A Musical Exploration of Choreographic Structure

*Passacaglia*, to my mind, is the greatest of Humphrey's dances because of its exuberance, scale, and life-affirming qualities, the reasons I chose to stage it for the Humphrey Centennial in 1995. The chance finding of Stokowski's orchestration, at the time out of print, was a particular thrill because the nature of the orchestral sound ideally matches the magnificence of the choreography. That this was Humphrey's preferred version of Bach's music was even more important. I wanted to explore the dance from a fresh perspective and to do so from within the Humphrey tradition, so I needed to make historical, evidence-based connections. Collingwood's ideas played an integral part in making these connections and, in broader terms, contributed to the development of a directorial stance rooted firmly in the present. On first encountering these ideas, I noted parallels with my rehearsal process for *Passacaglia* in 1995. Collingwood's "what history is" model provided a framework that was at once fixed and fluid, "fixed" because the work is at the core of the exploratory and interpretive process, and "fluid" because the process itself can embrace the elements of change and choice. Further points of identification were apparent with Benedetti's liberal category in terms of the "essential spirit of the play, transmitted by but not entirely bound in the text."[28] By approaching a work with the intent to "interpret" rather than "produce," the director can freely access the evidence. Many reconstructors already look beyond a Labanotation score when approaching a work. My approach was driven by the intent to interpret and, therefore, encompassed the "actual/potential" evidence base suggested by Collingwood alongside directorial imagination.

Recognizing the structural relationship between choreography and music is an intrinsic part of staging this dance, whatever the directorial context. Exploring the dynamic relationship created by the interplay of choreography and orchestration has created a further layer to my understanding. In turn, these insights have enabled an engagement with the dance from a perspective that has a greater emphasis on interpretation and directorial choice than the reconstructive parameters of earlier productions. I consider the Stokowski orchestration as primary or actual evidence because Humphrey preferred this version. The sound created by Stokowski's arrangement has a dimension I had not hitherto experienced. The augmented array of dynamics and tempi on offer in the orchestration ranges from subtle nuances to major climactic occurrences. The act of interpreting this sound elicited a creative relationship with the choreographic vocabulary that is not possible with the organ version, with its more limited dynamic range and "geometric" tempi.

Humphrey's letter to John Martin in 1943 is also regarded as actual evidence, with the interpretation of her remarks influencing my recent directorial process. In the passage cited earlier, at least six ideas can be identified that are open to interpretation: "I picked Bach for music because I still think he has the greatest of all genius for these very qualities of [1] *variety held in unity*, of [2] *grandeur of the human spirit*, of [3] *grace for fallen man*; not only this, but I sincerely believe [4] *the music has movement in it*, based on [5] *dances of forgotten men and women* who are the [6] *authors* (of much of the music) *of this or any other age*" (my numbering and emphasis).[29]

I chose to draw on two of these ideas. "Variety held in unity" is applied to the ensemble in terms of "what" it represents and how this could best be conveyed. For me, the dance, in part, is about a community of individuals moving with and through each other in an ongoing progression. The ensemble, therefore, collectively creates a visual and structural democracy. The Labanotation score indicates a clear hierarchical structure for casting the ensemble: four of the sixteen ensemble dancers have particularly prominent roles, and four dance only with the larger group. As with a number of Humphrey's dances, cast size can vary. In *Passacaglia*, cutting up to four roles can create a significant shift of emphasis within the ensemble. The dance becomes more egalitarian with two soloists and an ensemble of twelve. In reassigning certain movement phrases, each member of the "community" can have a more substantial role. In turn, this conveys a more democratized individuality throughout the ensemble. "The music has movement in it" was the second idea I chose to focus on, and this allowed me to interpret "what is heard" in the music in conjunction with "what is read" from the notation score and create an additional layer of dynamic possibility. This idea, in fact, became my central focus and is defined as interpreting the sound of the music. These examples illustrate the value of fluid material, of deciding what is important and the consequence(s) of making choices. A different production process could elicit different choices from this same evidence base and produce a different interpretation.

In choosing to explore the dance from a musical perspective and interpret the Stokowski sound in conjunction with the Bach score, it became apparent that choreo-musical relationships could exist on two levels: first, in a structural relationship between choreography and music, and second, in a dynamic relationship between choreography and orchestration. The synergy of these two interacting levels becomes an intrinsic part of the interpretive process. Figure 11 illustrates the structural relationship between choreography and music and shows how Humphrey layered her choreographic structure over Bach's musical structure. The work is in 3/4 meter, with the passacaglia section musically arranged in twenty-one eight-measure phrases. The fugue section, following musical convention, is more asymmetric. Bach adopted a structure comprising twelve phrases of differing length and a coda. Table 1 indicates the musical phrases by number with the choreographic action alongside. For the fugue, the number of measures in each phrase is also included. Individual roles are identified by letter in the Labanotation score and are incorporated in the table. The titles given to certain variations, such as "Lyric" and "Turns," are Humphrey's own, and the brief movement descriptions are from my directorial notes.

Humphrey's adherence to Bach's structure is more open than it may appear, with choreographic phrasing crossing over the musical structure in a number of instances. The first occurrence comes in Passacaglia 8, 9, and 10, "Processional." The movement is a nine-beat phrase repeated a number of times, first by the two soloists and then by the ensemble. The movement vocabulary begins

*Passacaglia*

| Phrase | Choreographic action |
|---|---|
| 1 | Unison hold, upstage facing |
| 2 | C turns |
| 3 | CD travel |
| 4 | Unison turn, downstage facing |
| 5/6 | CD, EF double duet |
| 7 | A and B, solo/duet |
| 8 | AB state processional |
| 9 | AB diagonal theme, group processional |
| 10 | AB side leaps, group processional |
| 11 | AB upstage/downstage tilts, group hold |
| 12 | AB processional leap and tilts, group processional |
| 13 | "Bell Theme," B and A with JL |
| 14 | AB duet, group canon |
| 15 | "Lyric" variation, CDEFG |
| 16 | "Turns" variation, A |
| 17 | "Jump" ("Men's") variation, ROP |
| 18 | "Chicken" variation, CDGL |
| 19 | Processional in canon, AB and group |
| 20 | Bell turns, unison |
| 21 | Bell turns and transition into the fugue, unison |

*Fugue*

| Phrase | Choreographic action |
|---|---|
| 1 (5) | K solo, with FGQ |
| 2 (7) | O solo, with PC |
| 3 (5) | L solo, with RE |
| 4 (6) | G solo, with BFJD |
| 5 (6) | B solo |
| 6 (11) | Walk on diagonal, BRL |
| 7 (12) | B solo, "Leaping Quartet," FGJD |
| 8 (13) | A with RL, group in canon |
| 9 (12) | Falling trio on boxes, CEP |
| 10 (10) | A with group falling in canon |
| 11 (16) | AB, with group |
| 12 (14) | Bell turns in canon, AB with group |
| Coda (7) | Final tilts/falling, AB with group |

Figure 11. Musical structure with corresponding choreographic action (abbreviations C, CD, etc. identify individual roles) in *Passacaglia*.

from a stance that has a sense of nobility, an adjective much associated with this dance. The arms are held in soft curves behind the body, with torso and focus lifted and open. Three purposeful steps on a circular spatial pathway are followed by a plié turn in to center, the right arm and leg extending upward in a progressive, arcing, expansive motion. The apex of the arc/suspension comes on beat 6, then releases down into a deep plié, arms in a simultaneous upward/downward press to meet each other before the final suspension on beat 9 as the body breathes in and turns, opening outward with the arms pulling back into the low curve to resume the procession. The "Processional" recurs in Passacaglia 12 and 13 with a variation in the concluding movement, and again in Passacaglia 19 in twelve- and six-beat forms.

A different kind of example occurs in Passacaglia 13 (the "Bell Theme") and in Fugue 6. Here, three measures of four beats (dance) are set against four measures of three beats (music). In addition, Humphrey creates a visual counterpoint by having a small group dance "three fours" against the ensemble dancing the "Processional" nine-count phrase in Passacaglia 13 and "four threes" in Fugue 6. In Fugue 9 a "falling" 9/8 phrase is repeated three times. Here again, Humphrey gives the falling phrase to a small group, a trio in this case, while the ensemble dance within the "four three" structure. In the 9/8 phrase, as in the "Processional," the dancers travel on a (semi)circular spatial pathway but

Figure 12. The "Bell Theme" trio, Passacaglia 13. Arkè Compagnia d'Arte, Turin, Italy, 2006. Photographer: Alberto Sachero.

Figure 13. The "Bell Theme" duet, Passacaglia 13. Arkè Compagnia d'Arte, Turin, Italy, 2006. Photographer: Alberto Sachero.

this time by way of falling, swooping, and expansive turning around the body's axis, an invigorating example of Humphrey's fall and recovery theory in action. A further device Humphrey employs is the accenting of particular beats. In Passacaglia 7, the ensemble's phrase is structured in four measures of six beats (rather than the standard eight measures of three beats). Within this, the movement's rhythmic pattern emphasizes beats 1, 2, 4, and 5. Following this, a similar pattern is seen in Passacaglia 11, with the accents here on beats 1, 2, and 5. The effect is subtle in Passacaglia 7, with small arm/torso shifts from side to side. In Passacaglia 11, the movement again involves shifting but this time through full body lunges, forward and back, side-on to the audience. In both variations, the movement material is quite different, but the effect of the ensemble moving rhythmically in unison is equally striking. These examples illustrate Humphrey's continual exploration of the oppositional pull between constancy and the unexpected and the play between symmetry and asymmetry.

That Humphrey created this work hearing the "sound" of the Stokowski orchestration makes great sense. Her passion and respect for Bach's music are well documented; however, the connection to Stokowski has not been considered in any depth other than in Jordan's work.[30] Sondra Fraleigh ventures into the area of musical/directorial interpretation through observations by former

Limón dancer Susannah Payton-Newman on her staging of the work based on Limón's interpretation.[31] Payton-Newman favors the Stokowski orchestral arrangement, finding the organ version "too sweet for the stately unsentimental style of the dance."[32] Her comment, interestingly, demonstrates how differently two listeners can hear the same sound. My own impression of the organ is that it has a dirgelike quality that pulls the dance inappropriately downward.

Interpreting the sound of the music became central to my interpretation of the dance and produced a creative relationship with the vocabulary that was not possible with the organ version. Jordan observes that Stokowski's interpretation is "flamboyant."[33] I would describe it as "wild" because it is exhilarating and unpredictable through the ever-changing textures and dynamics, some of which verge on the uncontrollable. There is a direct parallel here with Humphrey's Apollonian/Dionysian philosophy of an underlying groundedness coupled with complete abandon. There is color and drama in the Stokowski orchestration, aspects that are intertwined in the sound of the music. The sound gives the dance an added dimension, the identification of which has been both liberating and revelatory. The combination of orchestra and orchestration blends seamlessly with the Humphrey principles of suspension and expansive movement. As one example, the orchestration becomes more luminous and layered throughout the opening four variations, in direct contrast to the ponderous chordal sounds produced by the organ. The opening bar of Passacaglia 4 creates a unified optimism through the dual aspect of the strings picking up the theme and a purposeful increase in tempo at the very moment, choreographically, that the group moves as one for the first time. The movement, a unison pivot turn from upstage to downstage, is a powerful moment for the ensemble, whatever the accompaniment, because the combination of the movement with resulting color change (as the two-sided costumes reverse) conveys the start of something significant. Stokowski's orchestration gives this moment a greater resonance than the organ in two specific contexts. From the dancer's perspective, the pivot turn feels more uplifted and energized by adopting the dynamics produced by the sound of the strings. This heightened sense of suspension is manifested aurally and visually for the audience and increases the impact of the first sighting of the ensemble and the possibilities of who or what this group might be.

As noted earlier, I regard the recording or arrangement used during Humphrey's choreographic process as "actual" evidence. The arrangement conveys the phrasing and dynamics Humphrey heard while creating the dance, and this, in turn, offers clues to the execution of movements and movement phrases. One example is the degree of contrast in Passacaglia 15, "Lyric," and 16, "Turns." The former has a distinctly quiet, gentle quality, preceding the sweeping, booming sound that accompanies the technically virtuosic turn sequence. The progressive contrast in the sound adds to the dramatic progression of the work. More specifically, the qualities heard in the sound can translate to the movement. A further example is the opening-arm gesture preceding a jump sequence in Passacaglia 17, "Jump." The musical timing and sound of the Stokowski orchestration is a long, resonating dotted eighth note releasing into a staccato sixteenth note. By adopting this timing, the gesture can be pulled out and suspended, allowing the jump to burst forth. Other recordings do not have a comparable degree of resonance or staccato, so the sense of suspension is less pronounced. This particular emphasis appears in numerous passages throughout the work and is significant because suspension is a fundamental stylistic element in Humphrey's work.

The time frame of the musical work, for organ or orchestra, ranges between eleven and fifteen minutes, with the majority of recordings being eleven or twelve minutes. My first production in 1981 used an organ recording by Lionel Rogg, with the fugue section decelerated by electronic means, which brought the pitch down by a minor third, as it transpired. I felt the musical "tampering" was justifiable because the dancers in Venable's film clearly had time to fully execute the movement material. Venable worked with organist Richard Grant and was in a position to give him directions on dynamics and appropriate tempi. Venable's time frame of fifteen minutes seemed a credible gauge, therefore, on which to base the time frame and tempi for my own production. The Stokowski orchestration is at the slower end of the time frame spectrum because the stylistic aspects of his interpretation have resulted in decreases in tempi within a number of variations in the passacaglia and generally throughout the fugue. One example, early in the dance, comes in the final two bars of Passacaglia 8, as the two soloists execute a forward lunge to respective downstage corners, then pivot around and upward in an expansive suspension before releasing into a falling run to bring them back together center stage. The climactic moment here is the suspension on beat 3 in measure 7, as Stokowski pauses for some time at this "high point." His pause on that particular note and beat is ideally matched with Humphrey's suspension. It is an exhilarating passage to dance because of this synthesis and because of what precedes and follows. The dancer is both musically and choreographically drawn up to that climactic point through a deceleration in tempo and then allowed to fall out of the suspension in a corresponding acceleration, which creates a seamless flow into the next suspension, leading into the next variation.

The previous example illustrates the choreo-musical relationship in its dynamic context between choreography and orchestration and is a recurring feature throughout the work. When this same movement is danced to the organ, the suspension does not have the time to breathe and fully expand as it could because the tempo remains constant throughout the variation. This constancy has implications for the rest of the phrase, as the steps into the lunge do not have the decelerando Stokowski provides; instead, it retains the tempo of the preceding movement, the first occurrence of the "Processional" walk. The run out of the suspension, likewise, maintains the tempo. The regular tempo and lack of dynamic contrast, in comparison with the orchestration, produce a quite different movement experience, to dance and to view, an observation that is reflective of the complete work. Overall, the organ version produces a feeling of gradual progression in contrast with the dramatic and unexpected surges created throughout by Stokowski.

Important in performance terms is that the drama and scale of Stokowski's sound is matched by the dancing. The central idea given to the dancers, therefore, was to "get inside" the sound, to use and embody its dynamics to counter the danger of becoming submerged. The particular vocabulary of *Passacaglia* lends itself well to this idea, with its emphasis on lyrical movement and phrasing; with recurring motifs employing variations of curved, expansive motion; with fluid transitional movement permeating individual phrases; and, more generally, with the transitions from one variation into the next. Payton-Newman observes that *Passacaglia* has "the kind of completeness in itself through its formal constructs and full-bodied movement, its forward momentum, its warmth and deep character, that continue to fulfil [today's audience]. It is a wonderful dance to do and to watch because it is a full-bodied dance."[34] Her reference to "full-bodied" movement parallels my own experience of Humphrey's movement style, which Stodelle refers to as "wholeness of movement" and of "dancing from the inside out." The sensation is that every part of the body is "alive" and engaged in the movement activity with a simultaneous internal/peripheral connection. Payton-Newman also refers to *Passacaglia* itself as "full-bodied," which I would correlate with the idea of the dance having the innate expanse and resonance referred to earlier.

In relation to the idea of "resonance," the film version by Venable is a thrilling and idealistic representation of the dance. Venable was able to give the dance expansiveness because she had the space to do so on the vast stage of the New York State Theater at Lincoln Centre. Having access to such a performance space meant that she did not have to contend with the confines of the more conventional dance theater space Humphrey would have encountered on tour and at Juilliard and Connecticut College. "Space" is significant, because the amount available to the individual dancer has a direct correlation with how one can execute Humphrey's vocabulary. Space is especially relevant for the ensemble dancers, clustered together in close proximity. Venable's ensemble

Figure 14. Fugue 11, Momenta, Oak Park, Illinois, 2007. Photographer: Lisa Green (Steve Green Photography, www.sgreenphoto.com).

dancers have space to move that is generally more comparable to that of the two soloists, who dance apart from the main body of the ensemble for much of the work. In one sense, seeing the film representation leaves today's director frustrated because it is clear from the film what the dance can do. That aside, Venable's production illustrates the expanse of the work that a director can aspire to, although the means of achieving this will differ. While the physical space available to Venable would be difficult to replicate at this time, the Stokowski sound can create a metaphorical expanse. The directorial challenge lies in achieving this sense of expanse within a more limited physical space.

My approach was twofold: first, the dancers learned the material without spatial restrictions in order to fully experience the movement. Once they had reached the point of "dancing" rather than "learning," we went through a process of transposing what had become familiar sensations into a different spatial context. This new context involved some restriction but also added a further dimension, with the dancers being directed to extend the movement "upward." The upward image is not as simplistic as lifting either the focus or body parts higher in space but is based more on the direction of energy rising out of the body surfaces. This approach allowed the dancing body to maintain a sense of expanse as the "outward" dimension, directly surrounding the body, became more restricted.

Further challenges lay in the relationship between musical timing and technical execution. There are numerous examples of disruption throughout the work that contrast with the steadier tempo of the organ. The consequence of dancers losing the tempo is disruption to phrasing, flow, and unison, significant in a work where the music-dance relationship is intrinsic. Furthermore, when dancers stay in unison but lose the tempo collectively, the effect is equally disruptive because of the visual jarring produced in relation to flow, phrasing, and design. One example is Passacaglia 18, "Chicken," a quartet for four women. The dancers begin in a square formation with the choreography comprising a syncopated step/turn pattern with upper body tilts that shift side to side as the variation progresses, first in a circular pathway around the stage and then along linear pathways as the quartet breaks into two pairs. With the music-dance relationship intact, the eye is drawn to the overall spatial design and how the movement patterns unfold across the stage. When that relationship is disrupted, the sense of the "whole" is similarly disrupted. This is a useful example because it highlights a problem the contemporary director must address. Dancers have to keep a number of contrasting works in repertoire concurrently, and while a certain familiarity will come through performing a work over time, the dancers need to be given sufficient musical signposts during the rehearsal process. In the case of this particular quartet, the solution came in cueing the dancers to follow

Figure 15. The "Chicken" variation, Passacaglia 18. Arkè Compagnia d'Arte, Turin, Italy, 2006. Photographer: Alberto Sachero.

the flute line rather than the more emphatic bass line. The flute emphasizes the "pick up" on the first step of each measure, whereas the dancers had been losing the tempo and rhythm of the choreography by going with the bass.

Stokowski employs a midphrase ritardando liberally throughout his orchestration. In Passacaglia 9/10, the first instance of the "Processional" walk, the nine-beat phrase is repeated five times. Dancers need to be aware that the third repetition slows considerably during beats 4, 5, and 6 and that the tempo picks up swiftly going into the fourth and fifth repetitions. A slightly different example is Passacaglia 11, where the choreographic suspension into the next phrase has to come at a specific point. The musical tempo slows down, so that the beats become obscured. The dancers were directed to go with the timpani roll and to pick up the suspension from the oboe entry in a "rising" sense, much like the violin/pivot turn juxtaposition in Passacaglia 4. A notable example of dealing with ritardando from a technical perspective is the deceleration in Fugue 12, in the final set of bell turns for the soloists. These are challenging to execute at a steady tempo, and Stokowski's orchestration requires each of the four sets of turns to decrease in speed. The solution for the dancers, in conjunction with technical practice, was to embody the idea of "getting inside the sound" and going with it.

## Centennial Celebrations and Beyond

The inspiration for my 1995 production lay primarily in the music and in creating a work that would speak to a contemporary audience. There were two further contributory factors. The first was the occasion of Humphrey's centenary itself, with the work being chosen because it epitomizes Humphrey's legacy and demonstrates how accessible her work can be to today's audience. The second factor was a statement she made in 1943 that appears in the letter to dance critic John Martin, defending her use of Bach's music for *Passacaglia* and other works. The sentiments seemed particularly appropriate for the centenary, being reflective of both the individual work and her artistic credo as a whole. She wrote, "Now is the time for me to tell of the nobility the human spirit is capable of, stress the grace that is in us, give the young dancers a chance to move harmoniously with each other."[35] Alongside the more obvious emphases on nobility, grace, and harmonious movement, a striking feature of this passage is Humphrey's specific reference to "young" dancers and not simply "dancers." She was forty-five years old when she wrote this and, while "older" in dance terms, was still performing regularly, so this was not a sentimental reflection. Her words could have more than one meaning, of course, but I took from this the idea of "youthfulness" and the raw edge this would bring to a work noted for its maturity. I wanted the dance to look young and fresh, to capture the abandonment of youth that Humphrey herself emphasized. The combining of these elements created a vibrancy I felt would work with the sound created by the music.

A further influential element in the 1995 production process was the creation of a more prominent role for the female lead. Existing documentation, including Venable's Labanotation score, her 1965 film of the dance, and various literary references, all depict the male lead as the prominent role, identified in the score as "A." The principal reason for switching the male and female lead roles in my interpretation was to create a "spirit of Humphrey" through the central figure. Structurally, it was possible to do so by assigning certain variations in the work to the female lead. The Labanotation score indicates that the virtuosic "Turns" solo—Passacaglia 16—can be danced by either of the leads. In addition, Venable's film version has the soloists dancing the variation together. This evidence suggests certain latitude for the director that I in turn applied to two further variations—Passacaglia 7 and Fugue 10. These are, arguably, the two pivotal variations in the work, as the leadership emerges from the ensemble in Passacaglia 7 and is emphatically reaffirmed in Fugue 10. To maintain a sense of partnership between the two roles, the male soloist retained his lead in Passacaglia 10 and the assigned solos, Fugue 5 and Fugue 7. By assigning the soloist material in this way, a complete role reversal was avoided that could have left the male lead somewhat emasculated and following the female lead throughout. The adjustments, while not being completely equal, did allow for the establishment of both leads as individuals within the partnership. The adjustments are also reflective of Humphrey's position on gender equality. Former Humphrey-Weidman dancer Nona Schurman describes this as follows: "Doris's great message . . . is the equality of the men and women. There isn't dominance in any of her work. . . . There is always this harmonious relationship. It shows choreographically. . . . [Y]ou don't have to look for it, it's right there. So, the men's and the women's lines are equal in weight. She doesn't throw the weight to the men, she doesn't throw it to the women. There is a harmonious relationship there."[36]

I had set out to create a production of this work that would be accessible to a contemporary audience, so the occasion of Humphrey's centenary in 1995 provided a number of opportunities for the "accessibility" to be tested, and with audiences ranging from the lay person to the Humphrey expert. I estimated that the "informed" end of the audience spectrum would appreciate the production, and this did prove to be the case when the work was shown as part of a joint event between the Doris Humphrey Foundation, Dance Umbrella, and the Society for Dance Research. Audience members included Selma Jeanne Cohen, Ann Hutchinson Guest, Bonnie Bird, Millicent Hodson, and Els Grelinger. Following the performance, Cohen observed: "They can't do 'bell turns' like that in New York," a comment much appreciated by the dancers. Dance critic Alistair Macaulay remarked that he had never previously "gotten" Humphrey's work until he saw this production of *Passacaglia*. His reaction is significant because it underlines the importance of these dances being performed by dancers who can dance the style. The cast comprised graduating students for the most part, but they all had three years' experience of Humphrey technique and had taken class with Stodelle in the run-up to the centenary performances.

I was less certain how a lay audience might react, and, in one sense, this was the more important test of the work's accessibility. The dance was performed twice at the Royal Festival Hall as part of a daylong event on Humphrey.[37] Audiences were transitory, the underlying principle of the venue being to entice those who may not have encountered dance in a more conventional setting. The audience response at the conclusion of the performances made clear how accessible the work still is. Many individual reactions were made known to me afterward, ranging from feelings of exhilaration, to being moved, to being overwhelmed. It was particularly interesting to observe that for the audience the most prominent aspect was appreciating the dance as an "experience" rather than being concerned with what the dance might be "about."

The examples given here demonstrate the kinds of issues the directorial process must address when approaching this work from a musical perspective. My exploration of the structural relationship between choreography and music alongside the dynamic relationship between choreography and orchestration produced an interpretation that was distinctive from my past reconstruction-based stagings. The increased range of music-dance interactions gave me fresh insights into the dance work and served as an illustration of the mutual impact one art form can have in conjunction with another. Within the directorial process, the dance did have a more specific meaning, as represented by the "democratized community." It was not imperative, however, that an audience read this meaning. The response at the Royal Festival Hall made clear that the work could be appreciated without such specific information. In my role as director, the interpretive process encompassed translating the sound of the music into the movement vocabulary; for the dancers, it involved transposing the dynamics created by the movement vocabulary collectively in time and space from within the sound; and for the audience, it involved receiving what could be described as a multi-dimensional sensory experience.

The production processes undertaken in 2007-8 represent the third key period of engagement with the work. During this period, I directed the dance for two companies, Arkè Compagnia d'Arte in Turin, Italy, and Momenta Dance

Figure 16. Fugue 10, Momenta, Oak Park, Illinois, 2007. Photographer: Lisa Green (Steve Green Photography, www.sgreenphoto.com).

Company in Chicago. I had gone deep into the work and the working process in 1995, but the actual interpretive approach has since taken on a different, subtler guise. The two ideas I chose to focus on back then continue to have currency, and I am not quite ready to move on. "Variety held in unity" remains compelling because there are so many possibilities. Each new cast and stage space brings a fresh opportunity to explore the balance within the ensemble and how this can be conveyed by a new set of circumstances. Each new production begins from the premise of the democratized community, with each individual having an identifiable role in one or more variations. My practice in early rehearsals is to set movement from a number of variations on the full cast and then to observe how individual bodies respond. The variation-based structure of the dance provides a certain freedom in casting that enables the director to respond to these responses. In a dance such as this, with its emphasis on the ensemble, there is little room or opportunity for the ensemble dancers to make any individual interpretive contribution. Acknowledging what the dancing bodies are instinctively saying in response to newly learned material allows individual voices to be heard and accommodated to a degree. The choreography in this dance is certainly within the grasp of well-trained professional dancers; thus, one could cast ahead of the first rehearsal. For my approach, however, acknowledging individual flair is important and worth the rehearsal time spent on such discovery.

Staging two productions concurrently was an interesting process and heightened my awareness of the choices being made. One example was the casting for the opening duet, Passacaglia 2–4 (see figure 10). As the opening statement of the dance, this duet is significant. It requires mature poise and a calm inner stillness that can radiate outward as each dancer pivots, one following the other, to greet the audience for the first time. The dancers must also work especially well as a pair because their unison movement around the space, opening up the stage for what is to come, must be seamless. It was important, therefore, to cast dancers who had the required individual qualities but who could also work well together. An example of contrast between the two productions was Passacaglia 17, the "Jump" variation. In Chicago I followed the traditional casting of three men, all of whom had impressive elevation and brought a mature gravitas to the movement. I favor the idea of the male dancing in *Passacaglia* resonating with the spirits of Weidman and Limón, expansive through the torso and extremities with a deep, grounded power that is contained where appropriate but can also be unleashed with explosive effect. This particular variation embodies all of these qualities within its eight-bar framework. Not having three such men available in Turin, I went instead for a different look, casting three of the younger women. They, likewise, had impressive elevation but also brought a

Figure 17. The "Jump" variation, Passacaglia 17. Momenta, Oak Park, Illinois, 2007. Photographer: Lisa Green (Steve Green Photography, www.sgreenphoto.com).

youthful exuberance and spark that worked well alongside the musical sound and rhythms that Stokowski chose to emphasize in this passage.

The Momenta production provided the opportunity to play with the idea of "variety held in unity" in a spatial context. The set of rising boxes was constructed to the full height specifications, with an eighteen-inch drop for each of the three levels. Stepping down smoothly, without lowering the gaze or "clunking" down on one foot, presents something of a challenge, notably from the topmost level. Generally, this top level is the domain of the two soloists or static positioning for the ensemble. While setting Passacaglia 13 and 14, I saw an opportunity to explore the uppermost space further. This passage contains the concluding phrases of the nine-count "Processional" walk for the ensemble as they reassemble on the boxes (Passacaglia 13), followed by a rising and falling canon for the whole group (Passacaglia 14). Venable's film and the score both indicate that the first two levels are used for this section. Having a single dancer in the center of the ensemble climb up to the topmost box for the final "Processional" movement simultaneously lifted the visual representation of the group as a whole and created a center point at its highest level. A moment of stillness follows the "Processional," further emphasizing the visual expanse of the group — from the two soloists, positioned center stage, through the ensemble layered in front of and on each level of the boxes, up to the single figure at its peak.

The rising and falling canon that follows (Passacaglia 14) retains this increased dimension to good effect. The movement here begins with a suspension, an expansive horizontal opening of the arms as one leg extends forward, followed by a descent to one knee as the arms and leg release and lower. In two scattered groupings, the dancers rise and fall in opposition, creating a contrapuntal image that falls forward off the boxes. The addition of the single figure on the topmost level brought something new to this section, creating a sense of soaring forward into space that does not exist to the same degree farther down because there are more bodies within the same vicinities, and there is not the same degree of separation and height. This moment is exhilarating, in part because it requires a level of daring for the single dancer (and, not least, a head for heights) that embodies Humphrey's idea of "playing the edge." A further reason, as discussed earlier in this chapter in relation to Venable's staging, is the increased expansion of the stage space made possible by the adjustment, and it would certainly be retained in future productions.

Arkè provided a contrasting experience. There were no men in the company at the time, and I was curious to see how an all-female cast would work. The "variety held in unity" idea had one less facet, but plenty of scope remained with a group of fifteen individuals. The directors of the company, Matilde Dimarchi and Annagrazia D'Antico, danced the two soloist roles, bringing a

Figure 18. Matilde Demarchi and Annagrazia D'Antico, Passacaglia 12, Arkè Compagnia d'Arte, Turin, Italy, 2006. Photographer: Alberto Sachero.

mature and assured presence as well as a natural leadership of this particular group. Having adjusted the balance between the two soloist roles in 1995 to privilege the female soloist and create a "spirit of Humphrey," I retained these adjustments for Cameron Jarrett in the Momenta production. In the Arkè context, however, it made more sense to create a balance between the two women. Further adjustments were made to create an equitable prominence for both soloists, with one "leading" the passacaglia and the other the fugue. There is no question that a female cast gives the dance a different feel, but the power of the dance was in no way diminished by the lack of a male presence. That *Passacaglia* was programmed alongside Graham's all-female *Steps in the Street* (1936) in Turin gave added impact and was a most striking example of the feminine power embodied in modern dance.

The next idea I took from Humphrey, "The music has movement in it," similarly continues to stimulate. Over time, new impulses and influences in the music become apparent; following a different line of instrumentation, for example, can alter timing and, in turn, emphasis. Uncovering fresh stimuli is not so surprising given that the musical score is rich and complex. Add in the complexities of the orchestration, and one can get a sense of the possibilities. When it comes time to move on from having a musical approach at the forefront, the next set of ideas is not far away. That same 1943 statement throws up two further ideas for exploration — the third idea, "grace for fallen man," and the fifth, "dances of forgotten men and women." Link these to a more narrative response to the rise of fascism and war, and a quite different scenario could unfold. Would the dance look any different? Yes, I believe it would — and should, given the sources — but not so different that it turns into an unrecognizable form. That would imply a shift beyond directorial interpretation into Benedetti's radical/creative sphere. Of broader importance is that there is continuing engagement with these dances beyond simply keeping them alive. The interpretive processes related here in relation to *Passacaglia* illustrate that possibilities beyond traditional reconstruction certainly exist. Moreover, when undertaken from the appropriate perspective — from "within" a stylistic tradition — such approaches can produce new knowledge from the existing evidence. The productions of *Passacaglia* in 1995 and 2007-8 all lay within Benedetti's liberal category. In addition to capturing the essential spirit of the work and not being bound by the text, the processes undertaken have allowed the work to live relevant to the present moment — perhaps the most crucial aspect of all.

# WITH MY RED FIRES

*Choreography*: 1936
*Music*: Wallingford Reigger
*Premiere*: August 13, 1936, Armory, Bennington, Vermont

*With My Red Fires* is an exploration of the destructive elements of possessive love. Humphrey structured the dance in two parts, each with indicative subtitles:

> Part One: Ritual
> I Hymn to Priapus
> II Search and Betrothal
> III Departure
> Part Two: Drama
> IV Summons/Coercion and Escape
> V Alarm and Pursuit
> VI Judgment

The theme of possessive love is depicted through the interrelationships between three symbolic characters: the Matriarch, the Young Woman, and the Young Man, who entices the Young Woman away from home. A large ensemble of men and women represents a fourth "character." This ensemble at first celebrates the young couple finding each other in Part One but subsequently turns against them in Part Two through increasingly manipulative hectoring by the Matriarch. The choreographic ideas intersperse rigid power and conformity with gloriously uplifting, if fleeting, moments. The dance is an exhibition of opposition, of contrasts in movement dynamic, in emotion, in confrontation and resolution. Its very darkness at once creates apprehension and exhilaration. Humphrey creates the world of an unforgiving, unbending society through an

106

ingenious series of configurations for the ensemble. Structural elements such as the "processional" and "wheeling star" are used to devastating effect in the dramatic context of this work. These same forms, in contrast, have a quite different connotation and impact in other dances, including *New Dance, Passacaglia*, and *The Shakers*. Wallingford Reigger's dissonant score was added after the choreography was set, and one can hear how his composition was influenced by the percussive angularity in Humphrey's choreographic vocabulary.

In 1999 a young American art student named Matthew Shepherd was the victim of a brutal homophobic murder. The sickening attack that led to his death was further compounded by religious fundamentalists who refused to condemn the act and planned a protest at Shepherd's funeral. A handful of protesters appeared at the funeral, but they were completely overshadowed by the thousand-plus crowd that turned out to celebrate this young man's life. I recall vividly hearing news of these events as they unfolded and feeling shock and outrage at the level of violence and bigotry but also a renewed hope that tolerance and acceptance came through in the end. At the time I was starting work on *With My Red Fires*, and there was a marked distinction in how I "read" the work after hearing this news. The climax of the dance became emotionally overwhelming where it hadn't before, and it is no coincidence that previously underlying themes of intolerance and bigotry became far more pronounced. The subsequent interpretation was not based on what happened to Matthew Shepherd, but it was certainly shaped by those events and the emotions that were generated at the time. I felt that Humphrey's dance had the capacity to make a potent social comment on the issues raised and behaviors highlighted by the manner of Shepherd's attack and the contrasting responses to it. Social injustice is the unwelcome side of humankind. The individual turned on by a mob element, a minority shunned by the majority, society held to ransom by extremism are not new but no less abhorrent when they occur. In a similar vein, the inherent optimism of humanity is never quite dimmed.

The idea of modern dance works commenting on sociocultural issues and events is a familiar one throughout the history of the genre. Examples include *Theater Piece* (1935) and *Passacaglia* (1938) by Humphrey, *Lynchtown* (1936) by Weidman, Graham's *Steps in the Street* (1936), and Taylor's *Last Look* (1985) — all created around or influenced by a particular issue or event. Weidman's *Lynchtown*, for example, depicted the scapegoating of an innocent man accused of assaulting a white girl simply because he was black and subsequently hanged by the white townsfolk. Humphrey's themes, conversely, were tackled in a less literal manner. By reinterpreting an issue from a contemporary perspective, a work's message can be made relevant for its current audience. I would go further again and suggest that the power of a work's message may be better served by reinterpreting the work itself to the extent that elements could alter or disappear. There are no precedents in modern dance for this form of interpretive practice, but there are in theater. As discussed in part 1, the staging of Shakespeare provides an extensive and diverse range of directorial processes that can be adapted or adopted within a dance context. I approached *With My Red Fires* for the first time, therefore, from the dual standpoint of Benedetti's liberal position (to "unleash the work for its contemporary audience") and Hayden White's notion of creating a "recognizable form." My intention was to privilege Humphrey's underlying themes by reducing the literal emphasis of the narrative and characterizations in order to make these themes more compelling in a contemporary context.

## Performance History

*With My Red Fires* is distinctive within Humphrey's body of work because its dark connotations give it a notably different color and tone from her other dances. Humphrey's choreographic canon was noted for a recurring theme of idealism. She had not ventured into the darker side of the human psyche until she created this work. Siegel observes that "Doris pulled back from the demonic theatricality she had uncovered, almost in spite of herself, in *Red Fires*."[1] Furthermore, Humphrey seldom ventured into this dark territory again. The work became a staple in the Humphrey-Weidman repertoire following its premiere at Bennington. Humphrey went on to stage the dance regularly throughout her life, including at Juilliard and Connecticut College. Humphrey considered the work to be the middle part of her *New Dance Trilogy*, despite its being choreographed last in the sequence. *With My Red Fires* was acclaimed repeatedly over the years as a work in its own right. At its premiere, John Martin was "mightily impressed."[2] Margaret Lloyd, in a critique of the *New Dance Trilogy* for the *Christian Science Monitor* (October 8, 1937), called it "not only the greatest dance composition, but the greatest artistic expression of present day life in any form that has come out of America."[3] This followed a performance in the Hippodrome in front of an audience of five thousand — an unusually large crowd for modern dance at that time. Martin wrote in a piece for the *New York Times* in April 1942: "The work has never seemed more beautiful or more intensely moving. Certainly it has never been so superbly danced."

The work's more recent performance history in the United States has been intermittent, however. Twenty years elapsed between a revival for the American Dance Festival, filmed in 1972 and commercially released with *New Dance* in 1978, and a reconstruction staged by Repertory Dance Theater in 1992 at the

American Dance Festival West in Utah. There was also a further reconstruction presented by Mino Nicholas in 1995 for the Humphrey Centenary in New York. The 1972 reconstruction, staged by Ruth Currier, caused both controversial and appreciative reactions to the casting of an African American dancer in the role of the Young Man. This was at a time when interracial relationships were less widely accepted than they are today. The casting added a further layer of meaning to the work and introduced a new dimension to the Matriarch's disapproval of the Young Man and to the motivation behind the ensemble's pursuit of the couple in the later passages of the work. Currier's action in changing that one element illustrates the capacity for a reconstruction process to embrace updated commentary. Today, Charles H. Woodford, Humphrey's son and executor, prefers this casting: "In 1972, Ruth Currier cleverly cast a black dancer in the male lead so that the prejudice would have contemporary relevance. I think further reconstructions should be cast the same way."[4] His comment also reflects how little times have changed, perhaps.

## Contemporary Perspectives

I was drawn to the idea of this dance because of its narrative and its scale. Humphrey used forty-seven dancers in the premiere at Bennington, and although it would be difficult to find a performance space as large as that at Bennington, there is still great scope for the ensemble. Humphrey was noted for her use of the ensemble in general and the visual drama created by a mass of moving bodies, *Passacaglia* and *With My Red Fires* being of similar scale. My initial responses to the dance were based on its Labanotation score and the 1978 ADF film.[5] I had also seen a black-and-white version some years earlier of Humphrey's staging for Juilliard in 1954 and recall being ambivalent about the work at that time, although my reaction was, in part, due to a recording of poor picture and audio quality.[6] Viewing the work again in its updated form and in a high quality recorded version allowed me to see the dance differently. I was inspired by the dramatic power but even more by the dance's potential to speak meaningfully within a contemporized context. Humphrey's narrative is based on possessive love, but underneath lie secondary and interrelated meanings, including intolerance, bigotry, and survival, that were open to being drawn out and given greater prominence.

*With My Red Fires* is regarded as one of Humphrey's major choreographic achievements.[7] Along with a continuing performance history, the work has undergone analytical exploration. Ramsay Burt reassesses the work in the context of contemporary experience, which has a parallel with my own directorial investigation.[8] Burt discusses the value of viewing this modernist work from a

postmodernist perspective and the resulting political metaphors and symbolism that such a perspective can generate. In his experience, the political aspect
has greater meaning and relevance for contemporary students of dance than
Humphrey's more dominant theme of possessive love. The parallel between
his reassessment and my own is the acknowledgment that the "work" as it once
was has something more to say today if it is examined and reinterpreted from
a position that incorporates contemporary known experience.

More controversial than Burt's analysis is a paper presented by Susan Foster at the Society of Dance History Scholars 22nd Annual Conference in 1999.
Foster uses the work and her reading of the personal relationship between
Humphrey and long-term associate Pauline Lawrence to argue that Humphrey
choreographed action that supported multiple contradictory interpretations.
Foster opens her paper by stating that Humphrey and Lawrence were lovers. At the conference, Foster was challenged about the evidence she had to
substantiate her claim.[9] The close intimate friendship between Humphrey and
Lawrence is documented in Marcia Siegel's biography of Humphrey, *Days on
Earth* (1993). Siegel had access to Humphrey's private letters but acknowledged
that there was no conclusive evidence to indicate that the relationship had been
sexual; instead, it may have been an example of the "romantic friendship" that
existed between women in the late nineteenth and early twentieth centuries.[10]
Foster's stance was perhaps more about illustrating her argument on multiple
interpretations. The lesbian angle is, however, further emphasized through the
choice of language. She talks about the Matriarch pushing the Young Woman
"gently to the floor where they lie together" and the Young Woman "yearn-
ing for the Matriarch" as she leaves, turning her head "longingly towards the
Matriarch" as she steals away into the night with the Young Man.[11] A different
choice of vocabulary to describe these same episodes in the dance might depict
a mother/daughter scenario, for example, "the Matriarch urges the Young
Woman to lie down and sleep" or the "Young Woman turns her head to make
sure the Matriarch is not following as she steals away."

I concur with the idea of several contradictory interpretations. It is not
difficult to see beyond the surface mother/daughter relationship of the two female characters. Indeed, Humphrey did not intend her characters to be literal
representations in any case, so the ambiguity noted by Foster is unsurprising.
Foster offers three interpretations: a "mother figure/child leaving home," a
more mythical "oracle/wise woman handing down knowledge," and the "older
lesbian/pretty young girl" relationship. The latter stance, which Foster privileged, became more overtly prevalent in the 1960s and 1970s; it is exemplified
in other media with characters such as June and Childie, played by Beryl Reid
and Susannah York, respectively, in the once infamous and celebrated film

*The Killing of Sister George* (1964). Maggie Smith's central character in *The Prime of Miss Jean Brodie* (1969), with her silent but devastated response to her young protégée's betrayal with an older man, depicts an unrequited romantic attachment. An ambiguous illustration from modern dance is the second movement of Paul Taylor's *Esplanade* (1975), which includes a trio comprising a single male figure with two female figures, one representing a mature woman and the other a young frivolous girl. As the scenario unfolds, the young girl transfers her allegiance and affection from the older woman to the man. The attire of the older woman is similar to that of the men in the piece, mannish belted trousers with plain top; thus, one could read the "older lesbian/pretty young girl" relationship next to the "mother figure/child leaving home" scenario Taylor actually intended. A more recent example is the central relationship depicted in Zoë Heller's *Notes on a Scandal*, shortlisted for the Man Booker Prize in 2003 and subsequently released as a major motion picture in 2007 with Judi Dench and Cate Blanchett in the leading roles. There remains dramatic mileage in exploring the complexities of same-sex relationships, sexual or otherwise, if not the idea of a happy ending.

Foster further suggests that the dance offers a glimpse of Humphrey's awareness of her own difference in terms of her sexuality. I'm not wholly convinced by this argument, although it ties in neatly with Foster's narrative. I would venture a broader view, that we see, rather, Humphrey's awareness of "difference" in general and the dangers presented by being different or on the outside. In fact, Foster herself highlights this notion when she comments: "What the Matriarch rages against is the prohibition against difference," a more open stance that better reflects Humphrey's predilection for social inclusivity.[12]

The issue of multiple interpretations was also raised by Ann Dils, who observes that the roles of the Young Man and Young Woman could be played by two men or two women.[13] Pursuing such an interpretation would undoubtedly take the work somewhere new and would work within the existing narrative parameters of the dance. The representation of a same-sex couple, however, could suggest the dance was "about" homosexuality. At the time I first engaged with the work, such a reading was too specific, because my real creative interest lay in exploring Humphrey's underlying themes of intolerance and ignorance in a broader context through the dance's existing framework. There are without doubt other possibilities: interpretations based on character exploration, relationships, and characteristics. The ambiguity highlighted by Foster is certainly present and enticing from a directorial perspective. Humphrey consciously created an ambiguous set of dramatic circumstances. The interpretive possibilities, therefore, are already present in the work, waiting to be reshaped into a new narrative.

White's "recognizable form" is a useful concept to work with when dealing with narrative because it offers a number of interlinking ways to consider and interpret evidence. He talks about history (the work) being "made sense of," "endowing what originally appears problematic with a recognizable, because it is a familiar, form," "translating knowing into telling."[14] To make sense of *With My Red Fires* for a contemporary audience means first identifying what that recognizable form needs to be. In this instance, I chose the theme of "society's intolerance of difference." The exploration and articulation of this theme, encompassing interpretation, direction, and staging, represent the translation of "knowing" into "telling," thus making sense of the recognizable form for the audience. As with *Passacaglia*, there will always be more than one possible interpretation, with Dils's casting, for example, creating a different scenario. Same-sex casting would be equally "recognizable" and powerful in terms of what the dance could express in a contemporary context with two men or two women and a mixed-gender ensemble. There are further permutations that offer more open interpretations, such as two men with an all female ensemble, two women with an all male ensemble, an all male or all female cast. Each would conjure up different images and potential scenarios.

The narrative aspect of *With My Red Fires* presents an opportunity for dramatic exploration that does not always exist with dance works. In part I, I identified parallels with Shakespearean production. In applying interpretive strategies and processes from the theater to dance, one question is, Is there any difference in the directorial context? And, further, should there be? I would suggest that it depends on the nature of the individual work. *With My Red Fires* is open to theatrical intervention because of its narrative, as would be Graham's *Clytemnestra* and *Steps in the Street* because they too have narratives. An important factor is that they share elements with a play text. Conversely, the strategies adopted for *With My Red Fires* would be inappropriate for *Water Study* and *Air for the G String* because these dances have less in common with stage plays, having a heavier bias toward form and rhythm and no narrative.

There are two aspects of theater practice, and specifically Shakespearean production, that I believe can work successfully in a dance context. The first is interpretation in relation to a work, and the second is cutting and reshaping. Interpretation in modern dance is nothing new, of course, because dancers have been interpreting roles throughout its history. Less commonplace, however, are directors who take an interpretive stance to the work itself because of the genre's "traditions" of reconstruction or restaging. I reached a point with the Humphrey repertoire where restaging practices were insufficient to deal with the contemporized perspective that was emerging in my work. Shakespearean production was a particularly useful source because of the range of models it provides. If one thinks through Jonathan Miller's question, "What does a fairy look like?," for example, the potential answers are unlimited, with each individual having an individual impression of a mythical magical being. The director decides what a particular "fairy" looks like and then proceeds to ensure that its "form" is recognizable. Miller's question does not simply relate to *A Midsummer Night's Dream*, the obvious example, but to the broader idea of interpreting allegory. How does one interpret intolerance or ignorance, bigotry, survival? The answers are found as the process of discovery unfolds, as one works through and considers each element in light of the evidence and with creative imagination.

The second aspect, cutting and reshaping, will also have an influence. Humphrey's work, I would suggest, is open to reshaping, and to a considerable degree with some dances. *With My Red Fires* is a pertinent example, given the potential interplay between the Matriarch, the Young Woman, and the Young Man and their respective relationships with the group. Cutting and reshaping a dance work may sound drastic and questionable, but, again, there are numerous successful models in theater production, particularly when one is dealing with contemporized interpretation. Robert Wilson's *King Lear*, referred to earlier, is a useful example: three separate scenes involving each of the three sisters were reshaped into one scene for all three. To audience members familiar with the play, Wilson's actions may have resulted in creating a new perspective on these characters. Would audience members new to the play even notice the reshaping? Whatever the individual's position, reviews from the time made clear that the play itself remained *King Lear*. There is a logical interrelationship between the idea of cutting and reshaping and White's recognizable form/making sense position, because the actions involved in one idea will create the other.

## Evidence from the Source

Having been inspired by the visual representation of the dance, I went back to the source to get to the core of her thinking before embarking on my own exploration. Humphrey gives a detailed account of her ideas for this dance in a letter to her husband dated July 12, 1936.[15] As she was en route to Bennington to begin work on the dance at the time of writing, it is more than likely that these ideas contributed to her creative process. Humphrey provisionally named the dance *Romantic Tragedy*. She wrote of a "hymn" to Greek and Roman gods of love and procreation, of "the excitement, the greatness, the rapture, the pain of, frustration that is love," of "ever willing victims responding with flutterings, stabbings, listenings, impatience, fire in the blood." She refers to putting "the force to work," of two lovers being sought out. There is the inference of a climax, but one that is not entirely resolved because of the emergence of a matriarch figure who tries to prevent the young woman going any farther: "You will do as I say, walk like me, talk like me." The young woman silently refuses and steals away to join her lover. Humphrey goes on to describe the Matriarch's reaction as "the old woman screaming from the top of the house"; she "whips up the force" until "they gleam with virtuous hate"; she sends them after the pair: "See that they're well battered . . . and I shall shut the door." These descriptions and the language Humphrey uses provide clear indication of the central themes of manipulation and possessive, destructive love that form the narrative of the dance.

There are several additional sources of primary or "actual" evidence beyond Humphrey's initial ideas that also stem from her. The first is the title, dramatic in itself and taken from William Blake's poem *Jerusalem* (1804), second chapter (lines 53–54): "For the Divine Appearance is Brotherhood, but I am Love; Elevate into the Region of Brotherhood with my red fires." While these particular lines are relevant because Humphrey used them as a program note, she created the dance first; thus, the words were ascribed to the finished work rather than being its inspiration.[16] Incorporating Collingwood's actual/potential viewing model allows one to privilege evidence, to choose which parts to accept. In this instance I chose not to use the full text of the poem as part of the interpretive process. On another occasion this might change, as would the interpretation, and therein lies the power of choice. A body of evidence that is considered fluid in idealist terms, rather than fixed in a positivist context, gives the interpreter freedom, and this freedom, in my view, allows the work to remain vital and living.

The lines from *Jerusalem* describe Part One, which depicts the ritualistic search for and anointing of two lovers by the group or "society." One interpretation could be that the group is representative of Blake's "Brotherhood." Taking a different slant, these lines could similarly describe the whole work, not in relation to the group, because it evolves into a distinctly unbrotherly entity, but in relation to the central duo, who come through an ordeal of some measure and are elevated to a new and finer place by the conclusion. For Part Two, Humphrey also found lines from Blake's *Jerusalem* in a verse that refers to the "Great Selfhood," which concludes: "Such is the way of the Devouring Power"—a wonderfully evocative image I chose to use in the new interpretation. In addition, parts 1 and 2 have subtitles, although evidence does not make clear whether these were devised by Humphrey or by the poet Paul Love, a contemporary of Humphrey who assisted her with such matters.[17] These subtitles could potentially influence an interpretation but have not done so in my case, as the interpretation has neither the context for the descriptive titles nor the need for such tight and delineated structuring.

Humphrey considered this dance part of a trilogy she called the *New Dance Trilogy*, comprising *Theater Piece* (January 1936), *With My Red Fires* (August 1936), and *New Dance* (1935). The trilogy was not generally performed as one complete work because of the scale of each piece. Despite this, Humphrey created a context in which all three works are connected, and it is this connection that is relevant. She describes the thinking behind the works:

> I had an accumulation of things to be said which could no longer be confined within the limits of a short dance. There was the whole competitive modern world in upheaval; it must be expressed and commented upon and it was too large a theme for fragments and episodes. Whether it was my personal life within this world or my sense of technical sureness that impelled me into these three dances is difficult to say. I believe it was both. In almost the entire dance world I had seen nothing but negation. Anyone could tell you what was wrong but no one seemed to say what was right. It was with this mental conflict that I approached *New Dance* first, determined to open to the best of my ability the world as it could be and should be: a modern brotherhood of man. I would not offer nostrums and I could not offer a detailed answer. It was not time for that, but it was time to affirm the fact that there is a brotherhood of man and that the individual has his place within that group.[18]

In the early 1930s, Humphrey came under repeated criticism from the Workers Dance League and others associated with the leftist movement for not taking an overt political stance in her work. The reception for the *New Dance Trilogy* marked a departure from this negative criticism.[19] Humphrey was tackling identifiable social themes but in her own humanist/formalist terms. Her frustration with the "negative" factions in dance is also clear to see in these remarks.

The following extract is abridged from Margaret Lloyd's description and is particularly useful because Lloyd saw all the dances firsthand. She observes that the dances give converse sides of the social picture: "*Theater Piece* shows the competitive zeal . . . the negative side, the ruthless self-seeking in civic and commercial relationships that hinders the realisation of a desirable, harmonious state. *With My Red Fires* deals with another hindrance, the destructive selfishness of possessive love in personal relationships. *New Dance* is an affirmation of faith in a possible democratic society, in which the individual could develop his own capabilities with, and to the benefit of his fellows."[20] A further aspect is that Humphrey actually choreographed the last part, *New Dance*, first. Thus, despite the "demonic theatricality" she would encounter in *With My Red Fires*, she already had the final resolution in place.

Humphrey's description of the narrative places the emphasis on possessive love and the relationships between the Matriarch and the two lovers. The description provided in the Labanotation score gives similar detail. I was interested in taking a broader, less literal approach to focus on the interlinking aspects of conformity and intolerance that Humphrey ascribed to the Matriarch, noted earlier ("You will do as I say, walk like me, talk like me"), qualities that are also reflected through the group movement and structure. In considering a shift of emphasis within the narrative, attention had to be given to the place and relevance of the central characters. Humphrey intended these to be symbolic rather than literal representations, which could imply a certain openness. A further consideration was whether a production claiming to be an interpretation of *With My Red Fires* could legitimately make that claim without the Matriarch figure, as this character is pivotal to the narrative. The presence of that central figure is integral to the development of the narrative, however one approaches the interpretation of this work. Whether the character actually needs to be defined as the "Matriarch" is a different question. A less definitive alternative, for example, would be the "Central Figure." Humphrey gives a clear indication of how the character influences the action and scenario when she talks about "the old woman screaming from the top of the house." This particular description is key because the action it refers to instigates a transition for the massed group from being a benign entity into something darker and more destructive. Humphrey's description certainly creates an evocative image for the director, but the issue here is how the image is dramatized. Part of the directorial challenge, therefore, was to discover the means by which Humphrey's image could be conveyed.

Clues came from five sources: Charles H. Woodford, Humphrey's son; Leo Woodford, her husband; dance photographer Barbara Morgan; the photographic collection of the Dance Notation Bureau; and Blake's line "such is the way of the Devouring Power." The specific reference is to the role of the Matriarch, but there are psychological lines that can be traced and considered in relation to the whole dance. In a recent correspondence, Charles Woodford offered these insights: "*With My Red Fires*, I think, has to be placed in the context of its time, the rise of Fascism and Nazism. The Matriarch is a female Fuhrer. The group is, at times, militaristic and, at others, a lynch mob. The Matriarch's anger is ultimately self-destructive, prescient of the fate of Hitler and Goebbels." This description of the group could, for example, be redefined as "controlled by an external force" (militaristic) and "capable of or driven to extreme intolerance" (a lynch mob). In transposing a more generic vocabulary onto these literal ideas, a contemporized reading can be created. Woodford continues: "Some have wondered if DH's mother resembled the Matriarch in any way, and I think there is evidence that she did, though not to such an exaggerated extent. There is the scene from her adolescence when she was forbidden to attend a Sunday matinee performance by Pavlova on religious grounds, but left the house anyway, with her mother screaming after her that she was a wicked child." His description makes me wonder if the image of the old woman screaming from the top of the house stemmed from this incident. He noted further: "Later, when the Denishawn Company went to the Far East for two years, her mother came along for the trip, but soon became so jealous of DH's friends in the company that she was sent home."[21] Humphrey's own experience of possessive matriarchal love was evident but not, in her case, allowed to dominate her.

Leo Woodford wrote to his wife in March 1942, after seeing her perform the Matriarch for the first time: "I'm afraid that I was so overwhelmed by your performance in the murder that for the rest of the evening I was unreceptive — numbed — or shall we say, just plain scared."[22] His is a subjective and personalized account compared to Lloyd's critical perspective, but he did write knowledgeably to his wife about her work, as evidenced in their correspondence over the years. There are a number of points in this letter that offer insights, including his reference to "being overwhelmed," which implies dramatic impact, and to "the murder," which to me was curious, as I hadn't read this scene so literally, although I am aware that others have. His comment is also reflective of the level of violence portrayed in that particular scene, Part Two, Scene VI, "Judgment," which sees the Young Man and Young Woman set upon by the group at the instigation of the Matriarch: "See that they're well battered . . . and I shall shut the door." My reading of this scene was that the young couple were attacked and ostracized from society because they did not fit in or conform, but they were able to rise above the prejudice to survive intact. Woodford's reading does not suggest survival but rather spirits rising after death. The survival image that I see very clearly may not, therefore, be what Humphrey intended, but it exists nonetheless as a consequence of the action she put in place. Woodford continued: "Yet the character is not by any means repulsive. Quite the opposite. The body under that beautiful vicious face is full of fire and grace, serpentine in its fascination — vulgar yet hypnotic."[23] Again, while the personal relationship has to be taken into account, Woodford's observation is worth considering because of the insights it gives into Humphrey dancing the role and to possible underlying facets of the character.

Woodford's observations tie in with two particular photographs of Humphrey as the Matriarch, one by Morgan and one from the Dance Notation Bureau collection. These photographs convey a suspended stillness that I think is integral to interpreting this role, not through the poses involved but through the images and emotional undertones created through the photographs. In the Morgan photograph, Humphrey is caught facing the camera, arms stretched wide to the sides, hands in fists, with the left holding the wide swirling skirt.[24] The motion of the skirt suggests she is in midturn, as the fabric swirls upward in a spiral from low on the right, around her back, and up to the left fist. There is a sense of suspension to the movement, which is bound, strong, and direct. These qualities are evident in the DNB photograph in which Humphrey is seen in profile, standing tall on top of the box that represents the Matriarch's house. In addition to the movement quality, the juxtaposition of set, costume, and movement further emphasizes the power of this character. The hemline of her dress falls at least a foot below the top of the box, with the overlap creating the illusion of an elongated and superhuman force.

The combination of movement qualities identified in both photographs induces the sense of suspended stillness referred to above. I would give prominence to these images over others because the psychological drama can be better conveyed for a contemporary context in a more subtle, internalized manner than the exaggerated and pantomimic portrayal of the role as notated and performed in the 1978 film. Photographs housed in the Doris Humphrey Collection by Thomas Bouchard, William Black, Martha Swope, and Morgan also depict Humphrey in the role, with these images portraying the outwardly twisted facets of the character through action. Such photographs convey how the character could be interpreted in a reconstructed context.

A further source of primary or "actual" evidence came from Humphrey's choreographic notebook from 1936.[25] This notebook contains a breakdown of what she called "Gesture Themes," the opening phrases of Part One for the men's and women's groups and for the ensemble as a whole (see figure 20). In one respect, these notes give an insight into how Humphrey perceived the differing roles of men and women in the work contrasted with their more egalitarian treatment in *New Dance* and *Passacaglia*. If one were engaged in a reconstruction process, this evidence would be of practical value because the level of detail does not appear in the score or its supporting documentation, particularly in relation to how the women react to each other as well as to their situation. The value for me exists in knowing that these ideas was part of Humphrey's early thinking about the dance. One idea I have incorporated is "emotional movement in body—no hands" from the "Design" section of the "Girl's Theme." Humphrey's meaning could imply that the movement is generated from the center of the body and not the extremities, since this would be in keeping with her broader stylistic principles. I have taken this to a deeper level still, in that the "emotional movement" is generated through a process of internalization, specifically in relation to the role of the Matriarch, scored and portrayed as outwardly driven and twisted. If these qualities are reinterpreted through internalization, the resulting action becomes less explicit. Through capturing the

Figure 19. Doris Humphrey as the Matriarch. Photographer unknown. Image reprinted with permission of Charles H. Woodford. Image reproduced by Aviv Yaron.

| | Rhythm | Dynamics | Design |
|---|---|---|---|
| Men's Theme | Tempo slower than women; masculine steadiness; increase in tempo — double, still below women; even time spacing; showing emotional control. | strong accents; no variation; showing steady & controlled advance. | broad lines of run (against small feminine movements); gesture of salute; one arm. |
| Girl's Theme | Tempo faster than men (feminine excitement); uneven time; space suggesting rise and fall of feeling; continuation of triplets & eighths, more varied time to mood than 8ths and 4ths; more spontaneous in effect. | eagerness; smooth rushes with sudden steps; increase of excitement in stronger accents during developments of phrase. | with head & torso, foot raised in anticipation; listening gesture in head; emotional movement in body — no hands. |
| Whole | Counterpoint of three groups — advancing like waves. | thrust of one group forward after another of girls against men's steady background, both contest each other. | three groups advance toward focal point of altar. Advance & retreat is development making dissonance last longer. |

Figure 20. "Gestures Themes" — opening phrases from Part One, as detailed in Humphrey's notebook, 1936.

sense of suspended stillness, as identified in the two Humphrey photographs, the insidious and chilling aspects of the character can be retained.

## Reshaping the Matriarch

At the outset of the production process, an initial thought was to cut the Matriarch's role because the melodramatic aspects of the characterization did not match the contemporized stance driving the interpretation. One option considered was to represent the character through a small, unified group. Subsequently, it became clear that a single Central Figure would better serve the dramatic and thematic contexts of a new interpretation. This realization became clear through observing how the large ensemble group responded and developed as an entity in early rehearsals, then imagining its further manifestation in later sections. In addition, the images I wanted to create through the single figure could become obscured or ambiguous if represented by more than one body. The most significant of these images was a sense of "presence" through stillness. The Central Figure symbolizes the power base of the society and could, theoretically, be played by either gender. An important aspect of the portrayal of this role relates to the juxtaposing of elements identified by Leo Woodford when he refers to "that beautiful vicious face . . . full of fire and grace." A female dancer is more appropriate because these qualities are not readily associated with a male persona. In addition, the costume is significant in creating the elongated, superhuman force suggested by the DNB photograph. Costuming a man in such garb would be immediately suggestive of a "high priest" type of figure and too literal for the image I wanted to convey. An audience might well come to a similar conclusion about a female figure so dressed. The difference is that they have reached that conclusion through their own reading of the work and, further, that it is but one of a number of possible conclusions rather than being the only one.

Using the central idea of presence through stillness, the choreographic vocabulary for the Central Figure was amended throughout the work and to varying degrees. The outwardly twisted, pantomimic emphasis was replaced with downplayed expression, using such devices as the "gaze" and the "stance" to create a more subtly insidious being. The gaze is an integral dramatic element. It should be clear to the audience that this figure is an abstraction of a sinister and malevolent force in the guise of elegant beauty from the intent in the eyes and stance of the body. Blake's line, "such is the way of the Devouring Power," conjures up the idea of an all-pervading, dominating presence. One can interpret this idea as Humphrey did, through exaggerated gesture and expressive melodrama. Alternatively, one can interpret this idea through more subtle means to produce an effect that is, arguably, even more chilling. An example is the first appearance of the character. Her entrance takes place in such a way that the figure is unseen until appearing on top of the column closest to center stage — a "superhuman" force appearing as if from nowhere. The entrance is timed with the departure of the main ensemble, exiting upstage of her position, and of the Young Man and Young Woman exiting to the downstage right corner. The Central Figure does not acknowledge the ensemble at all — she does not need to because she knows she can reassert her authority whenever she chooses. Her attention is focused intently and directly on the departing duo because of what they represent — individuals breaking from the norm, difference. The movement vocabulary for the Central Figure is minimal, standing quite still and erect, watching the duo all the time, so that the attention is drawn to her gaze. The image created here is reflective of the DNB photograph of Humphrey. The effect of the extended stillness at this juncture makes clear the intentions of the character without having to resort to the frantic action of later scenes.

In order for the new interpretation to make sense, the section following the character's first appearance was cut completely. Scene 4, "Summons/Coercion and Escape," includes the Matriarch's first interaction with the Young Woman. Here, the Young Woman is drawn away from the Young Man into the confines of the matriarchal domain and is the scene described by Humphrey as "you will walk like me, talk like me" in her account of the dance. The action has a strong literal and gestural emphasis. The accompanying music creates a wailing anguished sound that is a rhythmic match to the choreographic action. The instrumentation here includes a solo voice that is representative of the Matriarch's anguish on discovering the Young Woman with the Young Man. The second part of this section comprises the Young Man returning to persuade the Young Woman to leave and go with him while the Matriarch sleeps. There is no meaning for the action within the new interpretation because Humphrey's primary narrative has been supplanted by broader themes. The section was cut, therefore, except for those elements that remained relevant, principally, the Matriarch's motivation rather than her explicit actions.

There is likely to be a need to create coherent transitions if one considers cutting material. Trevor Nunn, for example, admits he enjoys writing a line or two himself for good technical reasons when directing Shakespeare, and he is sure no one ever notices.[26] While on one level this may seem questionable (or amusing, depending on one's point of view), it is also logical in terms of the importance of maintaining a coherent line through the work for the audience. Cutting an entire scene for two of the leading protagonists has consequences. When *do* they meet, for example? Is there any direct relationship between the two? As it turns out, there is no discrete relationship. The connection now is between the Central Figure and the pair of dancers as a unit. She observes the pair leaving, taking in the fact that they have separated themselves from society as represented by the main ensemble. The separation indicates the desire to be different, to buck tradition. The prolonged stillness and gaze emphasize her disapproval coupled with her steely resolve to quash the attempted breakaway. The difference in motivation between the Matriarch and the Central Figure is negligible. The change is in the means of expression, achieved through cutting action and reshaping the intention behind the action.

A further cut involved the original set design, a representation of the Matriarch's house positioned upstage left. The set comprised a number of domestic features, including a doorway that opens and a window frame with a curtain, as detailed in the score and used in the 1978 film. These elements no longer have meaning because the specified relationship between mother and daughter and the corresponding domestic association have been removed. The surrounding elements of this part of the set, however, do retain an important spatial purpose. A series of adjacent rising columns create a platform, or dimension, in which the Central Figure can exist above the level of the other protagonists, commanding the moral high ground, as it were.

## Creative Possibility

The primary distinctions between my interpretation and the 1978 film are the setting, the nature and character of the ensemble, and the portrayal of the central role. Some choreographic change is involved for the Matriarch, with the existing movement vocabulary for the ensemble and Young Man and Young Woman remaining as scored. The ensemble is not a "group" in the harmonious, community-based sense of *Passacaglia* and *New Dance*, and for this reason it is redefined as the Mass. In Humphrey's narrative, Part One comprises a ritualistic procession in which two individuals, the Young Man and Young Woman, are identified and celebrated. Humphrey's notes for the ensemble indicate such emotions as "eagerness," "excitement," "anticipation," which suggest that the ensemble is a benign force at this point, in contrast to the later malevolence induced by the Matriarch in Part Two. My intention is to establish the themes of conformity and intolerance early on in the motivation of the protagonists. A setting that is metaphorically sinister, dark, and rigid allows the malevolent nature and character of the Mass to come through from the outset.

The opening scene provides a further illustration of how new interpretation can evolve. For comparative purposes, this is the "Gesture Themes" scene detailed in Humphrey's 1936 notebook. The Mass enters in three subgroups, all from stage right. There is a serpentlike quality to the movement. While the vocabulary is different for each of the three subgroups, the dynamic and intention are the same, with the collective intent being to take over the space. The dancers were given the image of a force emerging into a murky space, as if moving through the type of green haze induced by wearing night vision goggles. The dancers had no direct experience of such apparel, but nightly news coverage of military action in Afghanistan and Iraq provides clear points of identification. Movement quality is bound and direct, and this directness is transposed to the gaze — for the individual, for each subgroup, and for the collective Mass. Power is generated as much through the gaze as it is through physical means. The gaze, similarly, becomes an integral aspect of the quality as used in the portrayal of the Central Figure.

Having exited as three groupings, the next entrance sees the Mass further subdivided into four, with two groups entering from each side of the stage in a processional formation. The increase in number, with the resulting spatial impact and the now unison movement, further enhances the sense of the space being taken over. The serpentlike quality of the patterns becomes more overt as the dancers move farther and faster through the space. This section has one instance of choreographic adjustment to create a greater emphasis on the gaze and the serpentlike meandering of the collective entity as the four subgroups traverse the space. The vocabulary here is an advancing, repetitive walking pattern. In the score and the 1978 film, the torso was held in a forward high tilt throughout. The head was held in line with the torso, and the gaze was focused correspondingly forward and low. The adjustment involved removing the tilt so that the body was upright. This did not detract in any way from the dynamic of the vocabulary, but it did, importantly, lift the gaze so that the sense of penetrating directness established in the opening section was not compromised. The dancers, now in lines, were directed to feel the line of their gaze running through the back of the head of the dancer in front and to imagine that this line continued to traverse the space linking one subgroup to the next.

Within the main ensemble, Humphrey identifies individuals at intervals during the action. I reinterpreted these individuals as "lone voices of reason," rising up and attempting to break through the rigidity of the Mass. In the processional section, the first "lone voice" emerges, represented by a single figure in the most contained of four episodes. Her movement reaches up and out with an expansive quality in contrast to the continuing bound/direct flow of the Mass. The lone voice dancer stays within her subgroup, and the line of resistance is upward — the only available option without actually leaving the structure of the subgroup. The subsequent lone voice utterances are interwoven within the main ensemble dance, extending an invisible boundary each time. The strength

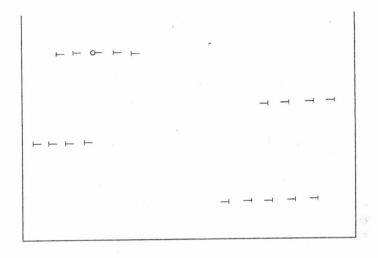

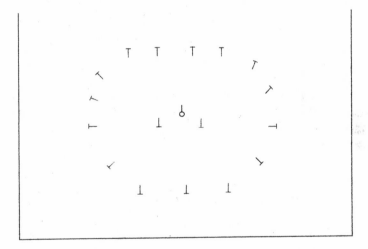

Figure 21. Floor plans to illustrate spatial patterns and first (*above*) and second (*below*) "lone voice" episodes.

of the Mass increases in this section as it merges into a single structure in the form of a circle, a powerful metaphor for "unity" but also for "enclosing." The second episode sees the lone voice dancers (trio) breaking from the Mass. The breakout is within limits, however, and extends only as far as the boundaries of the circle. The third episode (duet) is still within the confines of the circle, but the boundaries are further extended in that the movement is faster, lighter, and taken up into the air with expansive looping jumps. The movement vocabulary is the furthest removed yet from the dynamic qualities of the Mass. This third episode is also the first instance of human contact, through a recurring hand-clasp and direct gaze between the two dancers as they pass each other. The lone voices strengthen simultaneously, becoming more insistent and expansive and not dissuaded from trying to break out. The first lone voice solo dancer acts as instigator for each of the remaining episodes until she finds a partner willing to stand with her by the fourth episode. This pair of dancers become the Central Duo, formerly the Young Man and Young Woman.

Because Humphrey's roles were symbolic, there could also be an argument for creating a larger entity to represent the "nonconformist" duo. A trio or quartet, for example, would still appear minimal within the scale of the full ensemble. Such a group would create a different reading from that of the single female/male partnership, but one that would retain a similar breadth. As an idea, it has possibilities in structural terms but becomes problematic in relation to what would be lost in order to accommodate such a change. There are several instances through the piece where the interaction between the duo is particularly significant in emotional and choreographic terms. Adapting the choreography for a larger group would diminish the connection between them, a factor that contributed to retaining the female/male couple.

The examples analyzed above give some indication of the line taken with this work and in comparison with the processes used for *Water Study* and *Passacaglia*. The interpretation could still be defined as liberal within the Benedetti model, however, because the adjustments made and directorial decisions taken have resulted in a reshaping of the work. Benedetti's premise was that the act of re-shaping would "unleash the play for a contemporary audience." To "unleash" this work, the interpretive process encompassed a different and more extreme approach to counter the effects of Humphrey's primary narrative. Employing devices such as cutting action, redefining characters, and transposing the metaphorical setting produced a "new" interpretation of the work. While the interpretation discussed here would not entirely resemble the work as it would be if staged through a reconstruction process, the intention is that it would be recognizable as *With My Red Fires*. The Central Figure is, of course, a metaphor for intolerance and bigotry, just as the Matriarch was a metaphor for posses-sive, destructive love. What changed was the theme and the expression of the theme. Is the work still *With My Red Fires*? I would say so and hope so. The na-ture of the processes used to achieve this "recognizable form" further extended my participation as interpreter, evidenced through the degree of change that has taken place and, significantly, in the fact that the need for change was driven by directorial interpretation rather than adherence to choreographic narrative.

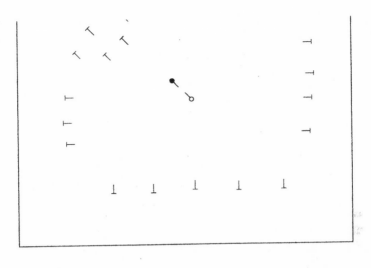

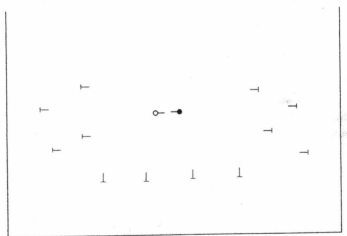

Figure 22. Floor plans to illustrate spatial patterns and third (*above*) and fourth (*below*) "lone voice" episodes.

More important than unleashing a work for oneself as interpreter, how-ever, is doing so for the contemporary audience. My interpretation was not "about" what happened to Matthew Shepherd, but it was driven by that event. A broader question is, Should contemporary art forms be bound to make so-ciocultural comment when they can? Relating this back to the leftist choreog-raphers versus Humphrey's stance discussed earlier, I would argue her corner on two counts: that Humphrey's drive to make work that was indigenous to being American was as socioculturally conscious as any overtly political artistic statement of the time; and, further, that her work had such depth and quality that it can continue to make profound sociocultural comment on contemporary times. Of those New York–based choreographers linked with the radical Left in the early 1930s, few continue to have their work performed today. An exception is Eve Gentry's *Tenant of the Street* (1938), performed regularly by Mary Anne Newhall.[27] Other surviving works, including Jane Dudley's *Harmonica Breakdown* (1940), make no politicized statement. By interpreting (certain) Humphrey works from a sociocultural standpoint, I would further argue that in so doing the work can be unleashed for a contemporary audience through its recognizable form, recognizable in this context by the sociocultural markers.

# THE SHAKERS

*Choreography*: 1931
*Music*: Traditional Shaker hymns, arranged by Pauline Lawrence
*Premiere*: February 1, 1931, Craig Theater, New York

Humphrey based *The Shakers* on a celibate religious movement that evolved out of the Quakers. The movement was founded in England and transported in the late 1700s to the United States, where it subsequently flourished. The name transpired through a particular swaying action the body took on during prayer rituals. Humphrey's dance reflects aspects of Shaker life, including a central philosophy that believers could shake themselves free from sin. The dance was originally titled *Dance of the Chosen* and subsequently renamed *The Shakers*. It is cast for a single female figure, depicting the Shaker Eldress, with six men and six women representing the community, and is loosely set at a prayer meeting.

Beginning from a place of reverence and stillness, the dance follows the progression of the meeting rituals. The Eldress leads her followers, first in an introspective contemplation, moving on through processional, wheeling, and linear formations as the "rituals" become more energetic and intense before culminating in a vibrant, collective release of ecstasy. Costumes are in the style of traditional Shaker dress, and the music is based on Shaker-type songs and accompaniment, harmonized by Daniel Jahn and arranged by Humphrey's associate Pauline Lawrence. Also radical for the time was Humphrey's inclusion of spoken text in the form of two "revelations." In an early section, a character identified as Man 1 calls out: "My life, my life, my carnal life. I must lay it down because it is depraved." Toward the climax of the dance, the Eldress proclaims to her followers: "It hath been revealed ye shall be saved when ye are shaken free of sin." Humphrey herself was said to "speak in tongues" when she

129

Figure 23. *The Shakers*. Re-created by Ernestine Stodelle for Silo Concert Dancers, 1986. Photographer: Jennifer Lester.

performed the role, mirroring the trancelike state reached by the Elder/Eldress figure as documented in historical accounts.

Picture, if you will, a standoff between two highly respected dance artists, Humphrey exponent Ernestine Stodelle and Labanotator Tom Brown, one adamant that "that's not what Doris did" and the other equally adamant that, "well, that's what the score says," with neither willing or able to give ground. This part of the *The Shakers* story begins in 1985, in Ernestine Stodelle's studio in Connecticut. She had asked me to reconstruct the dance from the Labanotation score to add to her company's repertoire of Humphrey works. Before we began working with the dancers I went through the various movements with her, and everything was fine until I demonstrated a phrase known as the nine-count phrase. "What is that?" she asked. "Are you sure that's what it says?," referring to the score. While I was relatively young and at the start of my career, I *was* sure, having worked on the dance as a college student in London some years earlier with notators Patty Howell and Sheila Marion. "That's not what Doris did" was the firm response, and we spent the rest of the afternoon working out what Doris did in fact do in 1931, which turned out to be so different that it changed the essence of the dance.

This scenario illustrates the "score versus person transmission" tension discussed in part 1. In this particular instance, Ernestine knew immediately that the movement I demonstrated that day was not the movement Humphrey had choreographed on her in 1931. She herself had related instances to me when she had been re-creating other Humphrey dances and couldn't quite remember what had been set or someone else had danced a particular role, so she used her judgment to fill the gaps. In this case, however, she was absolutely certain. She also conferred by telephone with Eleanor King, who played Man 1 opposite her Woman 1 in the original cast and confirmed Stodelle's memories. The telephone call itself is worth detailing as it is not documented elsewhere and involves two near-octogenarians in their respective living rooms in Connecticut and San Diego, retrieving what they instinctively knew had been given to them by the choreographer—which I can confirm, as I was holding the telephone to the ear of one because she needed both hands free to "demonstrate," and I could hear the other. Stodelle and King performed the work together regularly for years. In 1932 *The Shakers* and *Water Study* had been part of the Broadway revue *Americana 1932*, which ran for months. Their certainty, therefore, was based not only on memory but also on a repeated physiological exposure to the dance material.

When rehearsing the work with Stodelle in 1985, I became conscious that the sensations generated by her version of the nine-count phrase were different when dancing it within the formation required by the choreography as opposed to dancing it freely. The movement felt more contained within the linear formation, and I had to hold back from letting the movement go as far is it actually could. These sensations were perfectly appropriate given the dramatic and spatial contexts of the dance because one was meant to feel "contained" by those circumstances. However, I was also left with a mounting curiosity as to what would happen if the movement was allowed to "cross the line," to expand dynamically and spatially as far as it could. We will return to this part of the story in due course, but first we should look at the dance itself and the ideas that inspired Humphrey to create this work.

## Performance History

Audiences and a broad section of critics enthusiastically received the dance, from its premiere at the Craig Theater, New York, on February 1, 1931, through a number of tours in the years that followed, including Philadelphia, Detroit, Chicago, and Boston. One drama critic wrote: "a stunningly historical passage. It strikes deep and strangely at the very core of art and ecstasy."[1] John Martin acknowledged the striking originality of the subject and treatment of *The Shakers*, observing that it was "more a purely theatrical form than a dance, for it involved spoken phrases in unintelligible jargon and a hint of a linear plot."[2] At the time, Margaret Lloyd called it "a dance of outward brilliance and inward grace."[3] In early performances, the dance was also described as "a passionate and almost violent dance."[4] A review in the *Boston Transcript* read: "The widest appeal lies in the more pictorial compositions. *Water Study* and *The Shakers* are remarkably effective excursions into something that resembles American ballet."[5] In the Philadelphia tryout for *Americana 1932*, *The Shakers* was regarded as "the talk of the town," which was ironic, as the producer had threatened to pull it from the program because Humphrey refused to change the "drab" gray costumes for something more colorful, purple and white being the producer's preference.[6] The inclusion of both dances in the *Americana* revue allowed them to reach a much wider audience than would have been possible on the more formal dance concert circuit Humphrey and Weidman followed. For Humphrey, there was a double edge to the reception of the dance as time went on. In 1935, while on tour in Chicago, she wrote to her husband: "But another cross to bear is the fact that all attention in the press and social function is riveted on *The Shakers* and *Water Study*. It's just as though Charles and I hadn't danced at all. My big healthy children are beclouding me."[7]

On that same tour, Detroit critic Ralph Holmes commented: "It is less as dancers than as a social symptom that Humphrey and Weidman are significant—because they have the courage to mock at tradition and because of the response which they awaken. . . . [T]he younger people in the audience responded to the tortured twistings, the hard groupings, the preoccupation with angles, thrusts, staccato movements, and that is what interested me."[8] In a similar vein, Martin wrote in the *New York Times*: "The vast majority of the audience comes not from the diamond tiara sector but from the colleges where there is manifest an eagerness to participate in vital contemporary activities and to retrieve the arts from ostentatious sedatives. This is largely a balcony audience, but its potential numbers more than make up for its lack of wealth; it is aware of itself and capable of experiencing vigorous reactions without demanding hearts and flowers, symphony orchestras and scenic effects. Ultimately it is *the* dance audience, whether in New York or on the road."[9] These two contemporary observations say as much about the development of the dance audience of the time as they do about the response to individual dances. Eighty years on we are accustomed to and have indeed been part of that "balcony dance audience." Holmes's and Martin's observations acknowledge the first-time emergence of this type of audience, alongside the emergence and development of the genre itself.

From the original cast, King's early memory of the dance is of "an ecstatic theme . . . which was primitive American": "When we first started working on it we thought the movements hilariously funny. The crisp marching steps, the hopping with hands shaking lightly from the wrists, the bouncy rhythm, seemed singularly primitive, yet light and happy. But we soon ceased being amused and in no time were caught up in the compelling mood so masterfully built to an ecstatic climax."[10] Stodelle, similarly, recalls the rehearsal period, describing first the "Eights" section toward the end of the dance:

> The scene is a rehearsal in the 18th Street Studio, where the whitewashed walls appropriately set the stark mood of the dance. The combined cast of men and women were struggling with the abrupt, ejaculatory motions of the hands illustrative of "shaking away one's sins." The directions for the two separated groups of men and women, who were facing each other across the stage, were to advance with short hops on each foot until they reached an invisible dividing line, and then to turn sharply to face front and retreat to their own sides with staccato sideways steps, still vigorously flicking "the sins" from their down-pointing fingers.

In a broader description of the dance, Stodelle continued:

> Doris did not have to use the word "logic" for our understanding of her approach to *The Shakers*. Everything in it spoke of her choreographic attempt to interpret the spiritual purposes and worldly designs of Shaker life: the square of our meeting-house with its divisional center line; the pinwheel encircling of both groups on each side of the stage, once the men and women had risen from their kneeling positions; the hopping-shaking ritual as intensity increased; and then a man's impassioned outburst of a personal sense of guilt followed by the Eldress's revelation, "Ye shall be saved when ye are shaken free of sin!" The rhythmic dance that flowed swept across the stage with its powerful falling, rebounding, suspending, and thrusting movements. In a surge of fervor, both men and women shot upward into high split jumps, only to drop to their knees in prayer at the stage's edge as the music comes to an end in a resonant "Amen."[11]

Of the completed work, King wrote:

> *Shakers* was the most infectious of all Doris's compositions, because the simple rhythms to drum beats were so well built. These decorous Shakers controlled within fine boundaries the tension inherent in their lives, clearly stated in the pull and attraction to the straight line down the center of the room, the movements always drawing toward or away from it as an irresistible magnet. It was good Americana, good religious ritual, excellent theater, and just long enough to establish the mood, make its point and build to an exciting climax. It would have been easy to prolong it and spoil it, but Doris often said "all dances are too long," and she knew when to stop.[12]

An abundance of evidence exists on this dance, unlike some others, because the actual subject was well documented historically. Primary/actual evidence comprises Humphrey's own notes, which include references to the dance and to the Shaker movement.[13] Film and video recordings of the work are further supplemented by comment from Humphrey's contemporaries.[14] A salient starting point for understanding this dance is the history of the Shaker movement, its chronology and philosophies, and, following on from this, how the movement has been perceived by the wider world. By way of a brief summary, Mother Ann Lee founded the Shaker movement in England in 1769. She laid down the early principles of the movement in Manchester. When the group moved to New York in 1774, these principles remained at the heart of Shaker philosophy and have continued to do so, despite the major developments of the movement taking place after Lee's death. Her philosophies were centered on self-supporting, communal living as a basis for worship and included such mottoes as "hands to work, hearts to God." Singing and spontaneous dancing, led by Mother Ann and in the later communities by an eldress or elder, dominated prayer meetings. Between 1800 and 1820, communities became established across the United States, in New York, Massachusetts, Connecticut, Maine, New Hampshire, Indiana, Kentucky, Ohio, Florida, and Georgia, in what was regarded as the movement's most flourishing time.

On her initial thinking about *The Shakers*, Humphrey wrote: "The subject never is the point. Starting a new work on religious cults — the general theme being Shakerism. The subject is fascinating to read about — but is chiefly important as a starting point."[15] The dance is perhaps more reflective of Shakerism than she indicated, but the statement is revealing in terms of the position and significance of "the subject" to her creative process in general as well as for this particular work. Humphrey's notebook from 1931 illustrates how her thinking progressed, with references to "the strange group" and that "sin was a substance that could be shaken off the hands like a liquid. The shaking process took a rhythmic form." In what is a description of the final structure of the work, Humphrey noted: "The ritual begins with a rapt swaying of the believers and emerges into a rhythmic dance punctuated by revelations of the holy spirit in scriptural language. Led by the eldress they are at last purified and cleansed of sin in bursts of hysterical flying and jumping."[16] In structural terms, Humphrey adopted linear patterns associated with Shaker philosophy and construction. Shaker ceremonies included dancing in line formation, with men and women advancing and retreating from opposite sides of the meeting room. Shaker houses had an invisible "divide" down the center, including separate staircases for men and women. This invisible line was never crossed, and Humphrey's structure exemplifies this division throughout the dance.

Figure 24. "Opening," *The Shakers*. Re-created by Ernestine Stodelle for Silo Concert Dancers, 1986. Photographer: Jennifer Lester.

The history of the Shaker movement has been extensively chronicled.[17] A documentary made in 1990, *I Don't Want to Be Remembered as a Chair*, is based on the one remaining community at Sabbath Day Lake in Maine and contains a concise historical account alongside current perceptions from the wider community. The movement itself is regarded as something of a benign oddity, but there has been an enthusiasm for the collection of Shaker objects since the 1950s. The Shakers were responsible for mechanical and technological innovation, including farm equipment and the washing machine, but it is the more renowned wood-based "collectibles"—chairs, hatboxes, furniture—for which there continues to be a market. The film includes a telling scene that takes place at an auction of Shaker objects. A major television celebrity is seen near hysterical with delight at having secured a wardrobe for $100,000. At that same moment it begins to rain. The eldress at Sabbath Day Lake, Mother Frances, describes such instances as the tears of past Shakers, mourning what their offerings to God have become. A further aspect to this story is that the celebrity in question, while not coming over so well on this particular occasion, has an established history of generosity in her advocacy and support for young women of color, both in and outside the United States. An example, perhaps, of the dual aspect of the American psyche, on the one hand, generous, warmhearted, self-effacing, set against a brash, grabbing, ruthless, and materialistic persona. For Humphrey, at the time she choreographed *The Shakers*, making dances that were indigenous to "being American" was at the forefront of her mind, and this desire did not diminish as time went on. For those of us working to extend her tradition, it is important to acknowledge that this drive was central to her creative process. Humphrey went on to confront both aspects of this persona in 1935 through the brashness associated with the commercial business world in *Theater Piece* alongside the more idealistic representation of a humanitarian society in *New Dance*.

## Transmission Strategies

While the emphasis in my work is on moving forward, beyond what already exists, the influences are rooted in the past. In this instance, the experiences of others, namely, Stodelle, notators Ann Hutchinson Guest and Els Grelinger, and reconstructor Tom Brown, augmented my own. Stodelle's experience as a member of the original cast meant she was present during the creative process and performed the work regularly during subsequent years. Hutchinson Guest and Grelinger worked with the choreographer solely as notators, in comparison with the performing context of Venable's experience with *Passacaglia*. The notation process took place during a repertoire course in New York City in 1948, seventeen years after the work was originally created.[18] The score produced was markedly different from Stodelle's experience. Stodelle was certain that the version in the score was not the dance Humphrey had choreographed in 1931. Grelinger was equally certain that the version she notated in 1948 was what Humphrey had set.[19] It is probable, therefore, that Humphrey made changes to the work in the late 1940s. *Water Study* and *Passacaglia* are two further examples of works she is known to have changed after a period of years and that now have more than one version. In addition, by 1948 Humphrey was becoming crippled with arthritis, and I have often wondered whether the quite profound change in movement quality in the later version of *The Shakers* may have been influenced by her own physical pain and undoubted frustration at the disintegration of her extraordinary physical capabilities. I asked the question of both Stodelle and Grelinger, but neither was able to offer any direct insight. Humphrey was not given to sharing her personal circumstances and even less likely to do so with something as difficult as her diminishing dance ability.

The Stodelle/Brown standoff illustrates the broader issue of score versus person transmission discussed in part 1. Tom Brown's experience as a reconstructor was in the Labanotation system rather than in any specific choreographic style, in comparison with Venable, for example, who was an exponent of both system and style. His knowledge of the work was based on the Hutchinson Guest/Grelinger score, and his approach was indicative of the "score as all-encompassing document" philosophy held at that time. During the 1985 rehearsal period with Stodelle's company in Connecticut, the Dance Notation Bureau required that the production be checked due to the unorthodox combination of my reconstruction and Ernestine's re-creation. Brown questioned the changes she made and felt they should not be included because they differed significantly from the score. Stodelle felt just as strongly that the changes should be included because she was clear in her own mind about the movement Humphrey set in 1931. There was no resolution to the conflict within the rehearsal, which, in retrospect, was unsurprising, because Brown and Stodelle were working with two distinctive entities.

A danger with "person transmission" is that while an individual may know one part thoroughly, he or she may be less certain about other parts. One of the reasons the Stodelle/King version of *The Shakers* is credible is because they danced on opposite sides, so between them they had a sound grasp of the complete dance. When it came to reviving the work, Stodelle's subsequent transmission embodied King's experience as much as her own. The Dance Notation Bureau recognized the weight of Stodelle's experience, first, by not enforcing the changes Brown wanted to make and, in the longer term, by commissioning a score of Stodelle's version.

The combined experiences of Stodelle, Hutchinson Guest, Grelinger, and Brown provide a breadth of evidence that is also conflicting evidence. Given that conflicting evidence is not uncommon, the interpreter is faced with a choice. Collingwood's actual/potential viewing model works well in relation to conflicting evidence in terms of considering all the available evidence and then choosing to accept those experiences that best contribute to a process of discovery. The notion of discovery is important because it ensures that the directorial process is not about producing a copy, a version of what has already happened. This idea applies as much to a reconstruction process as it does to the kinds of stagings I am suggesting. Nothing will deaden a work more than steps learned from a video or score in isolation. The reconstructor must craft the movement and the ideas behind the movement into a configuration that holds meaning for the dancers as much as for the audience. The ideas, however, can be overlooked, and the reconstruction becomes a shallow regurgitation instead. On witnessing one of these regurgitations, my first thought would be to blame the score. I came to realize, however, that the deficiency was not in the score at all.

If one approaches a work with discovery at the forefront of the process, there is a strong likelihood that something new and fresh will be uncovered, and that really is the point, particularly in relation to process. What the audience eventually sees on the stage may seem similar to earlier versions of a work. The difference comes in how the work has gotten there, the ideas the director and dancers have worked through and embodied to realize their version of the dance. Fueling the process are those parts of the evidence the director has chosen to accept. Collingwood's idea in itself indicates that the power of choice can affect a work's interpretation. One needs to be sensitive, therefore, to the consequences of such decision making.

The primary choice for me was Stodelle's interpretation of the nine-count phrase. When the dynamic, drama, and emotion involved in dancing this phrase are considered alongside the documentary evidence, there is a clear and logical connection between the spirit Stodelle has captured in the movement and the spirit of the Shakers. Stodelle describes elements of this phrase in such terms as "impassioned run," "wheeling," "rushing," "tearing across," which was also evident in her 1985 rehearsal process.[20] The focus is outward and the feeling uplifted. This is in marked contrast to the inward rigidity depicted in the score and is the major distinction between the Hutchinson Guest/Grelinger score and Stodelle's version.

The nine-count phrase, in my view, contains broader reflections of the work in dramatic, dynamic, and physical contexts. The nine-count phrase is part of the "Eights, Nines, Tens" section and acts as instigator for the climactic resolution. Figure 25 indicates the structure of the dance, with subtitles taken from the score. The "Eights, Nines, Tens" section sees the central divide most tested as groups of dancers from both sides seemingly pound the "line" with the most energetic vocabulary of the dance thus far. By this stage, the dance has progressed from the opening floor-based section, through a processional walk that brings the two sides toward each other, into wheeling circles ("Pinwheels") and linear hopping formations ("1st and 2nd Hopping in Lines"). The leg action builds throughout, from a slow, sustained stepping in the processional, progressing

| Subtitles | Bar numbers |
|---|---|
| Opening | 1–13 |
| Processional | 14–17 |
| Pin Wheels | 18–21 |
| 1st Hopping in Lines/1st Revelation | 22–26 |
| 2nd Hopping in Lines/2nd Revelation | 27–34 |
| Eights/Nines/Tens | 35–48 |
| 20 count phrase | 49–51 |
| Jumps | 52–63 |
| Amen | 64 |

Figure 25. The structure of the dance.

from a minor to a major rebound, which then becomes a more vigorous hopping action, leading into the nine-count phrase itself. The phrase is danced first by a single male dancer downstage left. Others on the same side join him at nine-count intervals. On the opposite side, dancers start coming in after a six-count interval, two or three at a time, creating a contrapuntal image across the stage. This structural pattern is consistent in both versions. Earlier, I referred to Stodelle's nine-count phrase being so different that it changed the essence of the dance. The degree of difference will become evident through a comparative analysis of Stodelle's version and the Hutchinson Guest/Grelinger score.

The movement phrase begins on count 9, as an upbeat. Stodelle's version starts with an exhalation of breath as the hands, in fists, fall onto the chest, causing the body to hinge back suspended, with the focus high and lifted (count 9). Five steps follow (counts 1&2&3), performed with bent knees and retaining the suspended backward hinge.[21] The hands come together in a clasp in front of the chest, arms extending forward throughout the step pattern, increasing the feeling of suspension and with a sense of the soul being drawn out of the body. The steps culminate in a forward fall (count 4), a release out of the suspended run. The subsequent recovery rebounds up to a point of suspension to fall again, a quarter turn round, landing in a second-position plié; the focus is lifted, with the right arm opening down in a successional curve. The movement falls from a curve to a curve (counts &5). The phrase culminates with a three-quarter turn using the right arm (counts &6), followed by a falling run back toward the starting point (counts &7&8) and a final turn to the opening position (count 9). Stodelle's turn on count 6 is a sweeping, expansive movement in which the body is drawn round and laid open by the arm gesture, which has the same quality.

The nine-count phrase recorded in the score begins with the hands open, palms facing in, held up to the sides of the face, as if keeping something out, and the body tilts forward with focus down (count 9). The five steps (counts 1&2&3) are performed from a straight leg to a rise, retaining the slight forward tilt of the body and downward focus, creating a rigid staccato-type movement, and hands remain held up to the face. The fall (count 4) is an angular forward lunge with both arms piercing through to emphasize the forward low line. There is an angular transference of weight, rebounding from the forward lunge, through a quarter turn to a side lunge, right arm side low, taking the focus down with it. The movement strikes from a linear lunge to a linear lunge (counts &5). For the final counts in the phrase, the arm pulls round to a lifted angular position beside the head (counts &6). The back and chest are lifted also but with a sense of rigid, suspended tension and not the expansive quality described above. The falling runs retain the staccato-like quality from earlier in the phrase (counts &7&8).

Both Stodelle and the Hutchinson Guest/Grelinger score follow the same progression and structure. The distinction comes in the quality of the action, mirrored in the opening step pattern of the nine-count phrase. The score version retains a rigid, staccato feel throughout the dance, while Stodelle's movement, whether the knees are bent or elongated, has a more subtle weighted and fluid quality, inducing a greater emphasis on continuous flow. This, in turn, emphasizes the weighted aspect of fall and recovery. The arm and torso movement, as described in the falling lunges and final turn, are likewise indicative. In the score version, the sensation when executing the movement is an enclosed one, of being held firmly in, while the sensation from Stodelle's version is quite the opposite. The physical difference is in the shoulders and is felt particularly on the release of gestures. The dance contains many instances and variations of the hands being held in to the body and opening from a clasped position. The movement has a quite different feeling and reading, if the shoulders are held fixed or allowed to open unhindered.

The dramatic focus for the whole piece is reflected in the complete nine-count phrase but, I would argue, most particularly in the opening/final position. In the score, the movement pulls up and in, with a sense of anticipation but with rigid control, keeping everything at bay, and with a downward focus. In Stodelle's version, the movement falls into a backward hinge, with the focus lifted. As a part of the fall, the fists hit the chest and lay the upper body out, leaving it open and vulnerable but ready to go after whatever is waiting, despite the precarious position. One could argue the merits of both versions in terms of how they relate to Shakerism, with the score version conveying the inward, rigid, fixed qualities that we know are aspects of Shaker life. The energy generated by Stodelle's version embodies uplifting spiritual fulfillment but in addition creates a movement experience and connection that go beyond the dance and closer to Humphrey herself.

A further piece of evidence relates to Stodelle's 1985 re-creation. Having performed this version and witnessed its performance history over a number of years, I observed Stodelle making changes to the work. This is reminiscent of Humphrey's own practice of making changes over time and perhaps also reflects the assurance Stodelle had in her own relationship with the work. Stodelle was not the choreographer, but one could argue that she "stood in" for Humphrey because of her own long-term association and experience within the Humphrey tradition. Stodelle's changes were a conscious creative response to the work that evolved over time, whereas her reaction to the nine-count phrase was far more immediate and based on memory and performer instinct. Between 1985 and 1986, Stodelle staged four separate productions of the work—in the United States (Silo Concert Dancers), in London (London

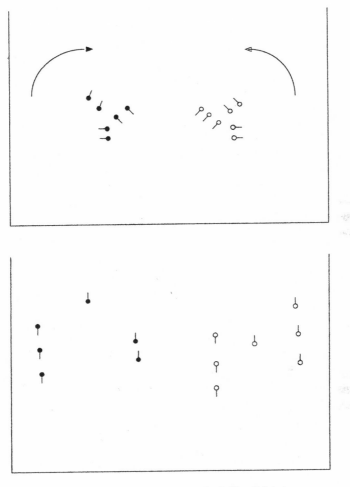

Figure 26. Floor plans for "Pinwheels" (*above*) and "Hopping in Lines" (*below*).

Contemporary Dance School), in Amsterdam (Danskern), and then back in the United States (Silo Concert Dancers). Aside from the first production, in which she focused on the work as a whole, Stodelle used the subsequent rehearsal periods to experiment with individual phrases and gestures. By the time of the fourth production, she had decided upon changes to the "Pinwheels" and the "Hopping in Lines" sections. The analysis below illustrates the ways in which Stodelle operated in what could be described as an interpretive capacity.

The "Pinwheels" section involves the two sides, each in a three-spoked formation wheeling in symmetrical converse circles. At certain points, the inward "spokes" pass close to each other. In the score, the outer dancer on the men's side would lunge and/or make an exaggerated gesture toward the women's side, with the outer female dancer responding by looking across. The men performed the pinwheel beating the left fist against the leg in time with the step pattern. Stodelle had initially changed the men's movement toward the women to a corresponding look because she did not recall the exaggerated lunging action as being what they had originally done. Her recollection was of a more subtle reaction, of the connecting force being exemplified by the power of the gaze and felt through the whole body before eye contact is made as the outer dancers begin to wheel in toward the center. Stodelle made further changes here, involving the arm gesture for the outer men. One did the original gesture, one beat the fist against the shoulder in a parallel position, and one beat across the chest toward the opposite shoulder. She considered it important to build a subtle contrast within the symmetry, an acknowledgment of Humphrey's ever-present concern about the interplay between symmetry and asymmetry.

Changes to the "Hopping in Lines" section were likewise made to break up the symmetry but with a further aspect of bringing greater expanse to the overall image. This section is repeated with minor variation and at a faster tempo the second time. The two groups of men and women move out of the pinwheel formation into six vertical lines of one, two, or three dancers. Each line has its own movement phrase of two or four counts repeated a set number of times. Originally, as in the score, dancers in the same line performed the same movement. Aside from the two single dancers, Stodelle made changes to the remaining four phrases, involving elements such as the angle of the head and upper body, alternating tilts and arm gestures, and adjusting counts for each dancer within the phrase so that "openings" would occur on different beats. The results did fill the space to a greater extent. Where originally three dancers would fall to the right, come up, fall to the left, the new version contained a forward, right, and left fall in unison. This created an "expanse" of movement that was in turn multiplied across the stage through the six individual lines.

Stodelle also made changes to the Eldress role in 1985 and 1986 and when she staged the dance again some years later. Following the "1st and 2nd Hopping in Lines," the Eldress breaks out of her repetitive phrase into a walking pattern that crosses the front of the stage to center, then upstage. On the upstage walk she performs a wrestling-type action in which the arms and upper body appear to be pulled and twisted by some external force. In the score, the movement is accentuated and percussive in keeping with the dynamic already described. Stodelle amended the movement to give greater emphasis to the suspension and breath. The movement became more fluid but no less powerful, and she treated the subsequent phrase in an identical manner. These two phrases are punctuated by a "revelation." The wrestling action depicts the body being possessed, culminating in the Eldress becoming subsumed. She calls the followers, speaks of her revelation, then collapses in a trancelike state, moving backward and forward repeatedly, as if the force is now being drawn out of her. There is a strong comparison here with the lunges and upper body action in the nine-count phrase, with the score indicating linear angles and Stodelle producing curved, weighted falls. The change involved the first of these phrases. Here, she removed the arm and torso movement completely from the upstage walk. She and Gail Corbin, who danced the role from 1985, both felt it was not working and that there was a better form of expression for that moment. This was achieved through the same idea of the gaze used in the "Pinwheels." The hands were held in a clasp in front of the chest throughout, with the "struggle" rising within.

These examples illustrate the impact of Stodelle's decision making on the dynamics, spatial configurations, movement vocabulary and quality, and dramatic interpretation of the work. Her decisions were based on two primary factors: her focus on the interplay between symmetry and asymmetry, and her responses to what was happening in rehearsal. The first has a direct link with Humphrey's own practice, and the second indicates Stodelle's willingness to allow the work to "speak" from and be influenced by its contemporary context. Stodelle was not out to contemporize the work. Her intent with all the works was to produce re-creations. She was secure enough in her roots, however, to trust the responses from herself and her dancers in the 1980s to movement

Figure 27. "Climax," *The Shakers*. Re-created by Ernestine Stodelle for Silo Concert Dancers, 1986. Photographer: Jennifer Lester.

material conceived in the 1930s. Relating Stodelle's approach to Benedetti's liberal category, the parallels are clear. He refers to a work "living relevant to its present moment and the essential spirit being transmitted by but not entirely bound in the text."[22] Given that Stodelle's intention was to produce a re-creation, one might think Benedetti's conservative/fidelity category would be more appropriate. It would be in relation to some of Stodelle's re-creations, *Air for the G String* and *Water Study* being two such examples. *The Shakers* is different because Stodelle's approach was different. She intervened and made changes — not filling in "gaps," as she had done with *Two Ecstatic Themes* and *The Call/Breath of Fire*, but making conscious creative changes to material she knew had come from Humphrey. Her actions reflect those of other performer-centered practitioners cited earlier. The pianist Wanda Landowska's comment, that Rameau had "nothing more to say" about his work, is true. Rather than accepting that nothing more could be said, however, both Landowska and Stodelle had the assurance to allow their own voices to emerge through the work itself.

## Crossing the Line

Stodelle's version of the dance influenced my own interpretation in two ways. In a broader sense, having danced with her for over twenty years, her movement style and quality, inevitably and implicitly, have an influence on whatever I do. In a more specific context and in line with Collingwood's model, I have chosen to accept her stylistic and dynamic interpretation of this work over the notated version because I see a correlation between the expansive qualities inherent in Stodelle's version and creative possibility. The presence of possibility creates the potential for new interpretation. Were I embarking on a reconstructive process, I would stage Stodelle's version as it is scored and produce a further version of *The Shakers*. Using Stodelle's version as a basis for interpretation, however, extends the parameters and allows the creative process to go further.

The production processes I discuss elsewhere in this book were concerned with contemporizing the whole work. The approach to *The Shakers*, in contrast, was driven by a creative exploration of specific aspects of the work, namely, the choreographic structure and vocabulary. I had long felt that Humphrey's vocabulary had more to say, but not in its existing form with a clearly specified setting. The intention, therefore, was to strip away the narrative, to discover what the movement and structure could say independently. My initial expectation had been that this approach would create a contemporized version of Humphrey's work. The ensuing exploration in fact resulted in the creation of a new work, in contrast with the interpretation of *With My Red Fires*, which produced a new reading. My role extended beyond the interpretive parameters of other productions, with the balance shifting in the degree to which I functioned as a creative artist more so than in a traditional directorial capacity. The resulting production had parallels with Robert Lepage's *Elsinore* (1996), for example, where *Hamlet* had been the stimulus for his new creation. Lepage's process involved taking aspects of Shakespeare's narrative and characters to generate a new configuration of the work embodied in a single character.

Other such examples include *Swan Lake*, *Giselle*, and *Dido and Aeneas*, all established works in contemporary consciousness with many distinct but recognizable interpretations. The interpretations by Matthew Bourne (*Swan Lake*), Mats Ek (*Giselle*), and Mark Morris (*Dido and Aeneas*) were so different, however, that each individual work attained a new facet that will remain in contemporary consciousness and has since become part of the work's performance history. Like Lepage, each choreographer/director took aspects of the "traditional" that had hitherto been unexplored. The central aspect for both Bourne and Morris was changing the gender of the leading protagonists. Ek chose to build his interpretation around Giselle's madness, setting the production in an asylum. There are certainly similarities in approach in all four examples, but there is also an important distinction. The three dance works had numerous productions and interpretations over many years. Bourne and Ek did not set out to reinterpret Petipa's work. They created new interpretations of the works that were also radically different from anything that had come before, and it is this radical difference that makes them stand out. Lepage, on the other hand, consciously took Shakespeare's play and changed it. My approach to *The Shakers* took a similar path.

A question that arises is, Why take such an approach at all? *The Shakers* as a dance work is complete in itself, with an extensive performance history that is likely to continue. What is the purpose, therefore, of playing around with it to the extent that I am suggesting? Looking at the broader context of a "dance tradition," I think the purpose is about exploration. In our society, there is a constantly renewed exploration of ideas in a myriad of contexts. It is a natural part of our advancement as human beings. In developing strategies to ensure our modern dance traditions continue to evolve, therefore, renewed exploration should be near the top of the list. In a process of exploration, working with familiar material in itself creates deeper understanding. Through deeper understanding, new trails and possibilities become apparent. In his definition of radical (creative) interpretation, Benedetti talked about returning to the source of a play to generate new forms and a new intuitive creative process. Benedetti's reference to "the source" could be interpreted in more than one way. Is the source Humphrey's choreography, the documented history of the Shakers, or both? Here again the element of choice is involved. My approach began from an impulse that arose from dancing the dance. The work drew me in through my responses to a particular movement phrase. I didn't set out to change the work for the sake of change but to explore where the movement seemed to be leading. To further that exploration, it was necessary to work with the body of evidence in order to create a credible foundation. In answering the question about the source, therefore, I drew on both Humphrey's choreography and documented Shaker history.

Broadly speaking, the evidence base I used comprised Humphrey's movement vocabulary and choreographic structure as embodied in Stodelle's version alongside a series of photographic images of Shaker artifacts by American photographer Linda Butler.[23] My impulse to explore the particular vocabulary of the nine-count phrase was linked to its structural context, from the literal urge to "cross the line that shouldn't be crossed," to a more physiological and dynamic response to the properties of the movement vocabulary. Ernestine often repeated a phrase Doris used in class when she was developing new movement phrases: "Take it and make it your own," acknowledging, perhaps, that the individual body responds to movement impulses in an individual way.[24] In taking this position, Humphrey encouraged freedom to follow an instinct in a creative rather than prescriptive manner that in turn allowed for fresh exploration.

As the Shaker movement developed and grew in the late nineteenth century, so did the emphasis on rigid discipline, rectilinear order and balance, relating to every aspect of the living and working life, and a constant aspiration to seek perfection in all things. Shaker invention and the resulting objects came to be highly regarded because of the quality of the workmanship coupled with a simple aesthetic beauty of design and form. The connecting factor for me relates to form, design, and structure as manifested through the objects. These aspects are exemplified through images created by photographer Linda Butler that contrast with more representational illustrations presented in other texts. Butler's interpretation adds a further dimension to the representations because of what she has *chosen* to capture in each photograph and the composition of each image. Her use of perspective, balance, and natural light further enhances the aspects of form, design, and structure. One example is *Photograph 37. Parallel Stairs 1*. Shaker houses traditionally had two staircases for separate use by the men and women of the community. Butler's image is shot from the midpoint of a landing at the foot of a pair of staircases. The image not only depicts the staircases and banisters as objects but also takes in the tops of the stairwells leading up from the floor below. At the opposite end of the landing, two adjacent windows face the camera, with parallel sets of chairs hung upside down on facing walls. There is a profound sense of symmetry and clarity of line, and there is also a sense of ascending, spiraling flow created by the position of the

Figure 28. *Photograph 37. Parallel Stairs 1.* Photograph by Linda Butler, from June Sprigg and Linda Butler, *Inner Light: The Shaker Legacy* (1985).

camera. Humphrey defines this form of flowing symmetry as "successional." While she was wary of an overemphasis of successional symmetry in relation to choreographic design, it is a device she used with great effect in *The Shakers* in an underlying capacity. In the dance, fleeting images emerge periodically, full of balance and repose, not unlike the images created in the Butler photographs, before the more electrifying and asymmetrical aspects resume.

The Butler images provided me with a fresh perspective on Shaker philosophy and the already familiar "historical" evidence base. In addition to successional symmetry, Humphrey's choreography contains a layering of asymmetrical movement design over symmetrical structural design. There is a corresponding play between symmetry and asymmetry in Butler's work, illustrated in the *Parallel Stairs* image through the curving swirls of the banister handrails against the mirror symmetry of the staircases themselves. The ideas expressed through these images in structural terms were especially relevant in relation to exploring the choreographic structure because of the emphasis on form. When I decided to explore the work "creatively," one of the first decisions I made was to cut all the narrative indicators. The idea was to abstract "what it is about" to leave "what it is," with the physical energy patterns following the route of the emotional/narrative patterns in the score-based and re-created versions of the dance. The Butler images provided an important link to the source, capturing the abstraction idea by removing the literal depiction of Shaker life (what it is about) and creating instead abstracted moments of stillness (what it is). The images provided contextually relevant examples of abstraction within an asymmetrical/symmetrical framework—precisely what I intended to do with the dance.

The exploration of the dance began with the nine-count phrase, with every other decision evolving from that point of origin. The physicality of this particular vocabulary is such that the body can experience the Apollonian/Dionysian aspects of Humphrey's fall and recovery philosophy to its fullest extent, but only from one or two specific positions within the group (Man 6, downstage left; Eldress, midstage right). I had long felt that the movement of the nine-count phrase had the capacity to go farther than it was able to when performed directly behind/in front of another body. There is a principle in the Humphrey tradition of letting the movement go as far as it can, embodied within the central concepts of "wholeness of movement" and "dancing from the inside out." The movement vocabulary for the nine-count phrase ("Nines") was retained intact for the new production process, but the structure of the section changed. The structure of *The Shakers* has the dancers in six horizontal lines, three facing three into center, with a traveling path for the movement that does not cross center because of the metaphorical divide in Shakerism. The first area for exploration, therefore, was discovering what would happen if the travel restriction were removed and the group were in a more open formation. Opening up the spatial form and structure involved allowing the center line to be breached and "loosening" the six horizontal lines so that no single body/entity was constricted. The result was twofold. Every body was able to take the movement as far as it could go, and, unexpectedly, a spatial form emerged that matched the new structure. As bodies from each side converge on/through center, the form of a cross appears, then separates throughout the section until the bodies come together as a single clustered entity. (I had deliberately stripped the dance of its religious connotations, so the irony of the cross did not escape me.)

The discoveries unlocked through exploring the nine-count phrase acted as a foundation for the broader exploration of the physical energy patterns of the whole dance. The intention behind the "Opening" section in the new work, for example, is to convey the image of energy emerging from stillness, rising up out of the ground to establish a grounded connection from the outset. The opening image of *The Shakers*, conversely, sees Man 1 in a standing lunge, pointing above and beyond the Eldress to an unseen vision, with the group, lifted up on the knees, inclining and reaching through a hand clasp in the same direction. As the music begins, the whole group lowers down to the floor in unison. The "Introduction" to the new work reverses this, not to create an intentional contrast but because of the significance of direction. The opening body position is a low kneel with the pelvis released, the head dropped forward, and the hands/arms resting on the upper legs. To begin, the body moves in an upward successional roll, initiated by the pelvis and in-breath, so that the spine unfurls completely. This upward lift is timed to flow, musically and physiologically, straight into the first phrase itself. In both dances, the body begins the first phrase proper from the same position.

## Navigating Narrative

Additional strategies adapted from theater production included cutting and reshaping existing material and relocating the setting of the work. Exploring the creative possibilities of these aspects helped frame the directorial process. One aspect of a play that is especially fluid and likely to change from director to director is its location or setting. Take a single Shakespeare play, say, *A Midsummer Night's Dream*, and consider how many diverse settings it has had over time. Alexander identified three categories of setting, as discussed in part 1. His "eclectic" category defines very well what happened with *The Shakers*. When taken in conjunction with Benedetti's radical category, a useful platform emerges from which to consider the degree of interpretation at play. Alexander talked about creating a world of the stage rather than a world of society and Benedetti about the source of a play generating new forms. Place these ideas alongside the idea of replacing what the work is about with what it is, and possibilities begin to appear.

Removing the narrative setting of the dance was perhaps the most radical act, as it impacted on all aspects of the work, including the title, casting, costume, and music in addition to the choreographic vocabulary and structure. The title of the dance, for example, became redundant because it was so specific. I wanted to create an ambiguous reading, to allow an audience to draw its own conclusion(s) as to what the dance was "about." Humphrey had originally titled the work *Dance of the Chosen*, less explicit but still suggestive of ritual. A further diminution to *The Chosen*, however, gives a more open title that allows for possibility within the creative process and conjures up the question, Chosen what? In approaching Stodelle's version from this standpoint and considering what abstract readings were possible, the idea of "energy" emerged. This energy became further defined as an "electrical force," manifest in the collective mass of bodies traversing around and through the physical space in a continuous and increasing flow of energy. The shift from sect-based to the less specific power-based energy force creates a greater emphasis on the structural aspect of Shakerism, to the simplicity and beauty of line and form as captured in Butler's photographic images. Humphrey herself acknowledged: "There was a center figure, yes, but by far the strongest and most important movement was given to the group, and it was their collective strength that gave power to the dance."[25]

Without the narrative, Humphrey's original casting of the Eldress, Women 1–6, and Men 1–6 became as redundant as the title. Casting can have various permutations—a male dancer as Elder, as men did take on this role in Shaker communities; a female lead with all male ensemble; a male lead with female ensemble. These permutations have possibility but are also limiting in terms of the readings they produce because of the presence of a central figure. *The Shakers* begins with the full cast onstage in a symmetrical, three-sided square formation, turned to the centrally placed lone figure making up the fourth side. The central figure is seated on a bench, placing her on a different level to the rest of the group, who are in a kneeling position on the floor. This image is immediately suggestive of a distinction between the central figure and the rest because she is alone and at a higher level. To create a more ambiguous reading in *The Chosen*, the lone figure and the bench have been cut and replaced by an upstage line comprising two dancers, a "connecting force" who replicate the kneeling position of the downstage group. A different, more uniform reading is created without resorting to the absolute symmetry of four lines of four. This new grouping takes over the spatial place vacated by the central figure but not as a dominant presence. The spatial consequences of having an even number of dancers (fourteen) allowed further exploration of the asymmetrical/symmetrical relationship. The floor plans in figures 29 and 30 illustrate some of these consequences and are placed alongside parallel moments from *The Shakers* for comparison.

Cutting and reshaping a play text is common practice in Shakespearean production. Having observed the robustness of a "work," it was important to explore how far the reshaping process could go beyond producing a new reading of a work, as I had done for *With My Red Fires*. All of the choreographic vocabulary in *The Chosen* is danced as it would be in *The Shakers* or with minimal adjustment. However, not all of the choreographic vocabulary of *The Shakers* appears in *The Chosen*. Alongside satisfying my explorative urges, it was important to me to create a recognizable form as described by White and Benedetti. In this particular instance, it is not important to the work's reception that an audience should literally recognize what the group is or is meant to represent. It is more about creating a coherent whole that can be recognized as such and that has meaning in and of itself. In order to create that coherent whole, cutting

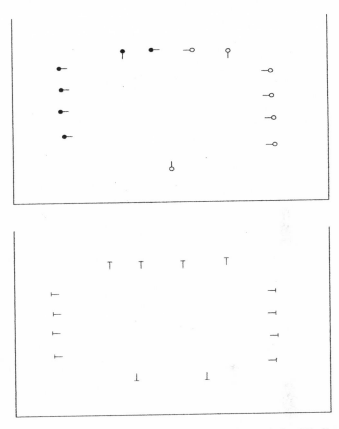

Figure 29. Comparative floor plans for the opening tableau for *The Shakers* (*above*) and *The Chosen* (*below*).

and reshaping material was more prominent than had been necessary for the interpretation of *With My Red Fires*.

The most significant cut was the "Eights" section, which leads into the nine-count phrase. This movement has a direct historic connection and is depicted in lithographs of Shaker ceremonies from the 1860s.[26] The elbows are held into the body, with lower arms out and forward, hands relaxed downward. The torso leans forward slightly, and the hands and arms take on the rhythmic rebound of the hopping action in the legs. It is a quite peculiar movement to perform, as King described earlier. Within a reconstruction or re-creation context, however, the historic connotation of the movement has a clear meaning and a direct connection to Humphrey's dance. In *The Chosen*, this connection no longer existed, and the movement looked incongruous and out of place. Cutting the section resulted in further reshaping of the structure leading into the nine-count phrase.

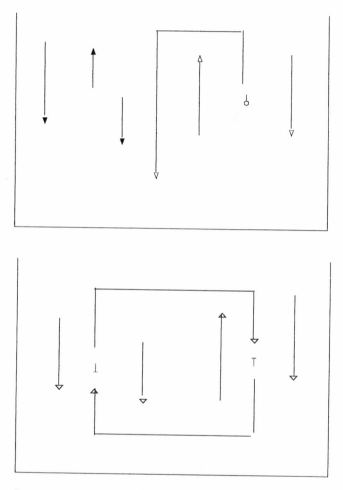

Figure 30. Comparative floor plans for the "2nd Hopping in Lines" pathways for *The Shakers* (*above*) and *The Chosen* (*below*).

Cutting the "Eights" also affected the musical score and structure. The original music is an arrangement of Shaker-type songs and accompaniment, harmonized by Daniel Jahn and arranged by Humphrey's associate Pauline Lawrence, and is scored for solo voice, drum, and harmonium. The development of the musical structure follows that of the choreography, gaining a similar momentum and dynamic as the piece progresses. The music for *The Chosen* was rescored for piano only because the sound has a more eclectic quality in comparison particularly to the harmonium and the voice. The piano has a "cleaner" sound that, to my ear, blends with the clarity I had sought to emphasize in the form and structure of the choreography. The instruction given to musical arranger Roger Cutts was to contemporize the score while retaining the melodic theme and phrase structure. The principal changes included subsuming the vocal line and replacing the drum part, both of which entailed new composition.

The most complex musical challenge lay in replacing the drum part in the "Eights, Nines, Tens" section because there is no other instrumentation at this point. It is also a lengthy section that bridges the first half of the work and the climax. Correlating the weighted, suspended qualities of the movement with the idea of an increasingly evolving force served as the instigator for new musical composition. The choreographic structure of this section, bridging the gap left by cutting the "Eights," had already been determined, so that it began with a seven-count phrase, originally danced in the "Nines" by Women 1, 2, and 3. The movement vocabulary has not been altered but is now danced by the whole group in a repetitive sequence from which the nine-count phrase itself emerges. The movement for the seven-count phrase comprises a three-step, arcing suspension and fall that travels side to side. The dynamic quality of this movement phrase acted as the catalyst for the musical development for the whole section. The seven-count phrase is more weighted and expansive than preceding sections and has elements that reappear or are developed in the "Nines" and "Tens." Two examples are a suspension on counts 1&2 (repeated on 3&4, 5&6), and a weighted fall on count 7. The suspension is seen in developed form at three points in the nine-count phrase and twice in the "Tens." The weighted fall is repeated in the nine-count phrase and developed in the final phrase of the "Tens." There are, therefore, clear dynamic connections throughout this section. The development of the musical composition began by capturing the qualities of the movement dynamic of the seven-count phrase, a suspension and fall, and in so doing established dynamic and melodic parameters for the remainder of the section that could, in turn, progress to the climax.

One aspect of exploring the work's structure was to do so from a different perspective in space as well as intention. Given the emphasis on structure, I was intrigued to see what would happen by introducing a viewing perspective from above the dance. The initial idea was to film directly over the stage space to capture the choreographic patterns from that position, but it was not possible to do so and keep all the dancing bodies in view. Filming from a thirty-foot tower, positioned some way back from the stage space, created a diagonal angle but kept the whole entity in view. This viewing perspective was used throughout the rehearsal process alongside the more traditional head-on, ground-level perspective. As the work developed, it became clear that cutting between the two perspectives would allow a further version of the choreographic structure to emerge.

The presence of the camera did not specifically influence creative decisions about the choreography, but the act of filming created a version of *The Chosen* that is distinct from the live version. The live action retains a "human" aspect that is less pronounced on the recording because the latter emphasizes the abstraction and form to a greater extent. With the live performance, one is conscious of bodies moving through space, whereas the predominant sense on the recording is of structure(s) moving through space, perhaps because the viewing mechanism through a TV monitor is decidedly more contained and framed than the open aspect of a performing space. The viewing perspectives of the camera added a further dimension, and the exploration has, in fact, created two works. One work is the dance as experienced by an audience that encompasses two perspectives — witnessing the live action and experiencing this action at ground level. The second work is an instance of the dance that has been created by the range of perspectives made possible through the camera and the processes involved in recording, editing, and transmitting these images. Humphrey herself had staged the dance with filmmaker Thomas Bouchard in 1940. He shot the dance in a studio setting, and his subsequent editing of the footage produced not a record of the dance but another version of the work.

An audience was invited to view *The Chosen* as a live experience. It was not an exclusively "dance" audience, and the audience members were given no indication of the setting of the work, but all were aware of my experience within the Humphrey tradition. A common response was of being drawn into the work and mesmerized by its evolving form. Examples of individual responses include the work being "architectural," "energizing," "emotional," "powerfully forbidding," "musical," "reminiscent of films like *The Battleship Potemkin* (1925) with its emphasis on the proletariat." No two responses were similar in terms of what the work was about. More importantly, however, all of the audience members felt that the work as they experienced it was complete in itself and had meaning(s) within their own individual perceptions.

To return to the "why do it at all" question, my response is that continued exploration extends a dance tradition and keeps it living, fresh, and creative. There are numerous examples from theater that indicate the robustness of a work. How many interpretations of *Hamlet, The Cherry Orchard, The Three Sisters* have there been, and how many more are to come? As importantly, consider what new knowledge has been uncovered about the works and their creators in the process. We should have confidence that our dance works can have this same robustness, as long as the approaches taken are rooted in the respective traditions.

# EPILOGUE

## Dancing the Past Tomorrow

The ideas and strategies presented in this book are intended to illustrate what is possible. The intention is not to replace existing practices, including reconstruction, but to extend current practice in the knowledge that the passing of time necessitates a new form of intervention.

In relation to the individual works, the impact of each central directorial choice determined the scale of change. The impact of the forward successional curve in *Water Study* was essential to the production process, to my own approach and what, in turn, I was able to convey to the dancers. Having consciously changed the internal focus, however, I made no actual adjustments to the work's choreography or structure. With *Passacaglia*, the musical emphasis affected the work in two ways: first, on the dancing in terms of movement quality and phrasing, and second, in relation to the work as a whole because the Stokowski sound generates a different, more expansive and resonant ambiance compared to other organ and orchestral arrangements. Secondary aspects such as creating a more prominent female lead and a democratic community further increased the degree of change. Privileging Humphrey's underlying themes in *With My Red Fires* required substantial reshaping. It may seem radical in one sense to cut scenes, remove the narrative, and redefine characters in a dance work. The work, however, both remains recognizable as Humphrey's *With My Red Fires* and, arguably, has greater meaning in a contemporary context.

*The Shakers* proved to be the most radical experience in relation to Benedetti's definition. The initial intention had been to explore what the choreography might reveal without its literal elements. The act of exploration, from its basis in historical documentary evidence, revealed, in fact, a new dance, despite much of Humphrey's choreographic vocabulary, structure, and design remaining unaltered. The extent of change may raise the question as to whether the new work can be defined as belonging to Humphrey at all. The artistic intention underpinning the production was to explore creatively rather than to create in itself. Humphrey provided the "words," I provided the context in which those words are uttered. The nature of that context is such that the "words" now reveal a quite different message. This may be taking interpretation to its edge, because the creative intervention on my part has produced a work that could not be categorized as "by" Doris Humphrey. However, to claim that *The Chosen* was "by" Lesley Main would also be inaccurate. Humphrey's dance was not simply a stimulus for my own creation. Her material forms a substantial part of the work, and to leave this unacknowledged would amount to choreographic plagiarism. The solution, in terms of public acknowledgment, is to include explanatory program notes.

None of the abstracted elements I chose in each of the dances were Humphrey's principal points of focus. She did, however, generate them all in some way. Approaching the works through elements identified from the present rather than engaging with the work in its past form had two consequences. First, it changed the nature of the directorial relationship with the work and the choreographer, placing it on a more even, triangular footing. Second, because the decision making evolved from the present, the interpretation could do likewise, linking with my desire for contemporized production. Positioning on the aforementioned continuum came about through particular choices being made in relation to the interpretation of evidence. It has been enlightening to see where on the continuum the individual dances lay, because each is distinct in nature and each has the capacity for more than one approach. Different choices, therefore, could result in different positioning—an intriguing prospect. The processes I have articulated here allow for further creative practice, contingent on a different selection and reading of evidence. I will undoubtedly revisit the Humphrey works discussed in this book, but my subsequent directorial processes will not necessarily include the same choices in terms of privileging one particular form of evidence over another. The Collingwood approach allows for that fresh look at the same documentation. With *Passacaglia*, the focus on the sound could give way to another aspect such as Humphrey's reaction to war, an underlying theme for her. Adopting such an approach could shift the emphasis from abstraction to a thematic or even narrative interpretation to discover what Humphrey's vocabulary can say within such a context. Similarly, new emphases could be identified in *With My Red Fires* in terms of the narrative and characterization, which, in turn, would elicit new readings. Having taken *The Shakers* to an extreme edge, I am now intrigued to explore its cultural-historic setting but from a contemporary perspective, from the present.

The ideas and principles I have developed in relation to Humphrey's dances are not intended to be exclusive to this particular tradition and would work as well in a wider context. Modern dance is in the early stages of developing its own history in comparison with the much older and established forms of classical ballet, music, and theater. Humphrey is a pertinent marker from which to develop processes that will both maintain and extend an artistic tradition. Of the major modern dance figures, Humphrey is the first whose tradition does not remain solely within the remit and responsibility of its direct descendant performers because the passing of time has necessitated intervention by the current generation.

Despite the ongoing work of these direct descendant exponents, there will come a point in the individual histories of the artistic traditions when the perpetuation of the repertoires and the underlying movement styles and philosophies will become the responsibility of artists who do not have that direct association with the choreographer. This will also be the point at which the existing body of evidence for a specific tradition will need to be drawn upon in ways that may not be required at this time because of the current prevalence of direct knowledge and experience. Graham was reluctant to have her dances notated during her lifetime, thus evidence of this nature does not exist to any large extent, although a small number of Labanotation scores have been produced in recent years.[1] A substantial body of evidence on her dances does exist, however, in the form of film and video recordings, photographs, and Graham's notebooks. Cunningham addressed the issue of his legacy in some detail prior to his death, putting plans in place for a final two-year tour of his company and the continued staging of his work beyond the company's closure. Taylor has embraced notation as a form of recording for years, with the majority of major works notated either during the choreographic process or during revivals for his own company.[2] His willingness to do so indicates not only a desire for his dances to continue being staged but also the acknowledgment that, someday, someone other than himself or his immediate associates will undertake this activity.

Such development is not imminent, but it is inevitable, and modern dance as a field should be ready for the transition in order to protect the great works that our major artists have produced. It is possible that Humphrey's *Passacaglia*, Graham's *Clytemnestra*, and Taylor's *Last Look* could have the longevity of *King Lear* and *The Cherry Orchard* because the strategies exist to keep the works alive and vibrant. As a result, dance audiences would become accustomed to seeing productions of the same work within a range of interpretations in the same way that theater audiences view interpretations of Shakespeare. Productions such as those presented by the Globe Theatre and by directors such as Peter Brook as well as the quite radical treatments favored by the likes of Peter

Sellars and Robert Wilson illustrate the capacity of a work to survive repeated and divergent intervention. Dance works have the same capacity. The issue is not just about the practical engagement with a work from an artistic perspective, however. It is also about the perception of a work and the processes through which we determine what a work is and, moreover, what a work can be. In a comparison with theater and opera, Siegel warned against the "wholesale transformation" of a dance work if artistic license is taken too far.[3] I agree if the intent driving a production is simply to produce a theatrical event. However, if the intent is to produce the work from within the stylistic tradition in a process that encompasses the body of evidence relating to that particular work, I suggest that the "work" as an entity is robust enough to withstand repeated and diverse interpretation. Whatever takes place during an interpretive process, the body of evidence will remain, as will the stylistic philosophy, and both aspects may be extended as a result of new interpretation.

The production processes discussed here and resulting performances have enabled me to both critique and develop existing theoretical approaches to reconstruction and to demonstrate that current practice can be extended effectively. The proceedings for "Preservation Politics," the last major international conference on dance reconstruction, contain reference to the "introduction of perspectives from Shakespeare edition, opera and theatre" and how "advanced thinking from other art forms poses a challenge to the dance community."[4] The findings drawn from my research demonstrate the application of such perspectives within a dance context and show that the art form can not only withstand external intervention but be enhanced by its presence. The four dances I staged along with accompanying analytical investigations indicate the scope that exists for directorial interpretation in relation to modern dance works. The principles that have arisen and been tested by these stagings have the potential to affect a wider field of creative practice and theory. Most specifically, however, by disrupting conventional notions of reconstruction, revealing the instability of a performance text yet retaining its stylistic imperatives, privileging the role of director as interpreter, and incorporating the imaginative manipulation of evidence, the dance works of history can remain accessible to future creators, performers, and audiences. The approaches that have been identified have the potential to produce a vibrant, grounded, and creative environment in which the individual works and the wider tradition can both exist and continue to flourish.

# NOTES

## Prologue: Negotiating a Living Past

1. See also Cohen (1982, 114–34) and Anderson (1987, 16–27) for further discussion on the nature of style as it relates to identity.

2. Others include Eleanor King (*Water Study, The Banshee, The Shakers*), Ruth Currier (*Brandenburg Concerto, Water Study*), Letitia Ide (*Day on Earth*), and Ray Cook (*Dawn in New York, Fantasy in Fugue*).

3. Further information on Gail Corbin's work can be found at www.humphrey weidman.com.

4. Karoun Tootikian worked with Ruth St. Denis from 1945 to 1965. She headed the faculty and Oriental Department of Miss Ruth's school in Los Angeles and gave classes in St. Denis's dance techniques and various forms of Oriental dance. She performed with Ruth St. Denis and Ted Shawn at Jacob's Pillow. In reconstructing many of Miss Ruth's early dances, Miss Tootikian was also able to consult with Ann Douglas, a former Denishawn dancer. Miss Tootikian's dance training included study with Adolph Bolm, Michio, La Meri, and Benjamin Zimoch, and she was a member of Lester Horton's first dance company. Many master teachers visited and taught at the St. Denis School during Miss Tootikian's years there: among them were Charles Weidman, Mary Wood Hinman, Harold Kreutzberg, Leon Destine, and Uday Shankar. Miss Tootikian was married to Robert Hawkinson, Miss Ruth's pianist and musical arranger.

5. For information on the Doris Humphrey Society, including details of the Humphrey Archive, recently collated into a single collection housed in the Newberry Library in Oak Park, Illinois, go to www.dorishumphrey.org.

6. This score is available for hire directly from the Doris Humphrey Society and is soon to be followed by the coaching DVD with Stodelle.

## Chasing the Ephemeral

1. Humphrey (1959, 106).

2. Doris Humphrey Collection, housed in the Jerome Robbins Dance Division of the Library for the Performing Arts at the New York Public Library (hereafter DHC), folder M65; Humphrey (1941, 189).

3. Siegel (1996c, 63).

4. As yet there is little reference in the literature on American modern dance acknowledging the significance of the contribution of these first-generation dancers.

5. See Topaz (2000, 102–4) and Thomas (2003, 110–11) for further reference to the evolution of the "dancing body."

6. Interview with Anne Went, former principal dancer with London Contemporary Dance Theatre, March 2010.

7. See Sherman (1995, 56), Siegel (1996a, 6; 1996b, 97), and Garafola (1996).

8. McPherson and Maxwell (1996, 110). The CORD special topics conference included concerts at Teacher's College and La Guardia High School.

9. Topaz (2000, 100, 103).

10. Brown (1993, 27).

11. Franko (1989, 57).

12. Manning (1993a, 12).

13. Archer and Hodson (2000, 1).

14. Stodelle (interview, 1986).

15. Marcia Siegel came upon this unidentified film in the DHC while researching her own book on Humphrey. Stodelle was then consulted regarding its identity and recalled Humphrey performing the pair of dances, *The Call* (1929) and *Breath of Fire* (1930), as one work regularly in the early 1930s.

16. Stodelle (interview, 1990).

17. Stodelle (interview, 1990).

18. Dils (1993b, 102).

19. Stodelle (interview, 1995).

20. Dils (1993b, 107).

21. Dils (1993b, 152).

22. Cook (1998, 75).

23. Archer and Hodson (2000, 12).

24. Dils (1993a, 226).

25. Topaz (2000, 101).

26. Dils (1993a, 224).

27. Dils (1993b, 172).

28. Collingwood (1993, 158, 231). Collingwood's views are reflected in more recent writing from the fields of history and philosophy: see White (1978, 1987), LaCapra (1985, 1989), Tosh (1993), Mink (1972), Goldstein (1994).

29. Collingwood (1993, xxii).

30. Eliot (1975, 39).

31. White (1978, 126).

32. White (1987, 1).

33. LaCapra (1985, 139).

34. LaCapra (1985, 14).

35. Collingwood (1993, 114).

36. Eliot (1975, 38).

37. Collingwood (1993, 7).

38. W. K. Wimsatt and Monroe C. Beardsley highlighted the notion of authorial intention in 1946 in their essay "The Intentional Fallacy." Although this was written in relation to literary theory, the ideas can also be applied in a performing arts context. They argue that "the design or intention of the author is neither available nor desirable

as a standard for judging the success of a work of literary art," with intention being defined as "design or plan in the author's mind . . . [that] has obvious affinities towards his work, the way he felt, what made him write" (Wimsatt and Beardsley 1971, 1015). Intention, in this instance, is acknowledged as an impulse-based, internalized experience that is essentially subjective. The question that arises is whether any outward manifestation can be determined by anyone other than the author/artist. There is, of course, the artwork itself, and Wimsatt and Beardsley do suggest that if the poet, in their example, is successful, the poem should reveal his intention. But, if this is the case, should this be regarded as *the* intention, or is it in actuality *an* intention, which in itself implies that there is more than one. They further argue that it is not necessary to know the artist's intention to judge a work and that this knowledge might, if it were available, even act as a distraction from the work itself. This may be so in terms of perceiving a work from the perspective of critic, spectator, and perhaps even performer. For the director and scholar, however, searching for traces of intent can be an illuminating part of the interpretive process. For more recent discussion on issues of "intention," see also Tanselle (1981), McLaverty (1984), and Shillingsburg (1991).

39. Collingwood (1993, 10).
40. Collingwood (1993, 10).
41. Collingwood (1993, 280).
42. Collingwood (1993, 420).
43. Stodelle (interview, 1985).
44. Taruskin (1995, 93).
45. Crutchfield (1988, 20).
46. Kenyon (1988, 14).
47. Quoted in Restout (1981, 407).
48. Quoted in Restout (1981, 406).
49. See Brook in Berry (1989, 1352).
50. See Miller (1986, 23).
51. See Miller in Berry (1989, 7).
52. Noble in Berry (1989, 167).
53. Mann in Cole (1992, 68).
54. Noble in Berry (1989, 165); Jackson in Benedetti (1985, 9).
55. Benedetti (1985, 14).
56. Benedetti (1985, 15).
57. Benedetti (1985, 15).
58. Brook in Berry (1989, 144).
59. Benedetti (1985, 15).
60. Orgel (1988, 7).
61. Miller (1986, 23); Strehler in Berry (1989, 122).
62. Humphrey (1978, 138).
63. Brook in Berry (1989, 132).
64. Berry (1989, 23).
65. Miller in Berry (1989, 2).
66. LeComte in Cole (1992, 98).
67. Bennett (1996, 46).
68. Bennett (1996, 46).
69. Nunn in Berry (1989, 79).

70. Brook in Berry (1989, 148–49).
71. Hall in Berry (1989, 216).
72. Bogdanov in Berry (1989, 225).
73. Berry (1989, 12); Ciulei in Cole (1992, 176).
74. Delgado and Heritage (1996, 275).
75. Holmberg (1996, 298).
76. Levine (1991, 177).
77. Orgel (1988, 3).
78. Berry (1989, 78, 152).
79. Mann in Cole (1992, 58).
80. Benedetti (1985, 223).
81. Benedetti (1985, 23).
82. See Hall in Berry (1989, 209), Miles (1995, 208), Maddox (2002, 49).
83. Linklater in Bennett (1996, 4).
84. Berry (1989, 178).
85. Benedetti (1985, 17).
86. Miller (1986, 121).
87. Benedetti (1985, 18).
88. Benedetti (1985, 15).
89. Charest (1998, 169).
90. Charest (1998, 170).
91. Brook (1968, 67).
92. Whitelaw (1995, 141).
93. Warner in Pitt (1995, 12).
94. Cole (1992, 190).
95. Sellars in Cole (1992, 189).
96. Cole (1992, 192).
97. Sellars in Cole (1992, 195).
98. Beckett (1984, 285).
99. Whitelaw (1995, 147).
100. McMullan (1994).
101. Warner in Pitt (1995, 12).
102. P. Lloyd (2000, 117).
103. Butler (1996a).
104. Manfull (1999, 53).
105. Billington (1994b).
106. Whitelaw (1995, 147).

## Exploring the Creative Impulse

1. Collingwood (1993, 114).

### *Water Study*

1. Siegel (1993a, 89, 85, first and third quotes; 1981, 27, second quote).
2. Jowitt (1988, 196).

3. The Dance Notation Bureau's publication *The Collected Works*, vol. 1, makes further reference to this in the introduction to the *Water Study* score, noting that "the dance contains the first full exhibition of the Humphrey principle of fall and recovery, the alternate yielding to and defying of gravity" (Humphrey 1978, 4).

4. Humphrey (1941, 189).

5. Humphrey (1941, 189).

6. M. Lloyd (1987, 89).

7. DHC, folder M73, 6.

8. DHC, folder M73, 6.

9. Humphrey in Cohen (1995a, 85).

10. Cohen (1995a, 86).

11. King (1978, 54).

12. King (1978, 55).

13. King (1978, 114).

14. Siegel (1993a, 151); King (1978, 202).

15. M. Lloyd (1987, 87).

16. Humphrey (1959, 142).

17. Humphrey (1959, 142).

18. Cohen (1995a, 116).

19. King (1978, 132).

20. King (1978, 305).

21. Stodelle (interview, 1985). Stodelle directed a video recording of *Water Study* in 1997 for the Doris Humphrey Society with Princeton Book Company, Hightstown, NJ. This is commercially available and contains reference to stylistic execution. It is an invaluable addition to the existing body of evidence on this work, particularly for Stodelle's own commentary.

22. Humphrey (1978, 5).

23. Marion (1992, 10).

24. A complete analysis of the differences can be found in Main (2003).

25. In 2002 I was asked by the Dance Notation Bureau to clarify and revise the performance notes for the Karen Barracuda score, with the score itself being checked by Lucy Venable. A final revision was undertaken in 2010.

26. There have been a number of analyses of the dance published since the late 1960s, including those by Davis and Schmais (1967), Kagan (1978), Siegel (1981), and Marion (1992). Each is distinctive in approach and focus, and collectively they provide a useful overview of the work.

27. DHC, folder M73, 6.

28. King (1977, 21).

29. M. Lloyd (1987, 87).

30. M. Lloyd (1987, 89).

31. Humphrey (1941, 189).

32. Siegel (1981, 31).

33. DHC, folder M65.

34. Stodelle (1995a, 15).

35. Stodelle (1995a, 15).

36. King (1978, 21).

37. King (1978, 135).
38. Stodelle (1995a). Successional movement: vertical, sideways, and with drop and gravitational pull (40–45). Change of weight with falling motion (48). Body bends (56). Figure eights: both arms (88). Horizontal torso swings: full circle with vertical thrust (93). Center drop, rebound, and circular successions (99). Thigh stretch (117), colloquially known as the "killer," performed on the floor as a preparation for falls, barre work, and *Water Study*. It is the principal conditioning exercise for the abdominal and quadricep muscles. Swings at the barre with circular successions and back fall (208).
39. Stodelle (interview, 1985); Humphrey (1959, 105).

### *Passacaglia*

1. In 1995 the Doris Humphrey Foundation UK produced a series of performance events to mark Humphrey's centenary in Great Britain. These included August 1 at the Royal Festival Hall, Ballroom Blitz Festival with Ernestine Stodelle; October 17 (Humphrey's birthday) at Middlesex University and Roehampton Institute London; and November 4 at the Place Theatre London in conjunction with the Society of Dance Research.
2. Reprinted in Stodelle (1995a, 263).
3. See Stodelle (1974, 1995a), King (1978), Morrison Brown (1980), Kriegsman (1981), Siegel (1981, 1993a), M. Lloyd (1987), Jordan (1993), Cohen (1995a), Hausler (1996b), Fraleigh (1996).
4. See Cohen (1995a); Siegel (1993a).
5. Humphrey's other dances set to Bach's music were *Air for the G String* (1928), *Gigue* (solo, 1928), *Gigue* (trio, 1929), *Decade* (1941), *Four Chorale Preludes* (1942), *Partita in G Major* (1942), and *Brandenburg Concerto* (1958).
6. DHC, folder M109.
7. Cohen (1995a, 150).
8. King (1977, 263).
9. Cohen (1995a, 256).
10. Johnson (1973).
11. Taruskin (1988) presents a detailed exposition of the vitalist/geometric argument.
12. Johnson (1973).
13. Including Stodelle (1974, 1995a), King (1978), Siegel (1981, 1993a), Jordan (1986, 1993), M. Lloyd (1987), Cohen (1995a), Fraleigh (1996).
14. Johnson (1973).
15. M. Lloyd (1987, 108, italics mine).
16. Stodelle (1974; 1995a, 262, italics mine).
17. DHC, folder M109.
18. DHC, folder C466.
19. Jordan (1986, 217).
20. Venable's experience is an earlier example of the "performer as notator" role discussed in relation to *Water Study*.
21. Reproduced in Manley (1998, 29).
22. Huth danced G. This role is assigned the "Lyric" (Passacaglia 15) and "Chicken" (Passacaglia 18) variations along with Fugue 4, which includes the precarious "walk

down the backs," and Fugue 7, the "Leaping Quartet." In addition, the dancer is placed at the front of the ensemble for the bell turns and big falling phrases.

23. One example is the opening movement phrase for soloist A in Passacaglia 7. This phrase comprises a series of forward lunges reaching out to and drawing in the audience. Wolenski's dancing in this phrase is overly precise and clipped, as is his execution of the "Turns" variation, Passacaglia 16, and the bell turns.

24. Fraleigh (1996, 213). During rehearsal with Momenta Dance Company in 2007, former Limón dancer Jim May also referred to "the gift" image, indicating that Limón retained this idea over time.

25. Payton-Newman in Fraleigh (1996, 218).

26. Varone (1998, 118).

27. Stodelle (interview, 1985).

28. Benedetti (1985, 15).

29. Reprinted in Cohen (1995a, 256).

30. Jordan (1986, 1993).

31. Fraleigh (1996).

32. Payton-Newman in Fraleigh (1996, 214).

33. Jordan (1993, 185).

34. Payton-Newman in Fraleigh (1996, 223).

35. Reprinted in Cohen (1995a, 256).

36. Quoted in Hausler (1996b, 45).

37. August 1, 1995, at the Royal Festival Hall, Ballroom Blitz Festival with Ernestine Stodelle and Gail Corbin.

## *With My Red Fires*

1. Siegel (1993a, 165).

2. Cohen (1995a, 142).

3. Cohen (1995a, 143).

4. Correspondence from Charles H. Woodford, September 2006.

5. The score was co-notated by Els Grelinger, Muriel Topaz, Karen Kanner, Rena Gluck, and Lucy Venable and published in 1964.

6. Ruth Currier and Lucy Venable assisted Humphrey in this production, in which Karen Kanner played the Matriarch.

7. See Kriegsman (1981), M. Lloyd (1987), Jowitt (1988), Dils (1993a, 1993b), Stowe (1992), Siegel (1993a, 1996b), Garafola (1996), Burt (1998a), Topaz (2000).

8. Burt (1995).

9. Foster (1999, 89). Foster's stance on Humphrey's sexuality was challenged at this conference by, amongst others, Humphrey's son, Charles Woodford, and Marcia Siegel, both of whom spoke vehemently in response and most notably about the lack of evidence that had been presented to substantiate this claim. See Carter (interview, 1999).

10. Siegel (1993a, 72).

11. Foster (1999, 91).

12. Foster (1999, 93).

13. Dils (1993b, 225).

14. White (1978, 126).

15. Reprinted in Cohen (1995a, 140).

16. For the program note, see DHC, folder M29.
17. DHC, "Programme," January 15, 1937.
18. Humphrey in Kriegsman (1981, 284).
19. Graff (1997, 33).
20. See M. Lloyd (1987, 95).
21. Correspondence from Charles H. Woodford, September 2006.
22. Woodford in Cohen (1995a, 172).
23. Woodford in Cohen (1995a, 172).
24. Housed in the DHC.
25. DHC, folder M28.
26. Berry (1989, 13).
27. Newhall (2009) discusses her work with Eva Gentry prior to the latter's death in 1994.

## The Shakers

1. Cohen (1995a, 116).
2. King (1978, 83).
3. M. Lloyd (1987, 89).
4. Siegel (1993a, 99).
5. King (1978, 208).
6. King (1978, 131).
7. King (1978, 200).
8. King (1978, 202, 203).
9. King (1978, 203).
10. King (1978, 73).
11. Stodelle (1995a, 257).
12. King (1978, 74).
13. Humphrey's notes are located at the DHC in folders C278–79, C300, C398, C442–43, C447, C466, C549, C648, M12–30, M150, and Z13–20.
14. Film versions include Stodelle's 1985 production at the Place with the London Contemporary Dance School. The remaining six are housed in the DHC, including a 1940 recording filmed by Thomas Bouchard. This film is not available for viewing without permission from the Bouchard estate, and this has proved to be elusive to date, which is regrettable, because this film is the only recorded version staged by Humphrey herself. The other films include a version staged by Helen Priest Rogers at Connecticut College (1955); a version staged by Carroll White at Ohio State University (1962); a complete production (1975); and excerpts (1984) by the Limón Company (1975). The Doris Humphrey Society produced the seventh and most recent recording (1997) in collaboration with Princeton Book Company, owned by Humphrey's son and executor, Charles Woodford. This recording is most useful for the commentary provided by Ernestine Stodelle on the staging of her interpretation of the work. Comment from Humphrey's contemporaries can be found in King (1978), Stodelle (1973), M. Lloyd (1987), Cohen (1995a). Further references include Youngerman (1978) and Siegel (1981, 1993a).
15. Humphrey (1959, 35).
16. DHC, folder M29, 4.

17. Key texts include Andrews (1953, 1967), Morse (1987), and Sprigg and Butler (1985).

18. The dance was notated in 1948 by Ann Hutchinson, assisted by Els Grelinger, during a repertoire workshop taught by Humphrey in New York City. Lucy Venable subsequently checked the score in 1955 at Connecticut College. The work has been staged regularly at college level as well as for professional companies in the United States, including the Limón Company.

19. Grelinger (interview, 1995).

20. Stodelle (1973).

21. The ampersand represents the "and count" of each beat.

22. Benedetti (1985, 14).

23. Sprigg and Butler (1985). This volume is currently available through www.linda butlerphoto.com.

24. Stodelle (interview, 1985).

25. Humphrey (1959, 92).

26. Held in the Bettman Archive and reproduced in Morse (1987, 166) and the 1990 documentary by Jane Treays.

## Epilogue: Dancing the Past Tomorrow

1. Stodelle (interview, 1985).

2. Kane (2000, 77).

3. Siegel (1993b, 15).

4. Jordan (2000, preface).

# BIBLIOGRAPHY

## Archive

Doris Humphrey Collection. Jerome Robbins Dance Division in the Library for the Performing Arts, at the New York Public Library. Folders C278–79, C300, C398, C442–43, C447, C466, C549, C648, M12–30, M65, M73–76, M109, M150, Z13–20, program notes from 1937.

## Sources

Anderson, Jack. 1987. *Choreography Observed*. Iowa City: University of Iowa Press.

Andrews, Edward D. 1953. *The People Called Shakers*. New York: Oxford University Press.

———. 1967. *The Gift to Be Simple: Songs, Dances and Rituals of the American Shakers*. New York: Dover. First published 1940.

Archer, Kenneth, and Millicent Hodson. 1998. "Seven Days from the Dervishes Diary." *Dance Theatre Journal* 14, no. 2: 35–43.

———. 2000. "Confronting Oblivion: Keynote Address and Lecture Demonstration on Reconstructing Ballets." In Jordan, *Preservation Politics*, 1–20.

Becker, Svea. 1984. "From Humphrey to Limón: A Modern Tradition." *Dance Notation Journal* 2, no. 1: 37–52.

Becker, Svea, and Joenine Roberts. 1983. "A Reaffirmation of the Humphrey-Weidman Quality." *Dance Notation Journal* 1, no. 1: 3–17.

Beckett, Samuel. 1984. *Collected Shorter Plays of Samuel Beckett*. London: Faber and Faber.

Benedetti, Robert. 1985. *The Director at Work*. Englewood Cliffs: Prentice Hall.

Bennett, Susan. 1990. *Theatre Audiences: A Theory of Production and Reception*. London: Routledge.

———. 1996. *Performing Nostalgia: Shifting Shakespeare and the Contemporary Past*. London: Routledge.

Berg, Shelley C. 1993. "The Real Thing: Authenticity and Dance at the Approach of the Millennium." In Palfy, *Dance Reconstructed*, 109–18.

———. 1999. "The Sense of the Past: Historiography and Dance." In *Researching Dance: Evolving Modes of Inquiry*, edited by Sondra Horton Fraleigh and Penelope Hanstein, 225–48. London: Dance Books.

Berry, Ralph. 1989. *On Directing Shakespeare*. London: Hamish Hamilton.

Billington, Michael. 1994a. "Foot and Mouth Disease." *Guardian*, March 16.
———. 1994b. "Foot-fault." *Guardian*, March 22.
———. 1995. "A Prince Too Far." *Guardian*, April 18.
Bloch, Alice. 1993. "Assessing History through the Dancing Body." In Palfy, *Dance Reconstructed*, 53–64.
Bookis Hofmeister, Eleni. 1993. "Balanchine and Humphrey: Comparing 'Serenade' and 'Passacaglia.'" *Choreography and Dance* 3, no. 3: 13–30.
Boucher, David, ed. 1994. *The Life and Thought of R. G. Collingwood*. Collingwood Studies 1. Swansea, Wales: R. G. Collingwood Society.
Brook, Peter. 1968. *The Empty Space*. London: Penguin.
———. 1993. *There Are No Secrets: Thoughts on Acting and Theatre*. London: Methuen.
Brown, Tom. 1993. "Documenting and Retrieving Nijinska's 'Les Noces.'" In Palfy, *Dance Reconstructed*, 27–40.
Bucek, Loren, and Ann Dils. 1996. Introduction to "Humphrey Centennial Edition." Special issue, *Dance Research Journal* 28, no. 2: 1–3.
Bunting, Madeleine, and Angella Johnson. 1994. "Exit for Life the Director Who Dared to Play with Beckett." *Guardian*, March 19.
Burt, Ramsay. 1995. "Humphrey, Modernism and Postmodernism." *Dance Theatre Journal* 12, no. 2: 10–13.
———. 1998a. *Alien Bodies: Representation of Modernity, "Race" and Nation in Early Modern Dance*. London: Routledge.
———. 1998b. "Re-presentations of Re-presentations." *Dance Theatre Journal* 14, no. 2: 30–33.
———. 2000. "Reconstructing the Disturbing New Spaces of Modernity: The Ballet *Skating Rink*." In Jordan, *Preservation Politics*, 21–30.
Butcher, Pat. 1994. "Play It Again Sam." *Guardian*, October 4.
Butler, Robert. 1996a. "Beckett Rescued from His Admirers." *Independent*, April 21.
———. 1996b. "Shakespeare and Company." *Independent*, March 31.
Calder, John. 1994. "Overstepping the Beckett Mark: Letter." *Guardian*, March 29.
Carter, Alexandra. 1998a. "The Case for Preservation." *Dance Theatre Journal* 14, no. 2: 26–29.
———, ed. 1998b. *The Routledge Dance Studies Reader*. London: Routledge.
Charest, Rémy. 1998. *Robert Lepage: Connecting Flights*. New York: Theatre Communications Group.
Cohen, Selma Jeanne. 1969. *The Modern Dance: Seven Statements of Belief*, Middletown, CT: Wesleyan University Press.
———. 1982. *Next Week, Swan Lake: Reflections on Dance and Dancing*. Middletown, CT: Wesleyan University Press.
———. 1995a. *Doris Humphrey: An Artist First. An Autobiography*. Middletown, CT: Wesleyan University Press. First published 1972.
———. 1995b. "Doris Humphrey: Moving from the Inside Out." *Dance Theatre Journal* 12, no. 2: 14–15.
Cole, Susan L. 1992. *Directors in Rehearsal*. London: Routledge.
Collingwood, Robin G. 1938. *The Principles of Art*. Oxford: Clarendon Press.
———. 1993. *The Idea of History*. Oxford: Oxford University Press. First published 1946.
Conlan, Tara. 1996. "Endgame." *Stage and Television Today*, April 25.
Cook, Ray. 1977. *The Dance Director*. New York: Dance Notation Bureau.

———. 1998. "Filling in the Gaps: *Dawn in New York—Fantasy and Fugue.*" *Choreography and Dance* 4, pt. 4: 75–92.

Cooper Albright, Ann. 1993. "The Long Afternoon of a Faun: Reconstruction and the Discourses of Desire." In Palfy, *Dance Reconstructed*, 219–22.

Coveney, Michael. 1994. "*Footfalls*: Review." *Observer*, March 20.

———. 1997. "Shakespeare Inc." *Observer*, August 25.

Crutchfield, Will. 1988. "Fashion, Conviction and Performance Style in an Age of Revivals." In Kenyon, *Authenticity and Early Music*, 19–26.

Davis, Martha A., and Claire Schmais. 1967. "An Analysis of the Style and Composition of *Water Study.*" *CORD Dance Research Annual* 9: 105–13.

Delgado, Maria M., and Paul Heritage, eds. 1996. *In Contact with The Gods? Directors Talk Theatre*. Manchester: Manchester University Press.

Denby, Edwin. 1968. *Looking at the Dance*. New York: Horizon Press.

———. 1986. *Dance Writings*. New York: Knopf.

Devries, Willem A. 1983. "Meaning and Interpretation in History." *History and Theory* 22, no. 2: 253–63.

Dils, Ann. 1993a. "Performance Practice and Humphrey Reconstructions." In Palfy, *Dance Reconstructed*, 223–28.

———. 1993b. "Re-conceptualizing Dance: Reconstructing the Dances of Doris Humphrey." PhD diss., New York University.

———. 1995. Review of *Doris Humphrey Technique: The Creative Potential*, by Ernestine Stodelle, and *Doris Humphrey: The Collected Works*, vol. 2, by Doris Humphrey. *Dance Research Journal* 27, no. 1: 40–41.

Donkin, Ellen, and Susan Clement, eds. 1993. *Upstaging Big Daddy: Directing Theatre as if Gender and Race Matter*. Ann Arbor: University of Michigan Press.

Donohue, Joseph. 1989. "Evidence and Documentation." In Postlewaite and McConachie, *Interpreting the Theatrical Past*, 177–97.

Dugdale, John. 1994. "Samuel Beckett vs. Deborah Warner." *Sunday Times*, March 27.

Eagleton, Terry. 1986. *Against the Grain: Selected Essays*. London: Verso.

Edsall, Mary. 1996. "Shakers in Cyberspace, Electronic Resources and the Bibliography of Dance." *Dance Research Journal* 28, no. 2: 60–74.

Edwardes, Jane. 1994. "Warner West End." *Time Out*, March 9.

Eliot, T. S. 1975. "Tradition and the Individual Talent." In *Selected Prose of T. S. Eliot*, edited by Frank Kermode, 37–44. London: Faber.

Finkelstein, Joan. 1996. "Doris Humphrey and the 92nd Street Y: A Dance Center for the People." *Dance Research Journal* 28, no. 2: 49–59.

Foster, Susan Leigh. 1986. *Reading Dancing*. Berkeley: University of California Press.

———, ed. 1995. *Choreographing History*. Bloomington: Indiana University Press.

———. 1999. "Narrative with a Vengeance: Doris Humphrey's *With My Red Fires.*" *Proceedings: Society of Dance History Scholars*, compiled by Juliette Willis, 89–93. Riverside, CA: Society of Dance History Scholars.

Fox, Ilene. 1993. "Strategies for Documentation and Retrieval: Panel." In Palfy, *Dance Reconstructed*, 167–84.

Fraleigh, Sondra. 1996. *Dance and the Lived Body*. Pittsburgh: University of Pittsburgh Press.

Franko, Mark. 1989. "Repeatability, Reconstruction and Beyond." *Theatre Journal* 41, no. 1: 56–74.

———. 1993. *Dance as Text: Ideologies of the Baroque Body*. New York: Cambridge University Press.

Gamson, Annabel. 1993. "Reflections on the Re-creation and the Interpretation of the Dances of Duncan, Wigman and King." In Palfy, *Dance Reconstructed*, 263–66.

Garafola, Lynn. 1986. Review of Carr/The Shakers. *Dance Magazine*, October, 34, 36.

———. 1996. Review of Doris Humphrey: A Centennial Celebration—Gala Performances, LaGuardia High School, New York, and the 1995 International Doris Humphrey Centennial Celebration, Pace Downtown Theater, New York. *Dance Magazine*, February, 119–20.

Genter, Sandra. 1996. "Reminiscences of the American Dance Festival." *Dance Research Journal* 28, no. 2: 35–39.

Goldstein, Leon. 1970. "Collingwood's Theory of Historical Knowing." *History and Theory* 9: 3–36.

———. 1994. "Conceptual Openness: Hegel and Collingwood." In Boucher, *The Life and Thought*, 44–59.

Graff, Ellen. 1993. "The Dance Offstage: Voices from the Federal Dance Project." In Palfy, *Dance Reconstructed*, 229–36.

———. 1996. "Dancers, Workers and Bees in the Choreography of Doris Humphrey." *Dance Research Journal* 28, no. 2: 29–34.

———.1997. *Stepping Left: Dance and Politics in New York City, 1928–1942*. Durham, NC: Duke University Press.

Gray, Louise. 1997. "Real to Reel." *Guardian*, March 28.

Harris, Joanna G. 1996. Review of Humphrey Centennial Celebrations. *DCA News*, New York, Spring, 4, 14–15.

Hausler, Barbara. 1996a. "The Influence of Francis W. Parker on Doris Humphrey's Teaching Methodology." *Dance Research Journal* 28, no. 2: 10–21.

———. 1996b. "Packaging Doris Humphrey or A Question of Form: Nona Schurman Shares Her Thoughts on Doris Humphrey's Choreography." *Dance Research Journal* 28, no. 2: 40–48.

———. 1998. "In the Long Line: The Teaching Work of Nona Schurman." *Choreography and Dance* 4, pt. 4: 41–60.

Herbert, Susannah. 1994. "Review: *Footfalls*." *Daily Telegraph*, March 16.

Hering, Doris. 1963. "Where Do They Come From?" *Dance Magazine*, October, 23–25, 66.

———. 1964. "My Words Echo Thus." *Dance Magazine*, February, 42–45.

Hodes, Stuart. 1993. "Dance Preservation and the Oral History Paradigm." In Palfy, *Dance Reconstructed*, 97–108.

Hodson, Millicent. 1986. "Ritual Design in the New Dance: Nijinsky's Choreographic Method." *Dance Research* 4, no. 1: 63–77.

———. 1987. "Sacre: Searching for Nijinsky's Chosen One." *Ballet Review* 15, no. 3: 53–66.

Holmberg, Arthur. 1996. *The Theatre of Robert Wilson*. Cambridge: Cambridge University Press.

Horton Fraleigh, Sondra, and Penelope Hanstein, eds. 1999. *Researching Dance: Evolving Modes of Inquiry*. London: Dance Books.

Hubbard, George. 1989. "Louisville Puts Shakers in Apt Setting." *Dance Magazine*, March, 10–11.

Humphrey, Doris. 1932. "What Shall We Dance About." *Trend Magazine* 1, no. 2: 46–48.

——. 1941. "My Approach to the Modern Dance." In *Dance: A Basic Educational Technique*, edited by Frederick Rand Rogers, 188–92. New York: Macmillan.

——. 1957. "Doris Humphrey Answers the Critics." *Dance and Dancers*, March, 21.

——. 1959. *The Art of Making Dances*. New York: Grove Press.

——. 1962. "Doris Humphrey Speaks (November 7, 1956)." *Dance Observer*, March, 37–40.

——. 1978. *The Collected Works*. Vol. 1. New York: Dance Notation Bureau.

——. 1992. *The Collected Works*. Vol. 2. New York: Dance Notation Bureau.

Hutchinson, Ann. 1972. *Labanotation*. London: Oxford University Press.

Hutchinson Guest, Ann. 1984. *Dance Notation: The Process of Recording Movement on Paper*. London: Dance Books.

——. 1989. *Choreographics*. New York: Gordon and Breech.

——. 1996. "What Exactly Do We Mean by Dynamics?" *Dance Theatre Journal* 13, no. 2: 29–33.

——. 2000. "Is Authenticity to Be Had?" In Jordan, *Preservation Politics*, 65–71.

Jackson, Naomi A. 1998. "Founding the 92nd Street YM-YWHA Dance Center 1934–1936." *Dance Chronicle* 21, no. 2: 193–228.

Jeschke, Claudia. 1999. "Notation Systems as Texts of Performative Knowledge." *Dance Research Journal* 31, no. 1: 4–7.

Johnson, Edward. 1973. *Bach Transcriptions* (sleeve notes). London: Decca Record Company.

Jordan, Stephanie. 1986. "Music as Structural Basis in the Choreography of Doris Humphrey, with Reference to Humphrey's Use of Music Visualization Techniques and Musical/Choreographic Counterpoint and to the Historical Context of her Work." PhD diss., London University, Goldsmiths' College.

——. 1988. "Eclectic Currents." *Listener*, September, 30.

——. 1993. "The Musical Key to Reconstruction." In Palfy, *Dance Reconstructed*, 185–90.

——. 1996. "Musical/Choreographic Discourse: Method, Music Theory, and Meaning." In Morris, *Moving Words*, 14–25.

——, ed. 2000. *Preservation Politics: Dance Revived, Reconstructed, Remade*. London: Dance Books.

Jowitt, Deborah. 1988. *Time and the Dancing Image*. New York: William Morrow.

——. 1996. "Form as the Image of Human Perfectibility and Natural Order." *Dance Research Journal* 28, no. 2: 22–28.

Kagan, Elizabeth. 1978. "Towards the Analysis of a Score: A Comparative Study of *Three Epitaphs* by Paul Taylor and *Water Study* by Doris Humphrey." *CORD Annual* 9: 75–92.

Kane, Angela. 2000. "Issues of Authenticity and Identity in the Restaging of Paul Taylor's *Airs*." In Jordan, *Preservation Politics*, 72–78.

Kaye, Meli Davis. 1995. "Doris Humphrey at Green Mansions, 1947." *Dance Chronicle* 18, no. 3: 405–18.

Kenyon, Nicholas, ed. 1988. *Authenticity and Early Music*. Oxford: Oxford University Press.

King, Eleanor. 1978. *Transformations: A Memoir by Eleanor King: The Humphrey-Weidman Era*. New York: Dance Horizons.

Koner, Pauline. 1984. "Working with Doris Humphrey." *Dance Chronicle* 7, no. 3: 235-78.
———. 1989. *Solitary Song*. Durham, NC: Duke University Press.
———. 1993. *Elements of Performance: A Guide for Performance in Dance, Theatre, and Opera*. Chur, Switzerland: Harwood Academic Publishers.
Kramer, Lloyd S. 1989. "Literature, Criticism, and Historical Imagination: The Literary Challenge of Hayden White and Dominick LaCapra." In *The New Cultural History*, edited by Lynn Hunt, 97-128. London: University of California Press.
Krausz, Michael, ed. 1972. *Critical Essays on the Philosophy of R. G. Collingwood*. Oxford: Clarendon Press.
Kriegsman, Sali Anne. 1981. *Modern Dance in America: The Bennington Years*. Boston: G. K. Hall.
———. 1993. "Keynote Address." In Palfy, *Dance Reconstructed*, 3-10.
LaCapra, Dominick. 1985. *History and Criticism*. Ithaca, NY: Cornell University Press.
———. 1989. *Soundings in Critical Theory*. Ithaca, NY: Cornell University Press.
Leech-Wilkinson, Daniel. 1984. "The Limits of Authenticity: A Discussion." *Early Music*, February, 13-16.
Lennard, J. C. 1993. "Making Plays with Shakespeare." *English Review* 4, no. 1: 11-13.
Leppert, Richard, and Susan McClary, eds. 1987. *Music and Society: The Politics of Composition, Performance, and Reception*. Cambridge: Cambridge University Press.
Levine, Lawrence W. 1988. *Highbrow/Lowbrow: The Emergence of Cultural Hierarchy in America*. Cambridge, MA: Harvard University Press.
———. 1991. "William Shakespeare and the American People: A Study in Cultural Transformation." In *Rethinking Popular Culture: Contemporary Perspectives in Cultural Studies*, edited by Chandra Mukerji and Michael Schudson, 157-97. Berkeley: University of California Press.
Lewis, Daniel. 1984. *The Illustrated Dance Technique of José Limón*. New York: Harper and Row.
Lister, David. 1994. "Review: *Footfalls*." *Times* (London), March 15.
Lloyd, Margaret. 1954. "Doris Humphrey: Yesterday and Today." *Dance Magazine*, November, 34-41.
———. 1987. *The Borzoi Book of Modern Dance*. New York: Dance Horizons. First published 1949.
Lloyd, Phyllida. 2000. "Interpreting or Remaking the Text? A Cross-Arts Panel." In Jordan, *Preservation Politics*, 113-19.
Lowen, Tirzah. 1990. *Peter Hall Directs "Anthony and Cleopatra."* London: Methuen.
Macaulay, Alastair. 1994. "Beckett's *Footfalls*." *Financial Times*, March 16.
Maddox, Fiona. 2002. "Interview with Sir Peter Hall." *London Evening Standard*, May 9.
Main, Lesley. 1995. "Preserved and Illuminated." *Dance Theatre Journal* 12, no. 2: 14-15.
———. 2000. "The Staging of Doris Humphrey's *Passacaglia*: A Director's Perspective." In Jordan, *Preservation Politics*, 105-12.
———. 2003. "The Dances of Doris Humphrey: An Investigation into Directorial Process and Co-authorship." PhD diss., Roehampton University.
———. 2005a. "The Dances of Doris Humphrey: Creating a Contemporary Perspective through Directorial Interpretation." *Dance Research* 23, no. 2: 106-22.
———. 2005b. "A Musical Exploration of Doris Humphrey's *Passacaglia*, with Reference to How Musical Interpretation Can Influence Directorial Interpretation and Performance of a Dance Work." Proceedings of "Sound Moves: An International

Conference on Music and Dance," Roehampton University, London, November 5, 6, 118–24. http://www.roehampton.ac.uk/soundmoves/SoundMovesConference 2005_Proceedings.pdf.

———. 2005c. "A Narrative Perspective on Doris Humphrey's 'With My Red Fires': An Exploration of the Consequences of Directorial Intervention in the Staging of Dance." In *Systems Research in the Arts: Music, Environmental Design, and the Choreography of Space,* edited by George E. Lasker et al., 67–71. Tecumseh, ON: International Institute for Advanced Studies in Systems Research and Cybernetics.

Manfull, Helen. 1999. *Taking the Stage: Women Directors on Directing.* London: Methuen.

Manley, Mary Elizabeth. 1998. "Links and Lineage: Doris Humphrey's Influence on the Pedagogy and Artistic Work of Virginia Tanner." *Choreography and Dance* 4, pt. 4: 17–40.

Manning, Susan. 1993a. *Ecstasy and the Demon: Feminism and Nationalism in the Dances of Mary Wigman.* Berkeley: University of California Press.

———. 1993b. "Perspectives in Reconstruction: Panel." In Palfy, *Dance Reconstructed,* 11–26.

Marion, Sheila. 1987. "Beyond Accuracy: Authenticity and Interpretation in Dance Notation." *Dance Notation Journal* 5, no. 1: 33–40.

———. 1992. "Studying *Water Study.*" *Dance Research Journal* 24, no. 1: 1–11.

Martin, John. 1965a. *Introduction to the Dance.* New York: Dance Horizons.

———. 1965b. *The Modern Dance.* New York: Dance Horizons.

———. 1968. *America Dancing.* New York: Dance Horizons.

Martin, Randy. 1993. "Reasserting Dance in the Public Sphere: Toward a Critical View of Reconstruction." In Palfy, *Dance Reconstructed,* 119–26.

Matthiessen, F. O. 1958. *The Achievement of T. S. Eliot.* Oxford: Oxford University Press.

McConachie, Bruce. 1985. "Towards a Post-Positivist Theatre History." *Theatre Journal* 37, no. 4: 465–86.

McCrum, Robert. 1997. "The New Globe." *Observer,* June 1.

McCue, Jim. 1994. "Persisting or Not with Life and Beckett." *Times Literary Supplement,* April 1.

McFerran, Ann. 1994. "Interview with Deborah Warner." *London Evening Standard,* March 10.

McLaverty, James. 1984. "The Concept of Authorial Intention in Textual Criticism." *Library* 6: 121–38.

McMullan, Anna. 1994. "Letter." *Guardian,* March 22.

McPherson, Elizabeth, and Carol Maxwell. 1996. "Doris Humphrey: A Centennial Celebration, Celebrating the Past—Envisioning the Future." *Dance Research Journal* 28, no. 1: 107–10.

Miles, Patrick. 1995. "Chekhov, Shakespeare, the Ensemble and the Company." *New Theatre Quarterly* 9, no. 43: 203–10.

Miller, Jonathan. 1986. *Subsequent Performances.* London: Faber.

Mindlin, Naomi, ed. 1998a. "Doris Humphrey: A Centennial Issue." Special issue, *Choreography and Dance* 4, pt. 4.

———. 1998b. "A Humphrey Tutorial: Beyond Theory." *Choreography and Dance* 4, pt. 4: 123–34.

Mink, Louis. 1969. *Mind, History and Dialectic: The Philosophy of R. G. Collingwood.* Bloomington: Indiana University Press.

———. 1972. "Collingwood's Historicism: A Dialectic of Process." In Krausz, *Critical Essays*, 154–65.

———. 1987. *Historical Understanding*. Ithaca, NY: Cornell University Press.

Moore, Lillian. 1975. *Artists of the Dance*. New York: Dance Horizons. First published 1938.

Morris, Gay, ed. 1996. *Moving Words: Re-writing Dance*. London: Routledge.

———. 2006. *A Game for Dancers*. Middletown, CT: Wesleyan University Press.

Morrison Brown, Jean, ed. 1980. *The Vision of Modern Dance*. London: Dance Books.

Morse, Flo. 1987. *The Shakers and the World's People*. Hanover, NH: University Press of New England. First published 1980.

Mueller, John. 1979. *Dance Film Directory: An Annotated and Evaluated Guide to Films on Ballet and Modern Dance*. Hightstown, NJ: Princeton Book Company.

Newhall, Mary Anne Santos. 2009. *Mary Wigman*. London: Routledge.

Novack, Cynthia J. 1990. *Sharing the Dance: Contact Improvisation and American Culture*. Madison: University of Wisconsin Press.

Nugent, Ann. 1993. "The Limón Company: Review." *Stage and Television Today*, July 1.

Orgel, Stephen. 1988. "The Authentic Shakespeare." *Representations* 21 (Winter): 1–25.

Palfy, Barbara, ed. 1993. *Dance Reconstructed: Conference Proceedings: A Conference on Modern Dance Art, Past, Present, Future, October 16 and 17, 1992, Rutgers University, New Brunswick, New Jersey*. New Brunswick, NJ: Rutgers University Press.

Peter, John. 1994. "Who? What? Why? Pause. Curtain." *Sunday Times*, March 6.

Petty, Moira. 1996. "Happy with Beckett." *Stage and Television Today*, April 25.

Pforish, Janis. 1978. "Labanalysis and Dance Style Research." *CORD Dance Research Annual* 9: 59–74.

Pitt, Angela. 1995. "A Conversation between Deborah Warner and Angela Pitt." *English Review* 4, no. 1: 10–12.

Pollock, Eileen. 1994. "Overstepping the Beckett Mark: Letter." *Guardian*, October 4.

Postlewaite, Thomas, and Bruce A. McConachie, eds. 1989. *Interpreting the Theatrical Past: Essays in the Historiography of Performance*. Iowa City: University of Iowa Press.

Restout, Denise, ed. 1981. *Landowska on Music*. New York: Stein and Day.

Rosen, Lillian. 1978. "A Doris Humphrey Celebration." *Dance News*, December, 13, 16.

Savery, Helen. 1984. "Dancing in the Depression." *Dance Chronicle* 7, no. 3: 279–93.

Schurman, Nona, and Sharon Leigh Clarke. 1972. *Modern Dance Fundamentals*. New York: Macmillan.

Shaw, Fiona. 1994. "Being True to Beckett." *Guardian*, March 25.

Shearer, Sybil. 1993. "A Comparison: Doris Humphrey and Trisha Brown." *Ballet Review* 21, no. 4: 15–17.

———. 1995. "The Limón Company: Review." *Ballet Review* 23, no. 2: 9–11.

Sherman, Jane. 1995. "Doris Humphrey Centennial." *Dance Magazine* 69, no. 10: 56–59.

Shillingsburg, Peter L. 1991. "Text as Matter, Concept and Action." *Studies in Bibliography* 44: 31–82.

Siegel, Marcia B. 1981. *The Shapes of Change*. Boston: Houghton Mifflin.

———. 1993a. *Days on Earth*. New Haven, CT: Yale University Press.

———. 1993b. "Perspectives in Reconstruction: Panel." In Palfy, *Dance Reconstructed*, 11–26.

———. 1996a. "Humphrey's Legacy: Loss and Recall." *Dance Research Journal* 28, no. 2: 4–9.

———. 1996b. "Matriarchal Mysteries." *Hudson Review* 49, no. 1: 97–103.

———. 1996c. "Visible Secrets: Style Analysis and Dance Literacy." In Morris, *Moving Words*, 26–37.

———. 1998. "Bridging the Critical Distance." In Carter, *The Routledge Dance Studies Reader*, 91–97.

Simisky, Karim. 1998. "The Genius behind *The Call/Breath of Fire*." *Choreography and Dance* 4, pt. 4: 109–16.

Slater, Ann Pasternak. 1982. *Shakespeare the Director*. Sussex: Harvester Press.

Smith, A. William. 1993. "*Flickers*: A Fifty-Year-Old Flicker of the Weidman Tradition." In Palfy, *Dance Reconstructed*, 245–62.

Sorrell, Walter, ed. 1951. *The Dance Has Many Faces*. Cleveland: World Publishing.

———. 1986. *Looking Back in Wonder*. New York: Columbia University Press.

Spencer, Charles. 1994. "Review: *Footfalls*." *Daily Telegraph*, March 18.

Sprigg, June, and Linda Butler. 1985. *Inner Light: The Shaker Legacy*. New York: Alfred A. Knopf.

Stodelle, Ernestine. 1959a. "The First *Duo-Drama*." *Dance Observer* 26, no. 10: 154–55.

———. 1959b. "A Lifetime's Text of Creative Artistry in the Dance." *New York Herald Tribune*, October 18.

———. 1960. "A Heritage Made Visible." *Dance Observer* 27, no. 2: 23–24.

———. 1961. "Humphrey–Weidman Theory of Movement." Unpublished paper presented at the University of North Carolina–Greensboro, June.

———. 1972. "Elements of Modern Choreography." Unpublished paper presented at Yale University, spring.

———. 1973. "Flesh and Spirit at War." *New Haven Register*, March 23.

———. 1974. "Lyricism and Logic Rejoined." *New Haven Register*, February 3.

———. 1984. *Deep Song: The Dance Story of Martha Graham*. New York: Schirmer Books.

———. 1994. "Deaths and Remembrances." *Art Times* 10, no. 7: 1, 9.

——— 1995a. *The Dance Technique of Doris Humphrey and Its Creative Potential*. 2nd ed. London: Dance Books. First published 1978.

———. 1995b. "Doris Humphrey: The Time Has Come." *Dance Now* 4, no. 3: 54–58.

———. 1998. "A Life Relived in Dance." *Choreography and Dance* 4, pt. 4: 3–16.

Stowe, Dorothy. 1992. "Review: Repertory Dance Theatre." *Dance Magazine*, March, 81.

Tanselle, Thomas G. 1981. "Recent Editorial Discussion and the Central Questions of Editing." *Studies in Bibliography* 34: 23–65.

———. 1986. "Historicism and Critical Editing." *Studies in Bibliography* 39: 1–46.

Taruskin, Richard. 1982. "On Letting the Music Speak for Itself: Some Reflections on Musicology and Performance." *Journal of Musicology* 1, no. 3: 338–49.

———. 1984. "The Limits of Authenticity: A Discussion." *Early Music*, February, 3–12.

———. 1988. "The Pastness of the Present and the Presence of the Past." In Kenyon, *Authenticity and Early Music*, 137–210.

———. 1992. "Tradition and Authority." *Early Music*, May, 311–25.

———. 1995. *Text and Act*. New York: Oxford University Press.

Taylor, Paul. 1987. *Private Domain*. New York: Alfred A. Knopf.

———. 1994. "Way out of Line." *Independent*, March 18.

Temperley, Nicholas. 1984. "The Limits of Authenticity: A Discussion." *Early Music*, February, 16–20.

Terry, Walter. 1978. *I Was There: Selected Reviews and Articles, 1936–1976*. New York: Marcel Dekker.

Thomas, Helen. 2000. "Reproducing the Dance: In Search of the Aura?" In Jordan, *Preservation Politics*, 125–31.

———. 2003. *The Body, Dance and Cultural Theory*. New York: Palgrave Macmillan.

Thompson, Ann. 1994. "Sexuality and Textuality in the Editing of Shakespeare." Lecture, Roehampton Institute London, June.

———. 2000. "Shakespeare: Preservation and/or Reinvention?" In Jordan, *Preservation Politics*, 120–24.

Thompson, Ann, and Neil Taylor. 1995. "Wanamaker's Dream: Achievable Authenticity and the Reconstructed Globe." Modern Language Association Convention, Drama Division, Chicago.

Todd, Arthur. 1957. "Limón for London." *Dance and Dancers*, September, 11–14.

Tomko, Linda. 1999. "Dance Notation and Cultural Agency: A Meditation Spurred by Choreo-graphics." *Dance Research Journal* 31, no. 1: 1–3.

Tomlinson, Gary. 1988. "The Historian, the Performer and Authentic Meaning in Music." In Kenyon, *Authenticity and Early Music*, 115–36.

Topaz, Muriel. 1993. "Perspectives in Reconstruction: Panel." In Palfy, *Dance Reconstructed*, 11–26.

———. 1998. "Three Dances by Doris Humphrey: Reflections on Style and Performance." *Choreography and Dance* 4, pt. 4: 61–74.

———. 2000. "Reconstruction: Living or Dead? Authentic or Phony?" In Jordan, *Preservation Politics*, 97–104.

Tosh, John. 1993. *The Pursuits of History: Aims, Methods and New Directions in the Study of Modern History*. 2nd ed. London: Longman. First published 1984.

Van Zile, Judy. 1985. "What Is the Dance? Implications for Dance Notation." *Dance Research Journal* 17, no. 2: 41–47.

Varone, Doug. 1998. "The Fourth Generation Speaks." *Choreography and Dance* 4, pt. 4: 117–22.

Venable, Lucy. 1965. "Passacaglia 1938–1968: The Art of Remaking a Dance." *Dance Scope* 1, no. 2: 6–14.

Wang, Yunyu. 1998. "Reconstruction of Humphrey's Masterpieces in the United States and Taiwan." *Choreography and Dance* 4, pt. 4: 93–108.

Warner, Deborah. 1996. "Exploring Space at Play." *New Theatre Quarterly* 12, no. 47: 229–36.

Wertkin, Gerard C. 1986. *The Four Seasons of Shaker Life*. New York: Simon and Schuster.

White, Hayden. 1973. "Interpretation in History." *New Literary History* 4, no. 2: 281–314.

———. 1978. *Tropics of Discourse: Essays in Cultural Criticism*. Baltimore, MD: Johns Hopkins University Press.

———. 1980. "The Value of Narrativity in the Representation of Reality." *Critical Inquiry* 7, no. 1: 5–27.

———. 1987. *The Content of the Form: Narrative Discourse and Historical Representation*. Baltimore, MD: Johns Hopkins University Press.

———. 1995. "Bodies and Their Plots." In Foster, *Choreographing History*, 229–34.

Whitelaw, Billie. 1995. *Who He? An Autobiography*. London: Hodder and Stoughton.

Wimsatt, William K., and Monroe C. Beardsley. 1971. "The Intentional Fallacy." In *Critical Theory since Plato*, edited by Hazard Adams, 945–52. New York: Harcourt, Brace, Jovanovich. First published 1946.

Winter, Robert. 1984. "The Limits of Authenticity: A Discussion." *Early Music*, February, 24–27.

Woodford, Charles H. 1985. Letter to Directors, Dance Notation Bureau, New York.

Youngerman, Suzanne. 1978. "The Translation of Culture into Choreography: A Critical Appraisal of *The Shakers* through the Use of Labanalysis." *CORD Annual* 9: 75–92.

## Films

*Doris Humphrey*. ca. 1935. Jerome Robbins Dance Division in the Library for the Performing Arts at the New York Public Library.

*Doris Humphrey: A Timeless Legacy*. 1995. Directed by Ernestine Stodelle. Live recording of centenary performance at LaGuardia High School for Music and Performing Arts, New York, October 22.

*Doris Humphrey Technique: The Creative Potential*. 1992. Directed by Ernestine Stodelle, produced by Dance Horizons Video, Princeton Book Company, Hightstown, NJ.

*The Four Pioneers*. 1965. Produced by John Mueller.

*I Don't Want to Be Remembered as a Chair*. 1990. Written and directed by Jane Treays, Timewatch, BBC 2.

*Ohio Impromptu*. 2002. Directed by Charles Sturridge, performed by Jeremy Irons for *Beckett on Film*, Channel 4, March 31.

*Students and Teachers at Bennington*. ca. 1939. Jerome Robbins Dance Division in the Library for the Performing Arts at the New York Public Library.

*Young America Dances*. ca. 1939. Jerome Robbins Dance Division in the Library for the Performing Arts at the New York Public Library.

## Dance Works

### 1928

*Air for the G String*. 1934. Featuring Doris Humphrey in the leading role, reproduced on *Doris Humphrey Technique: The Creative Potential* (1992), directed by Ernestine Stodelle, produced by Dance Horizons Video, Princeton Book Company, Hightstown, NJ.

*Air for the G String*. 1997. Directed by Ernestine Stodelle, produced by National Doris Humphrey Society with Princeton Book Company, Hightstown, NJ.

*Water Study*. 1985. London Contemporary Dance School, directed by Ernestine Stodelle, produced by the Video Place.

*Water Study*. 1997. Directed by Ernestine Stodelle, produced by National Doris Humphrey Society with Princeton Book Company, Hightstown, NJ.

### 1929/30

*The Call/Breath of Fire*. ca. 1931. Jerome Robbins Dance Division in the Library for the Performing Arts at the New York Public Library.

## 1931

*The Shakers.* 1940. Filmed by Thomas Bouchard, directed by Doris Humphrey. Jerome Robbins Dance Division in the Library for the Performing Arts at the New York Public Library (restricted access).

*The Shakers.* 1955. Directed by Helen Priest Rogers. Jerome Robbins Dance Division in the Library for the Performing Arts at the New York Public Library.

*The Shakers.* 1962. Filmed at Ohio State University, directed by Carroll White. Jerome Robbins Dance Division in the Library for the Performing Arts at the New York Public Library.

*The Shakers.* 1975. Performed by the Limón Company. Jerome Robbins Dance Division in the Library for the Performing Arts,, New York Public Library.

*The Shakers.* 1984. Excerpts performed by the Limón Company. Jerome Robbins Dance Division in the Library for the Performing Arts, at the New York Public Library.

*The Shakers.* 1985. London Contemporary Dance School, directed by Ernestine Stodelle, produced by the Video Place.

*The Shakers.* 1997. Directed by Ernestine Stodelle, produced by National Doris Humphrey Society with Princeton Book Company, Hightstown, NJ.

*Two Ecstatic Themes.* 1997. Directed by Ernestine Stodelle, produced by National Doris Humphrey Society with Princeton Book Company, Hightstown, NJ.

## 1935

*New Dance.* 1978. American Dance Festival, directed by Charles Reinhart and Martha Myers, produced by Dance Horizons Video, Princeton Book Company, Hightstown, NJ.

## 1936

*With My Red Fires.* 1954. Juilliard Dance Theatre. Jerome Robbins Dance Division in the Library for the Performing Arts, at the New York Public Library.

*With My Red Fires.* 1978. American Dance Festival, reconstructed by Christine Clark, produced by Dance Horizons Video, Princeton Book Company, Hightstown, NJ.

## 1938

*Passacaglia.* 1957. Silent black-and-white recording. Jerome Robbins Dance Division in the Library for the Performing Arts, at the New York Public Library.

*Passacaglia.* 1965. Directed by Lucy Venable, on *The Four Pioneers*, produced by John Muller.

### Labanotation Scores (produced and published by the Dance Notation Bureau, New York)

*Passacaglia*

Venable, Lucy, with Joan Gainer. 1955.

*The Shakers*

Hutchinson, Ann, with Els Grelinger. 1948, revised 1971.

*Water Study*

Barracuda, Karen. 1978.
Blum, Odette. 1966, revised 1998.

*With My Red Fires*

Grelinger, Els, Rena Gluck, Muriel Topaz, Karen Kanner, Lucy Venable (supervisor). 1954, revised 1964/65.

## Interviews

Carter, Alexandra. 1999, June. London.
Corbin, Gail. 1990, April. Connecticut.
———. 1994, June. London.
Garafola, Lynn. 2010, June. London.
Grelinger, Els. 1995, March. London.
Stodelle, Ernestine. 1985, between February and June. Connecticut.
———. 1986, various between January and March. Connecticut, London.
———. 1990, April. Connecticut.
———. 1994, June. London.
———. 1995, July and August. London.
———. 1997, July. London.
Went, Anne. 2010, March. London.

## Websites

www.dancenotation.org
www.dance.ohio-state.edu
www.dorishumphreyfoundationuk.co.uk
www.dorishumphrey.org
www.humphreyweidman.com
www.lindabutlerphoto.com
www.nypl.org/express
www.sgreenphoto.com

# INDEX

# Studies in Dance History
## A Publication of the Society of Dance History Scholars